Friendly Fire at the Veterans Hospital

The Conspiracy Concealing Malpractice and Mistreatment of US Veterans

J. B. Simms

Erik Publishing

Friendly Fire at the Veterans Hospital
The Conspiracy Concealing Malpractice and Mistreatment of US Veterans

Copyright © 2018 by Erik Publishing

All rights reserved. This book or any portion thereof may not be reproduced or used in any manner whatsoever without the express written permission of the publisher except for the use of brief quotations in a book review.

ISBN: 978-0-9795766-7-6 Paperback

ISBN: 978-0-9795766-8-3 EBook

Printed in the United States of America
First Printing, 2018

Names: Simms, J. B. (James B.), author.
Title: Friendly fire at the veterans hospital : the conspiracy concealing malpractice and mistreatment of U.S. veterans / J. B. Simms.
Description: Tampa : Erik Publishing, 2018.
Identifiers: ISBN 978-0-9795766-7-6 (pbk.)
Subjects: LCSH: Veterans' hospitals--United States. | Veterans--Medical care--United States. | Oncologists--Malpractice. | Physicians--Malpractice. | Whistle blowing--United States. | United States. Veterans Health Administration. | BISAC: MEDICAL / Ethics. | MEDICAL / Hospital Administration & Care. | LAW / Malpractice.
Classification: LCC UB369 .S56 2018 (print) | DDC 362.1086/970973--dc23.

Erik Publishing
6031 Bowen Daniel Drive, Apt. 103 Tampa, FL 33616
www.erikpublishing.com

Contents

Acknowledgments i
Introduction: "Do no harm" iii
The Informed Consent: What Veterans Must Know ix
American College of Radiology: Guidelines Reference xiii
Index of Individuals: Name and Position xvi
Chapter One: Intensity Modulated Radiation Therapy 1
Chapter Two: Sources of Evidence of Abuse and Corruption 5
Chapter Three: The Varian Incident 15
Chapter Four: The Varian Cover-Up is Born 27
Chapter Five: HIV, a Freckle, and Patient Abuse 41
Chapter Six: Filing Complaints to Protect Veterans 69
Chapter Seven: NY Times, OIG, and ACR 81
Chapter Eight: Doctor Denials and Fraud Conspiracy 85
Chapter Nine: More Patient Incidents, and the OIG 93
Chapter Ten: OIG Visits and Hagan's Betrayal 107
Chapter Eleven: 2011-Patient Abuse and Cover-Up 121
Chapter Twelve: Two OIG Reports- More Cover-Up 135
Chapter Thirteen: No Accountability for Abuse 161
Chapter Fourteen: Excuses by OIG; Schuder's Rescue 177
Chapter Fifteen: HR Bill 2104 June 11, 2011 209
Chapter Sixteen: Statement of Lynne Roy 213
Chapter Seventeen: Lana's Parting "Dear All" Shot 219
Chapter Eighteen: Lana Transferred, OSC in Denial 231
Chapter Nineteen: Exposing Corrupt Government Agencies 239
Chapter Twenty: Interview with Dr. Richard Robbins 255
Chapter Twenty-One: VA and ACR Put on Notice 257
Chapter Twenty-Two: Catching Up with Lana 285
Epilogue 291
Appendix One: Public Health Service Act HR 2104 293
Appendix Two: OIG Inspection-November 15-16, 2010 Report 309
About the Author 319

Acknowledgments

I want to thank Lana Miller Boyer for entrusting me to document this part of her life. Lana is one of the most brilliant, honest, and caring persons I know. Lana sets the bar for integrity far above the reach of the persons who had any authority over her, or any governmental agency employee with whom she came into contact.

I thank Dr. Suzie Schuder for referring her patient, Lana, to me. Dr. Schuder was more than a doctor for Lana; she was a friend and fierce defender. I am grateful for the trust placed in me by Dr. Schuder.

Nick Davies, Newport Beach, CA, was the film artist who videoed and produced the video of Lana in the office of Dr. Schuder for the presentation on YouTube. I wish Nick all the best in his continuing film career.

Lucas Schultz assisted Nick in the filming, and I am grateful to Lucas. Lucas and Nick are loyal and trusted friends of mine.

Mike Conner, retired US Army colonel, Vietnam Veteran, and West Point classmate of General Shinseki was instrumental in assisting me to reach into the higher levels of the Office of Veteran Affairs.

The two persons who gave me ongoing advice and critique during the writing were Dianne Helm, and Capt, Joe Simms.

Dianne Helm, my editor and friend from St. Petersburg, FL, always fed me advice. Dianne's experience as an editor and publisher, and her acceptance of my many phone calls, were very important to me.

I always thank my son, Capt. Joe Simms, USAF, for his support, his advice, and encouragement for my books. I also thank Joe for listening to his father's book stories. It is good feeling when one of your kids is smart enough to tell his "old man" what needs to be done. My respect for him has no bounds, and I am grateful for his help.

Introduction:

"Do no harm"

The mantra of "do no harm, " professed by physicians, and supposedly echoed by the administration at the Long Beach (CA) VA Hospital, was replaced by "hide the harm." The patients were receiving "Friendly Fire" at the VA Hospital; being "wounded" and worse by doctors who refused to heed reports and warnings from the Chief Radiation Therapist.

This is the story of the brave woman who sacrificed her career, mental and physical health, and her family relationships to save the lives of our Veterans. You will read the accounts, taken from volumes of email records, of the attacks upon the woman who tried to stop the abuse. You will meet this brave woman, Lana Miller Boyer.

From 2008-2014, cancer patients at the Long Beach VA Hospital were receiving inadequate and harmful radiation treatment. Uncertified and unskilled doctors, hiding behind their "Dr." were lying to patients, telling patients (Veterans) that the wounds suffered as a result of radiation oncology treatment was a "side effect of treatment." The truth was the wounds were caused by the indifferent attitude of radiation therapists and allowed by doctors because the doctors did not know how to appropriately delineate treatment to tumor areas. Thus, began the cover-up.

The company which created the machine used in the Radiation Oncology Department was Varian. The model of the radiation machine was a Clinax IX. I want to be clear to the readers that the Clinax IX linear accelerator was never found to be in error. Representatives from Varian inspected the machine and found human error. Copyright issues prohibited the publication of a photograph of the Clinax IX, but photographs can be easily found by searching "Clinax IX" on the internet.

Doctors hid the fact that they were not competent or conversant in many technical matters, and that they were unwilling to admit that they depended upon therapists and physicists to make the themselves appear to be competent.

The Chief Radiation Oncologist attempted to procure a falsified physical document of certification to present to an OIG inspection.

Doctors, administrators, and federal investigative agencies refused to confront and/or discipline persons responsible for wounding veterans in the hospital and concealed the evidence from the patient/Veterans and the American people. The policy of the Veterans Administration was that no one could be fired. This policy has changed under a new presidential administration.

The hospital had other problems. Members of the hospital administration resigned from their jobs under suspicious circumstances, including criminal acts of misuse of funds and simple theft, but no criminal charges were brought because "they retired."

During my 25+ years as a private investigator, I saw my share of cover-ups and corruption. My disdain for the criminal behavior of public officials, and government employees, was evident to all persons around me. The corrupt VA doctors and administrators hid behind bureaucratic shields. These people have no conscience, and no soul. The doctors and the administration of the VA hospital were more focused on concealing errors and lying to the sanctioning institutions than they were to furnishing proper and humane medical aid to Veterans. Lana Miller Boyer defended the Veterans and paid a price. They did not know that one person was going to expose their corruption.

Lana Miller Boyer saved lives at the VA, but it took years to make a change. Lana is one of the most intelligent, honest, and gutsy persons I have met. Lana sacrificed her health, and her job. This is her story.

As I write this book, I cannot escape the political climate in the United States, and the implications to this story. During the Obama administration, it was well known that "government employees" at the VA were hard to "fire"; people having a GS designation had a job for life, and the bureaucracy and "red tape" allowed persons, who Lana battled, to keep their jobs and have no accountability.

You will find in this book that people at the VA hospital in Long Beach never feared losing their jobs. After years of abuse at work and being ignored by the authorities who were supposed to protect the Veterans, Lana's psychiatrist had seen enough.

Below are outtakes from a letter which was sent from the psychiatrist from whom Lana was receiving treatment because of the abuse Lana received from doctors and administration:

June 6, 2011

Lana Miller is a patient in my care. She has been suffering with a work-related acute stress syndrome that has continued and evolved into a Chronic Post Traumatic Stress Disorder. The work- related stress is due to the continued harassment she has suffered at the hands of Dr. Samar Azawi, the chief of the Department of Radiation Oncology who is also Ms. Miller's direct supervisor. In addition, Dr. Azawi has had a great deal of influence on some of the other people in the department who have followed Dr. Azawi's lead in harassing Ms. Miller.

...[O]ne of the many examples of Dr. Azawi's harassment tactics occurred in the summer of 2009. Ms. Miller had asked Dr. Azawi to meet with her to discuss how they might improve treatment accuracy with the treating therapists. Ms. Miller had expected that Dr. Azawi would follow the basic protocol of a military facility honoring a chain of command.

... [M]s. Miller was informed of the new meeting parameters only about five minutes prior to the meeting time. The meeting then involved the therapist attacking Ms. Miller with comments saying that Ms. Miller lied about their inept and dangerous treatment protocols and that she did not know what she was talking about and was outdated. Their accusations were blatantly false as documented evidence showed.

Despite this, Dr. Azawi sat back and watched grinning from ear to ear encouraging the therapists in their attack of Ms. Miller. Ms. Miller sat in this meeting dumbfounded that her subordinates were not only allowed to debase her; they were encouraged to do so.

...[T]his incident, one many to follow, had totally undermined Ms. Miller's authority and prevented her from doing the job she was hired to do.

Whenever Ms. Miller tried to perform her duties and correct therapists' substandard patient treatments or point out inappropriate insubordinate behavior, the therapists in question would run and complain to Dr. Azawi who then told the therapists that it was no big deal and they should not worry about it.

...[S]he is also being harassed by other people in the department who are influenced by and would benefit from gaining Dr. Azawi's approval, by being the recipients of preferential treatment that includes salary increases. They took part in willful isolation of Ms. Miller especially during departmental events or meetings.

...[M]s. Miller has also been subjected to continued, unscheduled and unpredictable meetings with Dr. Azawi and Dr. Williams. This occurred and occurs almost on a daily basis without warning and without being given any idea about the topic that needed to be addressed so "urgently". It seems that the only purpose of these command meetings was in effect to intimidate, harass and demean Ms. Miller with false accusations and without allowing her to an opportunity to address any of the accusations.

...[A]lthough some types of PTSD are caused by a single trauma it can also be manifested by continued "prisoner of war" tactics. Examples of these tactics are described above and are insidious ways of harming another. Essentially Ms. Miller is being isolated and singled out as the only one to be harassed and "micromanaged" by Dr. Azawi who has bullied her and created an extremely hostile work environment as a way to exploit her power over anyone in the position of chief therapist.

...[T]he persecution, lead [sic] by Dr. Azawi, has caused Ms. Miller to suffer from insomnia, nightmares, fatigue, back pain due to muscle spasms, nausea, headaches, high blood pressure and anxiety along with the inability to concentrate.

She feels paralyzed, and has difficulty making decisions that had not been an issue for her in the past. Her health has been adversely affected by the hostile environment she faces on a daily basis. In that she has no more family leave time available and must be at work, I have advised her to take a few days off as sick leave because she will become ill to the point of being disabled.

[A]s a psychiatrist working with people with PTSD, I am appalled that such an abusive of power is allowed to exist in the health care arena causing poor health in employees. Furthermore it is ironic that a military hospital specializing in treating soldiers with PTSD allows an employee to harass her subordinates to the point of causing severe PTSD symptoms even without the trauma of being on the battlefield.

Suzie Schuder, MD

In August 2010, I met Dr. Schuder at an educational forum breakfast meeting at the University of California, Irvine. I was a morning speaker on the topic of my book, Don't Get Arrested in South Carolina, which is a book about a client of mine who was a victim of corruption of law enforcement and government officials' corruption in a criminal case. Two years later, during the spring of 2012, Dr. Schuder asked if I could write a book based upon the circumstances surrounding her patient who had PTSD as result of the actions at the VA Hospital in Long Beach, CA. With the permission and involvement of the patient, Lana Miller Boyer, I took on the task of writing Lana's story to empower and validate this outstanding lady who protected our Veterans.

Lana is a hero to many, and she is my hero, as well.

As this book was being reviewed and edited, it occurred to us that there would appear to be redundancy in events and facts presented throughout the book. You will see that the facts presented in the book are the same facts which were presented to persons in authority, governmental agencies which were to provide oversight of malfeasance, and to the Secretary of Veteran Affairs. These facts were directly presented to the Chief of Staff of the Secretary, both by Lana Boyer and my me. Please bear in mind while reading that you will hear many of the same facts being repeated, but to counter the appearance of repetition, you will understand that Lana was on a "hamster-wheel of denial and betrayal" as she was searching for someone to defend the Veterans from the persons who were directly harming the Veterans, and the persons who enabled the abuse for their personal benefit.

All Veterans, and/or family members of Veterans, who plan to or have received radiation treatment at a VA hospital, have a manner in which to address their fears: demand a copy of the digital and hard copy patient records and have these records examined by a qualified third- party. No competent physician or therapist will be offended by having their "work" reviewed. This is a Veteran enforcing "Peer Review" to protect themselves. This is discussed further in the following chapter.

Emails printed in italics are copied and are direct quotes. Typos and misspellings were not corrected, leaving the text original.

The Informed Consent:

What Veterans Must Know

The Office of the Inspector General (OIG), for the Office of Veteran Affairs, inspected the Long Beach VA Hospital twice in 2010; once in September (as the standard inspection which was mandated by Congress) and in November 2010 (which was a result of a hotline report submitted concerning improper care). The reports from the OIG were published on March 9 and 10, 2011. The hotline report revealed that at least one of the 10 patients had received "poor care," but this conclusion was not accurate; the report ignored the fact that deficiencies in medical records in nine of the ten radiation therapy patient files inspected constituted poor care and harmful "care."

The report results, stating "one in ten" patients reported to have received poor care, was misleading; nine in ten were found to have had deficiencies in medical records. When medical records are not complete and up to date, doctors cannot treat the patient effectively, and inaccurate treatment is given. The OIG dropped the ball, and other issues failed to be to be addressed.

As a result of the questionable conclusions published by the OIG, it became obvious that Veterans needed to be better informed about their radiation procedures and have confidence they were being told the truth. The following information should be noted by Veterans getting treatment at any VA hospital.

If you find that you have a question with respect to your treatment, side effects experienced, as well as the deficiencies in your records, we suggest you place an immediate request for your records, hard copy and digital, as well as for a copy of the "consent" you signed. If the Veteran chooses to show the records to another doctor, or certified Chief Radiation Therapist for consultation, that would be a good first step before consulting with the VA doctor.

The Consent: Side Effects to Expect and Occurrence

If your records are "deficient," this means your records could be missing one of several items: a list of treatments, treatment plan, doctor notes, and more. Your digital records will reveal if your treatments were accurate, and if your "side effects" were that; side effects, and not the result of misapplication of radiation. Digital records may show more information than hard copy.

If you feel uncomfortable, you should insist upon a prompt, thorough investigation of your allegations of mismanagement, poor treatment, lack of oversight, and incompetence of medical personnel, and demand immediate correction of deficiencies in your records.

Insist that persons found responsible be held accountable for their actions and lack of action.

In January 2010, Walt Bogdanich, along with Kristina Rebelo, authored a series of articles printed in the New York Times concerning the inadequate care of IMRT radiation patients in the hospitals in the United States.

http://topics.nytimes.com/top/news/us/series/radiation_boom/index.htm l?8qa

These articles prompted the US Congress to mandate that the VA Office of Inspector General (OIG) make on-site inspections of over 30 VA Hospital radiation oncology departments. Inspections began in 2010. The inspections were to verify the training of physicians in the highly complex planning and treatment of IMRT. In the case of the Long Beach VA Hospital, the OIG reports of the inspections of September and November 2010 never addressed the issues of lack of certification of physicians and lack of oversight by hospital administrators. You can read the full text of the OIG report of the Long Beach VA Hospital at:

http://www.va.gov/oig/54/reports/VAOIG-10-03861-119.pdf
Reports for all VA hospitals are available to the public at http://www.va.gov/oig/publications

Reports from all OIG inspections can be found at http://www.va.gov Scroll to the bottom of the page and enter any VA hospital name. On the bottom right of the page you will see the words "Inspector General" where you can click on that link.

Type in the name of your hospital into the search field at the top right of the page and you will see many articles of which you should be aware.

Below is information about an IMRT radiation therapy which you and your family should be familiar before being treated.

IMRT is a highly specialized form of radiation treatment which requires the utmost in knowledge, skill and understanding by the radiation oncologists and therapists. The oncologist (the physician) must have the ability to identify the tumor volume as well as healthy tissue adjacent to the tumor volume.

The treatment planning computer used by radiation oncologist and physicist can only calculate the treatment according to the skill level of the radiation oncologist, who must outline the anatomy of the tumor to designate the amount of radiation each bit of organ/tissue is supposed to receive. Radiation therapists, who deliver the treatment, must be extremely accurate in the setup and follow standards and requirements for treating each type of cancer.

If all the tasks are not performed correctly and accurately, each treatment (the dosage directed to the tumor) could be received by the wrong organ (rectum instead of the bladder, for example) and the treatment could give wrong dosage to the wrong body-part.

If you have been prescribed the correct dosage of radiation for your tumor, but the critical aspects are not performed with precision, side effects can be worse than old style radiation. IMRT allows a higher dosage to the tumor while sparing healthy tissue. In other words, there should be fewer side effects than endured by patients than patients long ago. If the procedures are not accurate, you will endure more side effects.

American College of Radiology:

Guidelines Reference

Every radiation oncology department in the VA Healthcare system was directed to be accredited by the American College of Radiology (ACR) for the Specialty of Radiation Oncology. These VA Departments must adhere to these guidelines to maintain their accreditation. Look for or ask to see the Certificate of Accreditation from ACR in your Radiation Oncology Department.

About the Informed Consent

Informed consent is a process and not the simple act of signing a formal document.

If a significantly prolonged time interval has passed, or if a significant change in the treatment has occurred, such as need for treatment of a different part of the body that was not a part of the treatment discussed at the time the original informed consent was obtained, the process should be repeated, and informed consent again obtained, and a new form signed.

Specifications within the Informed Consent

Diagnosis and known extent of the disease.

Type of proposed treatment, parts of the body to be treated, method of treatment to be given.

Complications or side effects of radiation treatment to the area being treated and considered "common" and likely to occur.

Complications or side effects of radiation treatment to the area being treated and may be RARE but serious. A reasonable patient would want to know about them before deciding to be treated since they occur with frequency. Doubts of the likelihood of experiencing a side effect or complication may be stated as appropriate.

Treatment Alternatives

Determine possible benefits of treatment and potential consequences of not receiving treatment.

For external beam radiation treatments, obtain permission for tattoos and photographs for setup and treatment fields if appropriate.

Research Studies

Two consents are to be signed: (1) The standard facility informed consent, and (2) A "study specific" informed consent.

The consent should include the Radiation Oncologist's name and signature, Radiation Oncology Resident's name and signature, patient's signature and witness's signature. Ask for a copy of the informed consent after form is completed.

Inherent to Quality Patient Care

The patient should have a clearly defined goal of treatment stated.

Anticipated interactions of combined treatments of radiation therapy with surgery, chemotherapy or other systemic therapies should be discussed with the patient prior to initiation of treatment.

The Radiation Oncologist should see each patient at least weekly (or as needed) and documents the evaluation.

Radiation oncologist are trained to: (1) Identify acute, sub-acute, late complications and side effects of the radiation treatments; (2) Notice effects of combined treatments (i.e. radiation and chemotherapy); (3) Notice recurrent disease detection and recommendations of diagnostic tests; (4) Recommend additional treatment strategies.

To avoid serious problems later, complications and side effects should be detected and treated early. If the radiation oncologist will not be seeing the patient during follow-up appointments, periodic updates on the patient's progress should be requested from the referring physician to ensure continuity of care.

This information was compiled from and can be read in its entirety at:

http://www.acr.org/~/media/ACR/Documents/PGTS/guidelines/Informed

_Consent_Rad_Onc.pdf

http://www.acr.org/~/media/ACR/Documents/PGTS/guidelines/Comm_R adiation_Oncology.pdf

http://www.acr.org/~/media/ACR/Documents/PGTS/guidelines/Radiation

_Oncology.pdf

Additional information on Standards and Guidelines from the American College of Radiology for Radiation Oncology can be found at:

http://www.acr.org/Quality-Safety/Standards-Guidelines/Practice-Guidelines-by-Modality/Radiation-Oncology

Index of Individuals:

Name and Position
Long Beach (CA) VA Hospital

Lana Miller Boyer- Chief Radiation Therapist

Dr. Azawi- Chief of Radiation Oncology

Dr. Williams- Assistant Chief of Radiation Oncology

Gail Francis- Radiation Therapist

Doug Hollins- Radiation Therapist

Lucinda (Cindy)Swan- Business Manager-Radiation

Dr. Sandor Szabo- Chief of Staff

Mary Beth McCartan- Director, Human Resources

Herb Moisa- Assistant Director, Human Resources

Isabel Duff- Director, Long Beach VA Hospital

Ronald Norby- Former Director, VISN Director

Donna Pikulsky- Head Nurse

Dr. Chun- Staff Physician

Dr. Tehranzadeh- Staff Physician

Mimi Mangohig- Front desk secretary

Steve Mills- Radiation Safety Officer

Lynette Fox- Chief Safety Officer

Dr. Hwan Park- Contract Physicist

George Dolla- Staff Dosimetrist

Dennis Aquinaga- Staff Radiation Therapist

Dave Fellion- Contract Radiation Therapist

Dr. Eric Frank- Contract Physicist

Rachel Alcocer- Fact Finder: Azawi attack on Dennis Aquinaga, June 10, 2008.

Esther Pittman- Employee Specialist

Michelle Kelsey Plummer- Fact Finder appointed 1/21/11 by Mary Beth McCartan

Dr. Schuldheis- Formal Grievance Report examiner

Steve Mills- Radiation Safety Officer

Joe Morse, Chief of Bio Med

Susan DeMasters, Manager of EEO/ADR, Long Beach, VA

Mina Behdad- Research assistant

Michon Dean- Administration Officer

Michael Conconi- Lab Manager

Leo Moons- Education Safety Coordinator

Charles Feistman- former Chief Financial Officer

Dr. Schiffner- Resident physician, approached by Azawi to obtain counterfeit IMRT certificate (radiation therapy)

Varian
Geraldina (Geraldine) Lauzon- R.T, Software Technical Support

VA Radiation Oncology Headquarters
Dr. Michael Hagan-Chief Radiation Oncologist VA

Wendy Kemp- Assistant to Dr. Michael Hagan

Chief Radiation Therapists
Patti Hall- Chief Radiation Therapist, Tampa VA

Jenni Inemer- Chief Radiation Therapist, Philadelphia

Robert Williams- the Chief Radiation Therapist- St. Louis, MO.

VA Office of Inspector General investigators
Mary Toy- OIG investigator, Los Angeles

Kathi Shimoda- OIG investigator

Douglas Henao- OIG investigator

Office of Special Counsel
Vivian Wells- Investigator

Bruce Fong- Investigator, Field Office Chief

Medical and Psychiatric Consultant
Suzie E. Schuder, MD- Newport Beach, CA

NY Times Reporters
Walt Bogdanich

Kristina Rebelo

J.B. Simms

Chapter One:

Intensity Modulated Radiation Therapy

Radiation Therapy, or Radiation Oncology, is one of the common methods used for treating cancer and some non-cancerous diseases, using very high energy, man- made radiation. The treatment is implemented using a treatment machine referred to as a linear accelerator. The procedure of IMRT (Intensity Modulated Radiation Therapy) is used to administer exact dosages of radiation to a more specific and more exact areas; beams of radiation conform to the shape of a tumor.

After a patient has consulted with the physician, the patient will be scheduled for the "simulation" phase, which involves placing the patient into the correct position, as if for a treatment of radiation. The patient needs to lie very still during the simulation as well as the treatment. Devices, some referred to as "chocks" are used keep the patient stationary. A CT or "CAT" scan (computerized axial tomography) will be performed after the patient is stationary during simulation.

Before the CT scan, marks, called temporary "tattoos," are drawn on the patient's skin to identify the center of the treatment area. The tattoos are used by the Radiation Therapist to aid in alignment for the treatment phase. All alignment information is documented in the chart for treatment. The physician (Radiation Oncologist) designates the treatment area, adjacent organs and structures, minimal margins of error (approximately .05-.07 centimeters), and the appropriate radiation dosage to be delivered to those specific areas noted on the CT scan.

Physics and dosimetry (study of dosage) personnel create the treatment fields and dosages, and the report is forwarded for the approval of the Radiation Oncologist; the doctor in charge.

Radiation should deliver a high enough dosage to kill different types of cancer. Not all cancers respond to radiation. Melanoma is resistant to radiation as well as nerve and muscle tumors.

Lymphomas, testicular, and benign pituitary cancers are treated with a lower dosage. If a high dosage is delivered to the tumor with a larger than needed area around it, the healthy tissue will be unnecessarily injured.

A physician prescribes a dosage and placement of the dosage.

Radiation Therapists deliver radiation treatments with a linear accelerator on a daily basis. If the patient were given the whole dosage in one day, it would probably kill the patient depending upon the treatment site. Given a small amount each day, the dosage becomes therapeutic.

The treatments must be reproduced precisely as planned; if not, this could cause the tumor and surrounding healthy tissue to receive a variance of dosage, which would create the potential of unnecessary or uncommon side effects and potential recurrence of the tumor. A physician could create a perfect plan, but if the plan is not delivered accurately by the Radiation Therapist, there will be problems, and harm to the patient.

Radiation Oncologists (doctors) are trained in the medical aspect of cancer treatment. Radiation Therapists are trained in the technical aspect of initial treatment position (simulation) and daily treatment delivery. Accuracy and replication of setup is paramount since measurements are in millimeters. The specialty of being a radiation therapist is based upon accuracy, attention to detail, honesty, judgment, and double checking. It also involves monitoring the treatment at the computer console when radiation is delivered as well as watching the patient on closed circuit TV while the patient is in the treatment room, adjacent to the room where the computer console is located.

The "treatment room" is the room where the patient receives the radiation.

The technicians administer the radiation from a glassed-in area where they observe the patient, but the technicians are not in close proximity to the patient. These are two distinct areas, separated by glass.

The therapists are supposed to position the patient, so the radiation is directed to the exact area as was determined during the simulation.

The "gantry" which is the mechanical device that circumvents the treatment table, or simply goes around the table like a construction boom, has to "clear" the table (not bump into the table or anything around the treatment table).

The gantry must have enough clearance to enable the radiation machine, which is named for the manufacturer (Varian), to deliver the radiation to a specific location.

Checking the clearance is performed before the radiation dosage is administered so the therapists know the gantry will travel around the table and deliver the dosage and be unobstructed.

Any number of dangers can occur while the patient is in the treatment room. The IMRT movement of "leaves" pulsing radiation can stick, causing dosage to be delivered in one concentrated spot instead of spreading across the organ being treated. The patient can become sick while a "mask" is secured, protecting unintended body parts from being radiated. At any point, one of the radiation therapists might need to run into the treatment room, from the control room, to "free" the patient to prevent further harm or stop the beam if the IMRT malfunctions. If the therapist leaves the control room, and makes any adjustment, this must be noted for future treatments and to examine the possibility of error.

A radiation therapist must be honest. If an error is committed by a therapist, such as failure to include a treatment device or a field of treatment being not delivered properly, the therapist must notify the physicist and the Radiation Oncologist. Often an error in dosage can be corrected if the error in treatment is admitted by the therapist. Integrity will protect the patient. Mistakes happen, therapist and doctors are human, but lies and cover-ups can kill a patient.

The doctor is the only person who can comment on the treatment or consult with the patient, not the therapists. If mistakes are made, and the doctor chooses not to tell the patient, the patient will never know his therapy was compromised, unless the "injured" patient receives results of test which reveal collateral damage, and since the patient cannot understand the reports, the patient is kept in the dark; knowing only what he was told.

J.B. Simms

Chapter Two:

Sources of Evidence of Abuse and Corruption

Soon after I met Lana, we arranged for me to pick up some reading material one afternoon in the parking lot of her psychiatrist, Suzie Schuder. When Lana arrived, she called me over to the back of her car. When she opened the trunk, I saw huge notebooks; she gave me at least five large three ringed binders which were stacked the trunk of her car. I put the binders in my car; they were heavier than I expected.

When I got home, I brought in the binders and spread them out on a huge dining table. I began looking through the binders and realized that the binders were full of letters, emails, and documents; the dated material was in chronological order and neatly organized. (I wish I could have had someone having Lana's organizational skills work for me during my PI years.) The contents of the binders dated from the beginning of 2008 through mid-2011. These emails were from Lana to Dr. Azawi, Mary Beth McCartan (HR), Office of Special Counsel, Office of Inspector General, American College of Radiology, and other employees and agencies who were aware of the uncertified physicians working at the Long Beach VA, the harm these doctors were causing the Veterans, and the cover-up.

These emails were shocking. The entire story was shocking. I did not know whether my anger for what happened to Lana caused me more anxiety than the fact that the physicians were causing harm to patients, who were Veterans. I was also incensed that the physicians covered up the story, and that persons in power protected their professional positions by the most unscrupulous means necessary.

I had the communication between persons which gave me context of time and direct quotes. I contacted Lana for a bit of explanation.

The emails mostly wrote the story themselves.

Within a few months, and after digesting the emails, making copies and notes, it became necessary for me to meet some of the persons who had been named by Lana in the emails, and who would give me their insight. These persons agreed to meet in a private, secret location. Lana called me late in the afternoon to advise me the location of the meeting.

Thursday, October 3, 2012

Lana called and told me that the meeting was going to take place in Long Beach, CA in a banquet room in the back of an Asian restaurant. I got there early and met a few people who had arrived before me. A few were seated at a large table in the banquet room; some were milling around talking to each other. I met more people as they trickled in. Lana was there when I arrived. When it appeared everyone was present, we sat around the and large table and people began telling their stories as I began taking notes. Persons from different departments in the hospital attended, and all of those who attended had something to say. They all knew the situation with the physicians in Radiology, and it was made clear that the corruption among the powers-that-be involved many people, which meant many secrets, in different areas.

There were at least eight people present. Some of the people were Veteran volunteers at the hospital and were aware of the day to day matters. Many were Vietnam War Veterans. Others had worked at the VA Long Beach for periods of time from a few years to upwards of over two decades. One of the volunteers was a medic in Vietnam and was highly decorated. People were brought to tears about the abuse to the Veterans and screamed at the same time about the civilians in charge who were stealing money. As with most large companies, the corrupt persons underestimate the "great unwashed."

All the persons present were supportive of Lana's effort to expose the rogue doctors and save the Veterans. All the persons admired Lana's courage, and expressed it openly during the meeting.

One person, who had worked at the Long Beach VA for over twenty-five years, asked me to sign a paper, indicating that I would never use their name as a participant of the meeting. This person was not only scared that they would lose their job, but they were scared they would be physically harmed.

J.B. Simms

The following is an outline of the information I obtained from the persons at the meeting:

The Long Beach VA hospital is part of a region or VISN (Veterans Integrated Service Network) – specifically VISN 22. The other VA hospitals in VISN 22 (Desert Healthcare System) are Las Vegas, Loma Linda, Greater Los Angeles and San Diego. The VISN 22 offices are in Long Beach (formerly at the VA hospital). The VISN office was moved from the VA hospital in Long Beach to a remote location. The Director (since around May 2011) of VISN 22 was Stan Johnson (formerly Director of the San Diego VA).

Ron Norby was Director of Long Beach VA Hospital when Lana was hired in 2007 and was shortly promoted to Director of VISN 22 in the spring of 2008.

As Director of Long Beach VA, Norby brought in several new administration employees and put them into positions which had not been posted as "available" as required by Human Resources policies - cronyism. Norby worked with HR to have his friends put into jobs. Favors bred loyalty. Most of Norby's hand-picked employees were not qualified for the positions.

A young man was referred by Norby to work in HR. This young man had no experience in Human Resources. It was learned that the young man used a home address which was the same as the home address for Ronald Norby. Norby had ended a romantic relationship with a male friend in favor of the younger man, and put this younger man into a job in HR.

One of the new employees was Isabel Duff, who was hired as a Nurse Executive from a facility in AZ and was now the director of the Long Beach VA Hospital.

When Norby transferred to the VISN 22 office, Duff was placed as Acting Director by Norby. Duff was promoted to Director of the Long Beach VA Hospital without anyone knowing that the opening for the position had been posted to allow for HR to make the decision of appointment. Duff had not obtained the designation of an SES (Senior Executive Service) when Norby made Duff the Director. The SES designation was said to be mandatory to have the Director job. Norby bypassed the regulation to secretly pave the way to have Duff in the Director position, with Norby as her supervisor. Duff owed Norby.

Because of Duff's inexperience, Norby ran the hospital through her.

There were also Associate Directors and Assistant Directors with no experience that Norby brought in. Hospital Administration kept getting bigger but accomplishing nothing.

Other key positions that would become involved in the corruption at the facility were:

Mary Beth McCartan- Chief of Human Resources (had insufficient experience for the job and not certified); McCartan was one of the primary persons involved in the cronyism and nepotism. She allowed and approved any person Norby wanted without question or regard to policies. McCartan's policy, encouraged by Isabel Duff, was to hire Duff's personal employee applicants, referred to as "slipping friends through" without proper procedures. Friends hiring friends created a tight web.

Most of Duff's referrals were for jobs that had not been published, which was in violation of the actual policy.

Herb Moisa-Assistant Chief of Human Resources, who came from Greater LA VA. The involvement of Herb Moisa in the hiring practices and other scandals was not clear. It was said that Moisa was marked to remove someone during one of the many scandals.

Chief of Staff, Dr. Sando Szabo- did not apply for the position like the other doctors who submitted applications and were interviewed; another Norby appointee.

Dr. Szabo was a pathologist and participated in research. He did not understand patient care. When Lana was hired, Szabo was the Chief of Staff, and he was also the Chief of one of the medicine groups, Diagnostic & Molecular Medicine (DMM) which encompassed the various types of Labs, Blood Bank, Pathology, Radiology, Nuclear Medicine and Radiation Oncology (Therapy). Many people saw this as a conflict of interest, because Szabo would be overseeing a medicine group which he was a member and controlled the money.

Another key employee was Charles Feistman, CFO. Feistman knew information concerning the finances of the VA hospital.

There are two "houses" on the campus; one for the Director of the hospital and another one for someone else. Norby had the "hospital" decorator redo both houses at great expense.

Not only did Norby decorate the houses, using VA money, but Norby also planned 2 new buildings which are now utilized. One is a 3-story outpatient building that also houses the Emergency Department and Outpatient Pharmacy on the first floor. The most recently completed building opened a few months ago houses the cafeteria, store, Human Resources, Education, large dividable meeting room and the Blind Rehab Center.

Approximately 2-3 years before, Norby wanted the VISN offices moved from the VA Long Beach hospital grounds, to the beach. Norby wanted to be near the beach.

One major hurdle was running a secure internet line (necessary to protect the identification of the Veterans pursuant to the HIPAA laws and regular government internet security) from the hospital to the beach which could be overcome, but it would cost one million dollars to install.

Charles Feistman, CFO, had documents detailing Norby's questionable financial dealings. Feistman reported the fact the Norby was trying to move the office and incur a million-dollar expense. It was believed Feistman reported this to the OIG attached to the VA; this became Feistman's undoing.

It was said that Norby found out about what Feistman was doing, and that the OIG had been notified of Norby's activity. Norby fired Feistman for using the "F" word on a conference call, but Norby knew the OIG was breathing down his neck.

The Office of the Inspector General for the VA arrived to do a less than thorough (called a "white-wash) investigation of the misdeeds reported by Feistman. (Later in the book you will see the lack of credibility of the OIG during other "investigations" detailing their work.)

In the summer of 2009 or 2010, Norby left as Director of VISN 22, under the guise of being offered a much better job in Orange County (CA).

J.B. Simms

The investigation continued, and it was anticipated that Duff, McCartan & Moisa would be fired for their part in the continuing soap opera and being part of the Norby connection. After 2 different departure deadlines passed, it was discovered all three would be staying. Norby bargained their freedom by saying he ordered them to do all the wrongs they committed. Norby was leaving the VA system; it did not matter to him. Norby fell on his sword to save the jobs of the persons he hired, and who knew of or participated in corrupt behavior.

While in a Supervisor's meeting with Dr. Szabo, he told "us" that Mary Beth McCartan had confessed to Duff that she had altered many records in Human Resources for protection of herself and others. Performance bonuses were being paid to persons who did not merit the payment. Cronyism with a supervisor was the best way to get a bonus in the tens of thousands of dollars. McCartan had to approve the bonuses and turned a blind eye to the validity of the merit payment submission.

The plans for the two buildings had been supposedly drawn up 5 years prior to construction. No one bothered to see if the plans were still appropriate prior to proceeding.

After one building was completed, but not occupied, offices had to be re-designed at physicians' requests and different furniture acquired for re-design.

Maintenance had changed fixtures in the hospital to one brand for ease of repair and inventory control. The new building had specs for different brands.

When moving into the new building was to begin, someone suddenly realized there was no fire sprinkling system installed.

They also forgot to draw a covered or enclosed passageway from the new building to the main building. They managed to create one later.

As is typical, the people who should be involved in a construction project (engineering, maintenance, electrical, HVAC, IT and BioMed) were never consulted about the building plans prior to construction start.

J.B. Simms

The person in charge of making sure the construction was performed and completed properly was Amy Cantor. Her claim to fame prior to this assignment was totally disorganizing the Radiology department as the Administrative Officer, followed by destroying operations in SPD commonly known as Central Supply at other hospitals. After being confronted with her deeds, it was told that she lunged over a table to attack someone at a meeting.

After those stellar performances she was promoted to work in Administration under one of the hand-picked Associate/Assistant Directors, Tony "D", who temporarily moved to the VISN office because Cantor had a fight with him.

Because of her "continued excellent employment history," Cantor is now one of the many Associate/Assistant Directors and hangs out in Duff's office.

The first building cost $1.5 - $2 Million more because of all the messes and unnecessary "improvements.";50 new computers were ordered. IT recently said they had to order 150 – 200 more because of poor planning.

The second new building had a few problems. The large meeting room, which was supposed to have built-in dividers, did not have the dividers, so an alternate plan had to be devised. Cantor was responsible for this building as well.

Then there was the paper towel dispenser escapade; someone ordered electronic hand towel dispensers (100) but someone did not like the model so the brand-new dispensers, still in boxes, were thrown in the dumpster. New ones were ordered.

About a year ago Dr. Szabo, (October 2011), Chief of Staff and Chief of DMM (Molecular Medicine), was told he had to give up one position because of the conflict of interest. He chose Chief of Staff for a year, then become Chief of DMM again. DMM was dismantled so the only position he could have would be Lead Pathologist. For some reason the VISN 22 decided to only have one Chief of Service and the other locations would have Lead Pathologists. The Chief of Pathology was in San Diego.

Szabo was getting close to 10 years as Chief of Staff which would give him a full year off paid vacation.

In December 2011 the Chief of Staff position was posted. Due to an EEO complaint of sexual harassment (now possibly sexual assault) against Szabo by another pathologist, Szabo was gone. The story was that he was on Permanent Annual Leave. Szabo was eventually given a title and an office away from the VA Long Beach hospital.

An investigation regarding misappropriation of DMM funds being used for Szabo's research projects began. Equipment and expenses were funneled to research projects far away from the VA Long Beach hospital to Hungary. Employees were being called in for questioning on the topic. At that point it was revealed the investigation would encompass additional events that would make the misappropriation issue small.

The Lab Manager who retired 4 years before, Ken "W", aided Szabo in improper dealings. "W" also tried to enlist the help of a newly transferred Chief Therapist in Radiology to become a participant in the wrongdoings. The Radiology Chief Tech refused. This Chief of Radiology was not Azawi. "W" was regularly rewarded by Szabo for aiding in the tasks. It was reported that Windle had received a $40,000 bonus using Szabo's recommendation. He had worked at the VA for 40 something years prior to retirement.

Approximately a year ago, Dr. Moran had informed Director Duff that Szabo was playing with research money. Nothing happened.

Was it any wonder why Gail Francis kept her job, and Azawi, was not afraid of Szabo? Everyone had the goods on other people; it was incestuous leverage.

An employee in the Education Department was looking at job openings listed for Long Beach. She saw her boss's job advertised. Dr. Herron was a psychiatrist who is ACOS in the Education department. The employee took the printout to Herron and asked if she were leaving. Dr. Herron said no.

Herron went immediately to Duff's office to find out why she was vacating her position. Duff told Herron she thought Herron would enjoy working as a psychiatrist more. Herron asked Duff which one of Duff's friends was being put in her position. Duff said it was none of her business.

J.B. Simms

The Acting Chief of Staff, Dr. Offstein, was the person who was removing Dr. Herron, so his "Partner" would be protected when Joint Commission came for their regular site survey.

Dr. Offstein's boyfriend is the Chief of CLC (Nursing Home). That is a terrible mess and has been investigated numerous times by the OIG, but nothing got fixed, so problems with patients there abound with regular "epidemics" of C-Difficile and scabies.

Patients seldom have clean scrubs to wear and some are so disheveled and uncared for they look like they are homeless instead in a facility that is supposed to tend to their personal hygiene. Some patients are filthy with layers of dirt on their necks, chests and arms that water and soap have not touched in a very long time. These Veterans would have to be soaked then be scrubbed so the layers of dirt and dead skin can be removed. There was no respect for Veterans.

Nancy Downey, Chief of Quality Management & Utilization Review, needed someone to manage Utilization Review. Her friend, who was the Nurse Practitioner in Employee Health, wanted out of that department because of the supervisor. Downey got her friend out of the Employee Health area and into the job to manage Utilization Review.

Downey's put her friend into the position, but the friend nothing about Utilization Review and certainly did not know that reports had to be given in person to Isabel Duff.

After attempting to give information to Duff and realizing she did not even understand what Duff was asking, she tried to get someone else in Utilization Review to give the reports in the future.

Prior to the above event, Duff was trying to "run off" Downey. Downey was isolated, ignored and marginalized to make her quit. Downey did not quit.

Human Resources attempted to avoid law suits by using, "the preferred method of dismissing someone who had committed no wrong; making their lives absolutely miserable, so they will quit." This was referred to as Constructive Dismissal. That was a creative term for "Wrongful Termination."

One person at the meeting called the VA Hospital a pit of vipers.

J.B. Simms

Chapter Three:

The Varian Incident

June 18, 2009 is a date Lana Boyer will never forget. The morning began as all do at the VA Hospital in Long Beach, California; Veterans were arriving at the VA hospital, some were going to receive radiation treatment. "June Gloom" meets the persons arriving, which is the name of the overcast atmospheric condition during spring, resulting from the dense, cool, morning fog rolling in off the Pacific Ocean.

On this morning, Lana arrived at the Long Beach Veterans Hospital, early as usual. Lana had been the Chief Radiation Therapist in the Radiology Department for the past year and a half; her job was to monitor and train (or correct) the persons who administer radiation treatment for cancer patients. Lana was trained and proficient in IMRT (Intensity Modulated Radiation Therapy.) The therapists supposedly had been trained in the discipline, but their job performance was to be scrutinized by Lana.

The job of Chief Radiation Therapist was to ensure that accurate radiation treatments were delivered to the patient. As stated in the previous chapter, The Chief (Lana)was comparing the CT scan conducted during "simulation" to the x-rays taken during the treatment. These are two separate procedures; the "simulation" established the benchmark with respect to establishing the position of the patient needed to deliver the effective radiation treatment.

Simulation and treatment films must match. The variance allowed is measured in millimeters, and most allowable variance would be 3 millimeters; sometime less. Radiation beamed to an unaffected area would damage a healthy organ and could burn the skin.

At 9:30am, Lana was seated at her desk, reviewing the previous day's CT and x-ray comparison of a patient's treatment and simulation.

As the Chief Radiation Therapist, part of her responsibility was to make certain the therapists were doing their jobs correctly, which involved reviewing treatment data.

Lana was comparing the x-rays (taken during a treatment of radiation) to the simulation film (which is done prior to the treatment). Both treatment films were supposed to match when laid one over the other. The patient was to receive three treatments of radiation. As Lana examined the film before her this morning, she determined that there had been a change in the treatment fields during the last two treatments; the films did not match. There was no explanation or notation in the file for this discrepancy.

Lana's experience told her that the treatment table must have been moved at least 3.0 centimeters, which is over an inch and a half during the treatment. (Remember, there are 2.54 centimeters in an inch.)

The patient had been treated with radiation in the wrong area.

No one said anything to Lana about this discrepancy until she read the charts. The therapists, Gail Francis and Doug Hollins, never came to Lana, who was their supervisor, to tell her there was a problem during treatment on the previous day, or that one of them moved the treatment table. Lana knew she had to confront the therapists because patients/Veterans could have been receiving incorrect treatment.

Lana contacted Gail and Doug, asking them to come to her office. Lana showed them the film, and pointed out that the two films did not match on two of the three treatments. Lana told them that the only way for there to be a discrepancy would be if one or both of them entered the area where the patient was being treated, and moved the table.

Neither admitted that either of them entered the treatment room while the patient was on the table. Gail Francis was quite a bit more vocal in her denial.

Lana was furious that the therapists must have moved the table, and lied. Lana knew better. Lana thought, "How could these therapists cover for each other and make a patient endure radiation treatment to an area which was not to be treated? These therapists had better be fearful for their jobs."

Errors did occur from time to time but admitting the treatment delivery errors usually allowed for a radiation dose correction.

Lana knew that Dr. Azawi, the head of the radiation oncology department, needed to know about this immediately. Lana grabbed up the file, including the two conflicting films, and went looking for Dr. Azawi. Reporting anything to Dr. Azawi was always an adventure because Lana never knew what kind of response or attitude she would receive from Dr. Azawi. Lana was not one of Azawi's favorite people. Many others in the Radiology Department had a history with Azawi, and it was not good. Lana was hoping that her own experience would convince Dr. Azawi that the therapists had lied to Lana, and Lana would be able to show Dr. Azawi that the therapists were caught lying. Lana became employed by the VA Health Care System on December 31, 2007 as the Supervisory Radiologic Therapeutic Technologist (Chief Radiation Therapist) in the Department of Radiology. Lana reported directly to Samar Azawi, MD, Chief Radiation Therapy, Diagnostic and Molecular Medicine Healthcare Group (DMM, HCG).

Lana's credentials were without question; Azawi's credentials were questionable. Azawi began her medical training in Iraq, moving to California after initial training in medicine. Lana was certified in IMRT technology; Azawi was not, and Azawi depended upon others to explain treatment results.

As the Chief Radiation Therapist, Lana oversaw all aspects of the performance of each therapist, as well as attendance, leave, pay, and performance appraisals. The therapists were too low on the food chain for doctors to have a social or professional relationship with a therapist.

Azawi was working at the Long Beach VA Hospital in December 2007 when Lana began working in the department. Azawi was the Chief Radiation Oncologist at the Long Beach VA Hospital. The Department of Veteran Affairs, located in Washington, DC, mandated that all radiation departments in the VA Healthcare System obtain accreditation by the American College of Radiology. Only two VA hospital radiation departments were not accredited; Long Beach (CA) VA and Puerto Rico VA Hospital.

On January 25, 2008, less than a month after Lana's arrival, Azawi, in her capacity as the Chief Oncologist at the Long Beach VA Hospital, submitted an application to the American College of Radiology for the hospital to become certified.

The process for submitting the application had begun months before. The application for accreditation was denied. That put Azawi under scrutiny, and she deflected the blame for the denial of accreditation to others.

Azawi was the type of person who considered herself blameless. She was an attacker if she were ever faced with accountability. It did not take long for Azawi to try to exert her authority and intimidation upon Lana and others which resulted in the immediate dismissal of a contract physicist who dared report Azawi for unprofessional behavior.

At the end of March 2008, approximately 4 months after Lana was hired, Azawi exposed her true self to Lana; Azawi accused Lana of refusing to simulate a patient with Dr. Venita Williams, resident physician, although Dr. Azawi had left it to the discretion of Dr. Williams and Lana. Azawi then attempted to have Lana fired for "refusing" her direct instruction by escalating the termination demand to the Chief of Staff, Dr. Szabo. Dr. Venitia Williams truthfully defended Lana to Dr. Szabo.

Azawi and Donna Pikulsky (head nurse) tried to drive a wedge between Lana and Lucinda (Cindy) Swan (Business Manager), by instructing Lana not to speak with Cindy. Cindy had been working at this VA hospital for decades, and knew more about the place than Azawi. It was clear that Azawi and Pikulsky had bonded, and were adversaries of Cindy Swan.

During the next month, Lana had to report the following things to Azawi: (1) a patient threatened to go to Consumer Affairs concerning his treatment in the department, (2) an incident occurred with respect to therapists "switching radiation fields" inappropriately, and (3) there was a backlog of patient files which had not been reviewed by the doctors. The backlog of files to be reviewed evidenced by the stack of patient files on the credenza behind Azawi's chair.

The most shocking revelation was on April 17, 2008, when Azawi sent an email to Lana, stating that Azawi:

"...wants [an] incident report written for 3rd time so someone without RT training can understand."

The person having no RT training was Azawi, herself.

It became apparent to Lana that Azawi did not know how to read the charts, x-rays, or CT scans with respect to the radiation treatment being given or understand the basic technical aspects of treatment delivery to the Veterans.

The hostile working conditions were affecting patient care.

On May 28, 2008, Lana sent an email to Cindy Swan and to Dr. Szabo, the Chief of Staff. Lana described the behavior of Azawi, the lack of knowledge, and lack of patient care. Szabo replied, *"Things will change."* Lana hoped.

Azawi's tirades became so disruptive and abusive that, within a week, a group of four, including therapists, and scientists, took a two-inch folder of disruptive incidents to Azawi's boss, Dr. Szabo:

Dr. Hwan Park- Contract Physicist
George Dolla- Staff Dosimetrist
Dennis Aquinaga- Staff Radiation
Therapist Dave Fellion- Contract Radiation Therapist

A folder which was at least two inches thick was given to Dr. Szabo. Inside the folder was incidents of abuse, and references to lack of professional knowledge on the part of Azawi. The four told Szabo that Azawi was destroying the reputation of the department, and endangering patients through her incompetence. These people independently confirmed to the chief of staff that Azawi was a danger to the hospital and to the patients.

After the "Szabo meeting,", all four employees left Szabo's office. The employees returned to the department following the meeting, Dr. Azawi was "lying in wait".

Azawi had been informed by Pikulsky that the employees had been seen going into the office of Dr. Szabo. Azawi approached Dennis Aquinaga and asked Dennis to come with her into her office. Lana waited.

When Dennis emerged, he appeared to be rattled, eyes red and watery, and he told Lana that Azawi yelled at him for meeting with Szabo.

After the meeting, Szabo obtained the blessing of the hospital director, Isabel Duff, and Ms. Duff demoted Azawi, pending an investigation, giving her Chief job to Dr. Williams on June 6, 2008. Dr. Richard Williams worked as second in command to Azawi. Azawi was no longer in charge of the department.

Lana fired off an email telling Szabo what Azawi had done to Dennis, who worked for Lana.

Szabo replied by thanking Lana. Lana copied Human Resources, and the head of HR, Mary Beth McCartan, on the email sent to Szabo. Lana was going to defend her people. Azawi had no right to pull Dennis into her office and intimidate him for meeting with Szabo without talking to Lana first.

As second in command, Azawi exerted power. The first act of retribution was to transfer Dr. Park, who was one of the persons who met with Dr. Szabo.

Dennis Aquinaga filed a report with HR concerning Azawi's "meeting" with him and her attack after he and the others met with Szabo. Dennis was the least powerful person, and Azawi attacked him as the weakest of the herd. HR assigned a "Fact Finder" named Rachel Alcocer to look into the incident. Ms. Alcocer requested a formal ROC (Report of Contact) from Dennis.

The department was abuzz that someone stood up to Azawi. Within a week of the demotion, Dr. Szabo met again with Lana with respect to Azawi. Lana told Szabo that little had changed, and that Azawi "ran over" the head of the department, Dr. Williams at every turn.

A few months later, Lana reported to Dr. Szabo that things were better since Azawi' demotion and people got along well with Dr. Williams (a different Williams than the person who had defended Lana against Azawi). Szabo replied, *"...Dr. Williams likes you..."*

Donna Pikulsky continued to be an ally of Dr. Azawi. Three months after the demotion of Azawi, Dr. Williams asked Lana to create a form which would better allow the department to keep up with patients. Donna Pikulsky sent Lana an email, refused to use the form, and Dr. Williams declined to enforce compliance from Pikulsky.

Dr. Williams was nice but had no backbone; he was a follower, not a leader.

On January 12, 2009, an announcement was made by The American College of Radiology that reported the radiation oncology department at the Long Beach VA Hospital was non-compliant "again," and that the department would not be accredited. Williams and Azawi could not get the hospital radiation department accredited. The reasons were that the department was non-compliant with respect to forms, meetings, and reports.

Accreditation was denied on January 12, 2009, and the application submitted in January 2008 had also been denied.

Patient records, which could be seen stacked behind Azawi's chair, and not reviewed, was one of the reasons for failing accreditation. These patient records were to be reviewed by the doctors after the radiation treatment, recommendations were to be made for treatment and/or medication and returned to be filed. Azawi was not just lazy; she needed someone to read and explain the file to her.

On February 17, 2009, within 8 months of Azawi losing her position as head of the department, an email was sent out by Szabo to persons in the department: Azawi had been reinstated as Chief of Radiation Oncology. Szabo was the same person who demoted Azawi. This was very suspicious.

After receiving the email, Lana and Cindy Swan immediately met with Dr. Szabo. Szabo told Lana and Cindy that the two-inch complaint file against Azawi which had been delivered to Dr. Szabo by the group of four, had been lost by the Human Resources Department, headed by Mary Beth McCartan.

J.B. Simms

The person in HR who claimed the complaint file was lost was said to be Herb Moisa. Cindy warned Dr. Szabo that Azawi would be trying to get rid of Lana by making her life a living hell.

How could the Human Resources office of a Veteran's hospital lose a 2-inch file? What did Azawi do to pressure the hospital to return her to the position as Chief Radiation Oncologist?

Azawi immediately resumed the same unprofessional behavior in the radiation department, many times gleefully rendering employees to tears.

Azawi had regained her position, and immediately filed a discrimination against Dr. Szabo, stating that Dr. Szabo had made a disparaging remark concerning the fact that Azawi was from Iraq (and had attended 2 years of medical school in Iraq). Azawi was awarded $50,000 in damages and basically, the "keys to the city." Azawi was even more untouchable.

Lana hated to have to deal directly with Azawi, but Lana would defend the Veterans at any cost. Lana had to report any therapist who was not performing well.

Below is part of the email Lana sent to Dr. Azawi:

March 31, 2009

4:20 pm RE: Gail

Francis

...not prepared for simulation when patient arrives

...Gail Francis was to remain in simulation for competency

...Simulation takes too long- patient uncomfortable. Needing help from Dennis Aquinaga and Doug Hollins to complete.

...Boyer had to work one on one with Gail Francis: films, pictures, treatments, simulation and trend charts.

...Gail Francis not paying attention to simulation schedule to turn on bath water in time for simulation

...Gail Francis making multiple masks for the same patient.

Gail Frances would be cited again for an incident on April 27 in which a patient was exposed to unnecessary radiation.

Only a few months later, on April 9, 2009 the American College of Radiology (ACR) denied accreditation for the radiology department after the onsite survey in January 2009.

This was the third denial in 18 months:

January 2008

January 2009

April 2009

This history led up to Lana's arrival for work on the morning of June 18, 2009, and finding that the therapists, Francis and Hollins, had treated a patient at least 3.2 centimeters from the prescribed location.

Lana was the recipient of some of the Azawi tirades, so Lana knew that taking this treatment error performed by Francis and Hollins would be a crap shoot.

Lana walked into the office of Dr. Azawi, unannounced, and hoped for the best. Lana was armed with two reports; (1) copies of the CT scans from the simulation, and (2) the film from the treatment, to show Azawi that the patient was treated on the wrong part of the body and that the films did not match.

Dr. Azawi was not certified in IMRT, nor was she proficient in the operation or the procedure of using the Varian Clinax IX machine (Varian was the manufacturer of the treatment machine); Azawi had to depend upon Lana, and others to explain the procedure, and to read the comparison of the simulation and treatment scans. It was a problem having Azawi in charge of a radiation department because Azawi had limited knowledge of the procedure. The fact that Azawi continued to have her job, not being able to read the charts, was as puzzling an issue as the fact that Azawi regained her position within a year of her demotion. Azawi must have had tremendous leverage, and she did.

Lana showed the reports of conflicting scans to Azawi. After having to explain the nuances of the procedure of IMRT (Intensity Modulated Radiation Therapy) to Azawi, Dr. Azawi's response was, "good catch," which meant Lana had done a good job catching the falsification of the report by Francis and Hollins. If Lana had left the file for Azawi to interpret, Azawi would not have been able to find the falsified information.

Lana was validated. Lana had done her job. The job of the subordinate is to make the boss look good, and the boss will take the credit. We also know that if someone directs blame on the boss, the boss will direct the blame to a subordinate. Lana was about to realize this, first hand.

The evidence revealed that the table had been moved during the radiation procedure. The therapists were denying guilt. Lana was left with limited options, which she explained to Azawi. The first thing to do was to report possible malfunction to the Radiation Safety Officer (RSO), Steve Mills, and then to the vendor (IMRT machine), Varian.

Azawi directed Lana to notify them both, and to send out emails to the appropriate persons advising them that the machine would be on "shut down" until Varian could inspect the machine and file a report.

Azawi told Lana that if the investigation revealed there was no problem with the Varian machine, Azawi would leave it up to Lana to recommend the removal of Ms. Francis and Mr. Hollins as therapists. Lana told Azawi that before recommending the dismissal of the therapists, a conference would be conducted with a fellow Chief Radiation Therapist, employed at another hospital, for a second opinion. Azawi agreed, so Lana's next step would be to contact her friend, the Chief Radiation Therapist in Philadelphia, Jenni Inemer. This consultation was sanctioned by Azawi.

As Lana emerged from Azawi's office, Gail Francis, one of the therapists, charged into Azawi's office and closed the door loudly.

What was that all about? Why would a radiation therapist be doing going directly to the chief radiation oncologists' office in such a frantic manner? Gail knew she was in trouble, but how did Gail have the authority to enter the office of the doctor as she did?

Lana sent the "shut down" within moments of returning to her own office. She sent emails to the Chief of Staff, Dr. Szabo, who replied remotely from out of office, as did Dr. Tehranzadeh and Dr. Chun. Lana contacted the technicians from Varian, and was told the representatives would be arriving later in the day.

Dr. Azawi and Steve Mills agreed to take the IMRT machine out of operation until the full investigation had been completed by Varian, which could take as many as four days. This was very serious, expensive, and time consuming. Patients who had been scheduled for a long time would have to delay their treatment.

Lana knew the therapists were not being truthful. It was terrible that this patient received treatments in the wrong area. The cavalier attitude of the therapists and their lack of truthfulness was harming the patients.

Within the next few days, the Varian technicians arrived to check out the IMRT linear accelerator and determine if there was any malfunction of the machine. Lana was ready to consult with her fellow Chief of Radiation

Therapist in Philadelphia, and then contact Human Resources to have the therapists replaced. It all seemed simple; then, all hell broke loose, and the innocent became the victim.

The Varian team worked around the clock, from Thursday through the weekend, conducting tests on the Clinax IX to determine if any machine error could have occurred. The Varian group was not only technicians, they were scientists.

J.B. Simms

Chapter Four:

The Varian Cover-Up is Born

The "Varian Incident" as it was to be referred, became a turning point in the future of the Radiation Therapy department of the VA Hospital in Long Beach, California.

All scheduled radiation appointments had to be canceled as a result of the error found by Lana. It was decided that that the IMRT linear accelerator would not be used again until the Varian people conducted their investigation.

Veterans had been scheduled for radiation. Staff had to call the Veterans and delay radiation treatment. Those who had been receiving regular treatment would have to interrupt their treatment. This was a major issue.

Lana knew the result would show that the table had been moved by the therapists and the therapists lacked the integrity to admit what they did. Lana thought the therapists would be found out, fired, and new people brought in. How could these therapists do this to a person who offered their lives for our country, and with such indifference?

Varian engineers arrived on site by 3:30 pm of June 18, 2009 which was the same day Lana had found and reported the problem. More engineers showed up during a 2-day period from different parts of the United States, and overseas. Varian NTS are the top-level problem/technical people who travel to any location needed to fix or report big issues. Lana had worked with a Varian tech named Geraldina Lauzon (Lana had known her in Florida, and referred to her as Geraldine), which gave Lana some comfort.

Lana wanted to know what happened in the treatment room.

Lana told Geraldine that she thought it was a therapist who moved the table, but could not be sure until they checked everything. Geraldine told Lana that it sounded like human error, but Varian was going to check everything because it could be a machine malfunction.

Geraldine and some of the others worked through the weekend doing test scenarios.

On Friday, June 19, the Varian personnel took statements from Gail Francis and Doug Hollins. Neither admitted leaving the control area to go into the treatment room to move the table.

After Dr. Azawi saw the statements, she was heard telling Dr. Chun, a staff physician, that"...there was a misreading, not a mistreatment." An email was sent to Lana from Azawi attesting to this conversion with Dr. Chun. Was Azawi accusing Lana of misreading a radiation result, and misreading the films? Lana was the person who had to explain the films to Azawi.

The therapists moved the table; Lana was sure the Varian report would show that. The therapists were not smart enough to know that the test which was going to be run on the machine would prove whether it was machine malfunction or human error. This was a very complicated machine, the latest in technology, and the therapists had no idea what they would be facing.

When Azawi said there was no mistreatment, but instead a misreading of the film, Lana was shocked but not surprised. Why was Azawi now coming up with a theory to present to Varian? Lana was the person who read the charts, and Lana was the one who brought this to the attention of Azawi, Szabo (the Chief of Staff), and the Varian staff. The Varian staff knew that Lana did not misread the film.

Lana showed Geraldine the binder with the setup problems and images. These images were CT scans taken from the simulation and the film taken from the treatment area. This was simple enough for a layman to understand; the grid from the CT scan is "over-laid" over the grid made from the treatment film. The grids did not match. The radiation was transmitted to the wrong area.

Lana did not misread the film. Azawi was beginning to find a scapegoat, because it was more acceptable to misread data than mistreat a patient. This way, supposedly and deceitfully, no one was harmed. Why was Azawi making excuses for lowly therapists?

Geraldine was horrified. She then told Lana about her first day working at the National Cancer Institute when the doctor told her that the worst thing she could do is lie or not point out a mistake she had made. Lana asked Geraldine to "please" bring that up in the final meeting.

The weekend had passed. Varian people had been at the Long Beach VA Hospital during the entire weekend.

Upon arriving at work on the following Monday (June 22), Lana was given guidelines to submit to the American College of Radiation (ACR). Azawi was submitting proposed guidelines to the ACR in an attempt to be accredited during the time that a major challenge to the integrity of the Radiation Department was occurring. Azawi's reality was incomprehensible. The department had failed accreditation three times in eighteen months, the Varian technicians are in the department, and Azawi is giving Lana ACR guidelines for submission to attain certification? On what planet was Azawi living?

It was embarrassing that the Long Beach VA Hospital was the only VA Hospital in the country which was not accredited by the ACR. The only other VA Hospital not accredited was in Puerto Rico. This accreditation affected moneys paid to the VA from many sources, including insurance and social welfare and entitlement programs. Since the "Varian Incident" was taking center stage, the guidelines would have to wait to be completed.

Later in the morning, Lana came upon Dr. Azawi discussing the issue of firing the therapists with a nurse, Donna Pikulsky. This matter had nothing to do with Donna; it was an HR issue, and Azawi was in violation by talking to Donna about the therapists. It was also learned that Azawi also was discussing this issue with Mimi Mangohig, a secretary at the front desk.

Lana approached Dr. Azawi and requested that no one be privy to the matters involving the therapists. Azawi agreed, telling Lana that she (Lana) was more familiar with the RT's (radiation therapists) than anyone else, and that Lana was to make the decision about their future.

Geraldine called a meeting with Azawi, the therapists, other NTS people, and Lana. Geraldine showed everyone the preliminary report which revealed "operator error."

Varian officials were waiting on some additional computer logs from Switzerland. The Varian officials worked all weekend running tests on the equipment. They kept checking and reviewing the data.

Geraldine and Lana showed the short log to Doug and Gail, the therapists. The log showed that the table was moved 3.2cm (centimeters). Doug's response was "It never happened."

Doug was questioning the findings that either he or Gail moved the table the mysterious 3.2 centimeters.

Dr. Azawi appeared to not understand what the Varian officials were reporting at the meeting. Azawi either did not understand, or she understood but did not want to admit an error had been committed. Geraldine repeated at the meeting, in front of Azawi, what she had been told many years ago; that "the worst thing she could do is lie or not point out a mistake she had made." Azawi did not get it. Geraldine signed the Varian report.

After the meeting, late in the day, Dr. Tehranzadeh discussed the matter with Lana. Dr. Tehranzadeh told Lana that Azawi had assured him that the patient "did not receive radiation treatment" in the incident. Now Azawi is making up a story that the patient did not receive treatment when the Varian officials had stated the treatment was done incorrectly.

The Varian inspectors stated the patient had received radiation treatment. Azawi denied it. Azawi said there was no treatment (radiation) given to the patient; it was a misreading. But first, Azawi stated there was treatment given and the therapists could be fired. Which story does Azawi want people to believe?

Why would Azawi need to lie? If you find an incompetent employee, just fire them. The fact remained that Lana, as the Chief Radiation Therapist, was certified and an expert, and more conversant with the radiation technology than was Azawi. Lana was now a threat to Azawi. Instead of using Lana's skill and intelligence, Azawi planned to discredit and disgrace Lana.

The final Varian meeting was held on the morning of Tuesday, June 23. It was clear from Varian's report; "the therapists moved the table and did not recalibrate the linear accelerator.

Radiation treatment was given 3.2 centimeters from the point designated in the simulation." A physics report was submitted, and the radiation dose given to the patient was noted.

Azawi had two lies to cover; one that the incident was a misreading and not mistreatment, the other that there was no dosage of radiation given to the patient. Why would she cover for a technician? What power did the technician have over the Chief Radiation Oncologist?

Lana gave Azawi the oral recommendation of the removal of the two therapists. The written recommendation would follow.

Lana knew that a problem was brewing. Azawi had been seen discussing the personnel matter with Donna Pikulsky and Mimi Mangohig, which was not proper, and a violation of policy.

A troubling incident occurred later the same day, Tuesday, June 23. At 3:45pm, Lana received an email from Azawi in which Azawi stated she was amenable to replacing the Radiation Therapists, but she wanted to run it by Dr. Williams, who was the associate head of the oncology radiation department. (Dr. Williams was temporarily head of the department during the time Azawi was suspended from her position as head of the department.) Azawi further stated she would contact Human resources about Gail Francis, who was the staff therapist. The other therapist, Doug Hollins, was employed by a staffing agency, and his termination had to be handled through his agency.

Thirty-two minutes later, Lana received an email from Azawi which was time-stamped at 4:26pm, in which Azawi was not enthusiastic about firing the therapists. What happened?

<u>Wednesday, June 24, 2009</u>
Geraldine Lauzon left the Long Beach VA Hospital, as did the engineers from Varian. Lana and the doctors had a copy of the preliminary report, but Varian was to print out their official report in a few days. The Varian Incident report was sent to Dr. Azawi and Dr. Williams. There was no denying the mistreatment, but Azawi was denying it.

Below are portions of the Varian Report on three separate patients. Patient A was the one caught by Lana.

J.B. Simms

Varian Medical Systems, Inc.
2250 Newmarket Pky, Ste 120
Marietta, GA 30067
tel 817.483.5417
fax 603.372.4706
www.varian.com

To: Richard Williams M.D., Samar Azawi M.D., Lana Miller RTT
Facility: US Vetarans Administration Medical Center
5901 East 7th St.
Long Beach, CA 90822
800-826-8000

Cc: Les Guyse, Joe Denzel, Ferd Weinhammer, Ervin Pon, Trevor Guest, Bob Richardson, Ian Hudson, Sheila Greenwood, Tina Morin
From: Geraldina Lauzon,
Date: June 26, 2009

Problem: Unexplained shifts on 3 patient treatment records with possible mistreatment.

Problem Synopsis:

Customer found 3 patient records during QA reviewing that on first analysis showed probable mistreatment due to wrong couch shifts by the OBI application and/or Clinac IX. VA Long Beach Radiation Safety officer suspended the treatment of patients until Varian confirms that there was no mistreatment or software is corrected.

Root Cause:

Treatment methodology and patient positioning on the couch contributed to the ambiguity of the data in the records. No evidence that supports equipment or software malfunction was found.

Corrective action:

We assisted the customer by answering applications questions related to the investigation of the affected patient records and demonstrating scenarios that were supported by collected and analyzed data from images, patient records, equipment functionality and application logs as part of a collaborative effort investigation by Service, Applications Helpdesk, National Technical Support and Product Support Engineering Lab in Baden Switzerland. Filed an Adverse Event Report when applicable.

J.B. Simms

Report Details

Existing conditions:

Customer had suspended patient treatment until Varian confirmed that there was no mistreatment or software is corrected. 3 patients were reported to have problems and for the investigation are identified as Patient A, Patient B and Patient C for privacy purposes.

Software versions:
ARIA 8.5.11.7
OSP 1.3.4.0
Treatment Admin 8.3.0 SP12
OBI 1.4.13.0
Clinac 7.6
MLC 6.8

1. Patient A had a couch lateral shift of +3.2 cm between treatment fields 3 (FLD 3 LAO1) and 1 (FLD RPO 1) during treatment session 4 on June 17, 2009 at 2:20:47 pm. This discrepancy was identified by the customer while doing a QA review of patient records in RT Chart and Off Line Review.

   - Based on the analysis of gathered data and logs conducted by Help Desk, NTS and PSELab in Baden Switzerland the sequence of events are described below:
     1. 13:56:32 Patient selected from Queue: Plan 'IMRTw/bolus' (UID 1.2.246.352.71.5.1190465974.43783.20090602111443) loaded via TreatDeamon to 4D Treatment
     2. 14:07:35 1st kV image acquired
     3. 14:07:39 2D/2D Match button pressed in OBI
     4. 14:08:23 2nd kV image acquired
     5. 14:08:28 Analyze button pressed in OBI
     6. 14:14:18 Apply Shift button pressed in OBI
     7. 14:14:18 Couch shift Vrt -0.3cm, Lng -0.2cm, Lat +0.3cm, Rtn 0.0deg sent to Clinac (This confirms that Offline Review shows the online couch corrections correctly.)
     8. 14:14:33 Done button pressed in OBI
     9. 14:18:09 Patient closed in 4D Treatment. Log entry in Treatment log: ERROR,"The user dhollins signed off on closing a patient with radiation remaining."
     10. 14:18:15 Patient selected from Queue again: Plan 'IMRTw/bolus' (UID 1.2.246.352.71.5.1190465974.43783.20090602111443) loaded via TreatDeamon to 4D Treatment
     11. 14:19:02 Field 'FLD 5 LPO' treated, but with error in Treatment ERROR,"IXMLDOMParseError: Line 0, Char 0, file= "(null)" Description: Element content is invalid according to the DTD/Schema.
     12. 14:19:55 Field 'FLD 4 LAO2' treated, but with error in Treatment log:ERROR,"IXMLDOMParseError: Line 0, Char 0, file = "(null)" Description: Element content is invalid according to the DTD/Schema.

At Number One, it stated of the +3.2-centimeter shift (error), was discovered by the customer; that "customer" was Lana Miller Boyer.

13. 14:20:47 Field 'FLD 3 LAO1' treated, but with error in Treatment log: ERROR,"IXMLDOMParseError: Line 0, Char 0, file= "(null)" Description: Element content is invalid according to the DTD/Schema.
14. 14:22:02 Field 'FLD 1 RPO1' treated, but with error in Treatment log:ERROR,"IXMLDOMParseError: Line 0, Char 0, file= "(null)" Description: Element content is invalid according to the DTD/Schema.
15. 14:24:10 Field 'FLD 2 RPO2' treated, but with error in Treatment log: ERROR,"IXMLDOMParseError: Line 0, Char 0, file= "(null)" Description: Element content is invalid according to the DTD/Schema.
16. 14:24:15 5 treatment records saved back to the database via theTreatDaemon
17. Note: ERROR,"IXMLDOMParseError: Line 0, Char 0, file= "(null)" Description: Element content is invalid according to the DTD/Schema. Is un-related to the event and has been present on all of the patient treatment sessions.

- Based on OLR time line a delta shows that there was a change of position of the couch see tables below:

Time Line Results (Actual Table Movements):

	kV Aq	Shift	5 LPO	4LAO2	3LAO1	Shift	1RPO1	2RPO2
Vrt	121.5	-0.2	121.3	121.3	121.3	-0.1	121.2	121.2
Lng	112.8	-0.2	112.6	112.6	112.6		112.6	112.6
Lat	96.2	0.3	96.5	96.5	96.5	+3.2	99.7	99.7
Rtn	180.0		180.0	180.0	180.0		180.0	180.0

Show online Matched (OBI expected results):

	Online Match
Vrt	-0.3
Lng	-0.2
Lat	0.3
Rtn	0.0

Test Patient Scenario 1
- Created a plan that matched patient A planned parameters
- Scheduled test patient in Time Planner
- Selected patient from the Queue
- Overrode SCIC
- Placed Headboard and patient mask on the couch
- Positioned the couch to match image setup parameter values
- Aligned marks to the laser
- Closed the treatment door
- Selected and moded up KV LAT setup
- On OBI download axis, move arms to position and selected technique
- Initiate radiographic exposure
- Pressed 2D2D button
- Moved gantry and arms to position
- Took second radiographic exposure
- Pressed Analyze Button

Notice the variance of +3.2 centimeters, a "Lateral Shift", which proves the table was moved. The therapists lied, and Lana caught the lie.

J.B. Simms

15. 14:25:28 Send couch shift: CouchVrt 0.0 / CouchLng -0.335 / CouchLat-0.139 cm
16. 14:26:06 Done button pressed in OBI
NOTE: At the 4D Treatment Console, it was selected to apply the shift permanently, which updates the plan data. (Note: This explains the records in the Patient Editing Log.)
17. 14:26:57 Acquire 3rd kV image 'PA KV' (to verify the match result)
18. Instance UID 1.2.246.352.61.3.5463423170869480486.3741447768668846756 with couch at position CouchVrt -12.2 / CouchLng 115.3 / CouchLat 3.3 cm
19. 14:28:07 2D Match button pressed in OBI
20. 14:28:10 Analyze button pressed in OBI
NOTE: At this point the customer was happy with the position the position and didn't see a need for additional matching. Therefore the match process was cancelled (see next step).
21. 14:29:25 Cancel button pressed in OBI
22. 14:36:05 Close Patient in Treatment. Modified Plan (with new couch
23. values) and 3 treatment records (2 for the 2 MV images, 1 for the treatment field) are saved back to the DB via the TreatDaemon.
24. 14:36:09 5 images (2 MV images, 3 kV images) saved back to the DB via the ImageDaemon.

Corrective Actions

1. Patient A had a couch lateral shift of +3.2 cm between treatment fields 3 (FLD 3 LAO1) and 1 (FLD RPO 1) during treatment session 4 on June 17, 2009 at 2:20:47 pm.

Root cause: Couch at the shifted position LAT 96.5 cm, VRT 121.3 LNG 112.6 would cause the gantry to collide with the couch for field 1 unless the couch is moved towards the center position (100cm). Because the patient treatment session was closed it close the OBI session clearing all the shifts. The couch values were acquired for that session only and the plan will not have updated couch values when re-loaded for treatment. The position of the couch was within tolerance for the couch LAT parameter of 10.00 cm and it did not require an override.

Solution: Follow Varian instructions of use provided in the equipment and software user manuals.
- Perform dry runs of treatment to anticipate and avoid collision risk
- Stop motions immediately if you suspect a collision may occur
- Always observe remote motions using closed-circuit monitors

The customer came into a decision based on the evidence and facts provided to handle this event as a mistreatment for treatment session 4.
An adverse Event Report has been filed.

2. Patient B treatment record had a couch longitudinal shift of -12.6 cm that was discovered after patient A discrepancy was found in Off Line Review that could not be understood

Root cause: Patient had to be repositioned and the couch had to be retracted in order to bring the couch longitudinal values to <158 cm. The shift is not possible if the couch actual positions are outside the limits that are set in Clinac Physics configuration for remote motions with arms retracted or extended. Patient was re-imaged at the new position, images analyzed and shift applied before beam on.

In Page 9 of the Varian Report, notice in the Corrective Actions, the movement (shift) was confirmed.

J.B. Simms

Solution: Make sure that patients are aligned and positioned verifying that the couch longitudinal position does not exceed 158 cm before OBI imaging.

3. Patient C had a couch longitudinal shift of -7 cm after the first set of acquired images.

   Root cause: The patient was aligned incorrectly on the first set of images. This was corrected by re-aligning the patient and moving the couch -7cm. Patient was re-imaged, another match was done and couch parameters were applied permanently. A last image was acquired to confirm that the patient was in the correct treatment position before beam on

   Solution: Not applicable.

Verification of proper operation

Equipment and software are functioning as designed.

Closing summary:

Patient B and C were treated correctly based on the investigation. Patient A was evaluated and a clinical decision was made by the customer to handle fields 1 and 2 as a mistreatment in session 4 because there is no confirmation that the patient was re-aligned to correct treatment position.

Geraldina Lauzon, R.T. (R) (T)
Software Technical Support
North America – Integrated Systems

On the last page of the Varian Report, Patient A (the victim reported by Lana) was "mistreated" by the therapists.

The evidence was clear: Lana had determined that the therapists had moved the table, the therapists lied, the test results were not misread by Lana, the dosage was administered, and Lana was correct in her assessment.

With the Varian people gone, Lana did not know what to expect from Azawi.

Lana gave her recommendation to Dr. Azawi, stating that the two therapists be fired. Soon after Lana turned in the recommendation, which was to be endorsed by Dr. Azawi (depending upon her mood or the phase of the moon), Lana noticed that Donna Pikulsky (the nurse) and Mimi Mangohig were in Dr. Azawi's office talking with Dr. Azawi. Later, Dr. Azawi was seen in the hall and heard talking to Donna about the two therapists. Lana reminded Dr. Azawi that this was a matter involving the therapists, Lana as their supervisor, and this was not a matter to be discussed with anyone outside the treatment area.

Soon thereafter, Donna and Mimi were seen coming into the treatment area. These women approached Gail and Doug, the therapists in question. The four appeared to be whispering, and then all of them left the treatment area and went to Donna's office, which was at the front of the department.

It was later determined that Dr. Azawi had been talking to more people about this matter, and that Dr. Azawi was also discussing the matter with Eric Frank, a contract physicist, and George Dolla, the dosimetrist, asking these two men if they thought the therapists should be fired.

Then came the fireworks: Gail Francis approached Lana and told Lana that Ms. Pikulsky told Gail and Doug that Lana wanted them fired. The environment became hostile.

The therapists were still performing below standard, making errors in machine parameters and alignment, but the therapists seemed unconcerned. Lana saw their behavior as inexcusable. The patients were being harmed but now the doctors were not listening to Lana.

J.B. Simms

Thursday, June 25, 2009

Lana checked her email to find a reply from Jenni Inemer, the Chief Therapist in Philadelphia. The following are excerpts from the email which Lana received from Jenni Inemer:

"I'm very sorry to hear of your situation. This is an unfortunate event, but what is most upsetting to me is that there is now definitive evidence of a "cover-up..."

"The therapists' actions warrant immediate attention because the entire patient population was affected by one error and their failure to admit it."

"...The Chief of your department should respect your decision for Removal [of the therapists]."

Lana had the endorsement of the Chief Therapist in Philadelphia, and at 8:22am, Lana sent a copy of the email to Dr. Azawi and Dr. Williams.

Lana was hoping this would be over soon, and Human Resources would take over and take it out of the hands of Dr. Azawi. Subterfuge was going to be the name of the game from this point forward. Donna (the nurse) and Mimi (the office worker) were blatantly involved in the drama concerning the blocking of removal of the therapists. Azawi brought these two persons into the conversation, violating Lana's authority over the therapists, and violating HR policies.

Soon thereafter, Donna Pikulsky was seen leaving her area, walking to the back of the radiation area. Donna was carrying a large envelope. Donna approached Gail Francis, who slipped paper(s) into the large envelope which Donna was holding.

The plan was to replace the contracting radiation therapist, Hollins, who, worked for an agency and was not a regular employee; The VA had to deal with the agency. Lucinda Swan, the Business Manager, contacted the employment agency at 10:32am at the direction of Lana, having been given the authority by Dr. Azawi. Dr. Azawi seemed to waffle a bit, but Azawi was shown by Lana and Varian that these therapists lied and were dangerous.

Within 30 minutes, the agency had contacted Cindy Swan, and Ms. Swan had received a resume sent to her of someone to replace Doug Hollins.

After Dr. Azawi and Lana received the email from Ms. Swan, Dr. Azawi sent a return email stating she (Azawi) did not believe Hollins needed to be replaced. A few minutes later Dr. Azawi sent out another email stating she was delaying her decision.

What was Dr. Azawi doing? She was waffling for no reason, but, there was a reason she was waffling. Azawi did not want the blame on herself for not noticing that the film showed the patient was treated 3.2 centimeters from the treatment target. She could dodge this by firing the therapists because they were the ones who moved the table during the treatment and lied about moving the table. But, from the beginning, the therapists have discovered that Dr. Azawi has less knowledge of the equipment than the therapists, and Azawi had no certification in IMRT. A stalemate was created at the cost of Veteran's health. Azawi was now a hostage of the therapists.

How could the VA hospital administrator or HR not know that Azawi was not certified?

Lana emailed Jenni Inemer, the Chief Radiation Therapist at the VA Hospital in Philadelphia. Azawi had agreed Lana would do this to get an opinion on the Varian incident from outside the Long Beach VA Hospital. Lana told Jenni that Dr. Azawi was waffling, and there appeared to be an effort to keep the incident from being known, especially to patients.

Lana was thinking that if Lana showed Dr. Azawi the independent validation from outside the Long Beach hospital, maybe she would agree (again) to fire the therapists. Communication had been established between the employment agency and Human Resources with respect to finding out if the agency had another person who had worked for a VA hospital (to replace Hollins), and another email came up to Lana concerning Hollins.

Dr. Azawi contradicted herself again by sending an email to Lana directing her to conduct her own investigation:

"... [V]arian Investigation, keep close supervision of the therapists [Lana had always done that], and develop a personnel plan for the replacement of the radiation technologists to ensure a smooth transition."

Azawi had changed her mind again. Now, Dr. Azawi wanted them fired. The afternoon before she had wanted them retained. Lana did exactly what she was asked by Azawi; Lana submitted the personnel plan along with the statements of the therapists to Human Resources.

Both therapists stated that neither of them left the control room and entered the treatment room to move the table, allowing the gantry to circumvent the table. The Varian investigative group proved the therapists were lying.

The biggest question was not if the therapists lied; they did. The biggest question is "Why was Azawi changing her mind 3, 4 and 5 times with respect to firing the rogue therapists?

What did Gail Francis say to Azawi when she rushed past Lana into Azawi's office on the day after the incident?

All the drama of the Varian people being in the hospital was over, and Lana knew the situation was going to get worse. Lana's authority was being eroded by Azawi. Lana could not review the performance of the therapists without being "dismissed" by the doctors Azawi and Williams.

Later in the day (Thursday, June 25, 2009) Lana received her midyear evaluation from Dr. Azawi. Dr. Azawi reviewed the evaluation, which was of no consequence. It was pretty much a report that Lana was adequate in her job performance, scoring high in all her performance categories.

Lana asked for a copy and Dr. Azawi told her she would get one for Lana. As Lana was preparing to leave the review, Dr. Azawi handed a piece of paper to Lana; it was a business card for the Employee Assistance Program. Azawi told Lana that Lana needed to seek psychological help. Psychological help? Lana was about to be experience "gas lighting." This was Azawi at her worst. And Azawi claimed Lana was crazy?

When Lana told Jenni about the incident with Azawi and the referral for counseling, Jenni agreed that that Lana was being the scapegoat for calling in Varian. That was bad publicity for Azawi, and a new application for accreditation with the ACR was to be turned in soon. How was Azawi going to keep the Varian Incident hidden from the ACR?

Chapter Five:

HIV, a Freckle, and Patient Abuse

Lana was alone. Lana defended persons who were abused by Azawi, even going to Szabo, the Chief of Staff, to defend them.

None of the persons who were allies of Lana had enough fervor to defend Lana or to go after Azawi. After Azawi was reinstated, and received the $50,000 in a discrimination suit, Azawi was untouchable.

Lana was not a confrontational person, but could hold her own in a debate about facts. Azawi tried to manipulate by power, leverage, and any other means to gain validation. Facts did not help Lana.

There were no complaints against Lana from anyone. Lana was respected by her peers, having been asked to be on national committees, and admired by co-workers. Lana was more tolerant than most.

Lana knew no "facts" were going to change the narrative at the VA hospital, and Lana was not looking forward to going to work on the following day.

Friday, June 26, 2009

One more day before the weekend and Lana was thinking she could get away from this mess for a few days. Lana was getting tired of Azawi changing her mind many times about the therapists being fired, denying the Varian report, and accusing Lana of needing counseling. Hopefully this could get behind everyone, soon.

Dr. Azawi had not changed her attitude since having her Chief designation removed by Dr. Szabo a year before, then regaining it in February 2009. How was Azawi getting away with this? What kind of information does Azawi have on Szabo?

The circumstances surrounding Azawi regaining her position had bothered Lana. Lana was not alone in the mistrust of Azawi; Lucinda Swan, and the four others who met with Dr. Szabo could not all be wrong.

This day Lana was greeted with a mid-morning email from Dr. Azawi. Azawi stated in the email that:

[Azawi]discussed the situation with "others" last evening, and things would be put on hold regarding the radiation therapists [the firing of them both]

Lana was to discontinue direct supervision of the radiation therapists, and "return to the supervisory role," whatever that was supposed to mean.

By removing Lana from direct supervision, Lana would no longer be correcting the Radiation Therapy reports. Azawi would allow errors because Azawi could not identify an error, and allowed patients to continue to be harmed.

What in the world was Azawi thinking? These people were dangerous and Azawi was protecting them. Did they know something about Azawi which protected them? What kind of leverage did the therapists have over Azawi? Was this an inmate/asylum scenario?

The department was being controlled by persons using leverage and blackmail rather than medical talent and patient care.

Who were the "others" Azawi supposedly spoke with concerning the therapists and the Varian incident? Did Azawi not realize that the Varian people pointed the finger at the therapists, Francis and Hollins?

Fewer than two hours after Azawi removed supervisory authority from Lana, the final report was emailed from Varian. As noted in the previous chapter, the patient had been moved 3.2 centimeters during the radiation therapy. Lana was smart enough to have been able to see this, and Azawi would now be attacking Lana for bringing in the Varian people and embarrassing Azawi.

Was Azawi wondering if this would affect the American College of Radiology certification of the Long Beach VA Oncology Department?

Lana had been vindicated. Lana caught the therapists moving the table. The Varian experts reported there was no malfunction in their equipment, and that the therapists would have been able to enter the treatment room and move the table within 63 seconds.

Lana wondered, "What is the hospital going to do with Azawi now that she is denying the Varian report?"

To compound matters, Gail Francis and Doug Hollins were found to be using the wrong chart to set up a patient, who had a problem on the previous day.

After Azawi removed Lana's authority to review therapist reports, Gail became out of control, refusing simple requests or direction given by Lana. Somehow Gail was empowered by Azawi. Gail reminded Lana that she heard from Donna Pikulsky that Lana wanted both Gail and Doug fired.

After receiving the final Varian Report, Lana found Doug and asked to talk with him. Lana reminded him of what he said when he was presented with the facts, and the statement Doug made that "It never happened." Doug was also reminded that a Varian representative was standing with Lana and Doug as he made that statement. Doug's response was, "I knew there was something wrong with her." That was a puzzling answer.

Lana's control of the department was taken from Lana by Azawi.

Azawi's retreat in her decision to fire the therapists was giving the therapists power over Lana, which was exactly what Azawi wanted. This was Azawi's way of paying Lana back for going to Szabo a year earlier.

Monday, June 29, 2009

A third request was made from Lana to Gail to have Gail change supervisor notation in her reports. Lana was no longer the supervisor. The therapists had no supervisor. Lana continued to be ignored and insubordination by Gail was rampant.

Wednesday, July 1, 2009

The sloppy and unsafe work practices of Gail Francis and Doug Hollins were becoming unbearable. Both continued to lie about things which were important, and some things which were not.

It had been established that Lana would not be able to perform any discipline, and the doctors would not follow through with Human Resources to fire them.

The big question was why was this being allowed? Did anyone give a damn for the Veterans who offered their lives for these people?

Radiation treatment continued to be inaccurate, ineffective, and injurious. Patients were not being healed; patients were being injured, and the injuries had to be treated either in the emergency room or in other facilities.

Radiation patients who suffered burns received inaccurate therapy, were taken to the emergency room. The records were altered as to deflect blame from the Radiation Therapists, or Drs. Azawi or Williams.

Lana asked for a meeting with Azawi and Williams to show the doctors what the errors being made were doing to the Veteran patients.

A meeting was held on July 1, 2009. This was the first day since the Varian Incident (June 18, 2009) that Lana had the opportunity to sit with Dr. Azawi and Dr. Williams concerning the unsafe procedures performed by the therapists, and the first meeting after the final report from Varian.

Lana was a bit scared to go to the meeting, knowing that Azawi had demoted Lana because the Varian Incident had (unintentionally) revealed to Varian and the hospital that Azawi was not a competent doctor. Lana was taking a big risk to her mental health by showing Azawi and Williams that patients were being abused and receiving dangerous treatment after Lana was removed as the supervisor of the therapists.

Printouts and images of misalignment and mistreatment were shown to the doctors by Lana. It was pointed out to the doctors that the images from a simulation were supposed to match the film of the set up for treatment, on the day of the treatment. The therapists were giving treatment even though the images did not match, which is how Lana "caught" the huge variation in the on June 18, the day after the Varian incident.

As Lana was showing the printouts and images to the doctors, it became apparent why the doctors had allied themselves with the radiation therapists; the doctors were not familiar with the icons in the "Timeline" section of the "Offline" review. The doctors exhibited no concern with the documentation although it showed mistreatment by misalignment.

The riddle of the conspiracy to avoid punishing bad radiation therapists had been solved: the doctors who were supposed to be supervising the radiation therapy department did not know how to read the reports generated from the Varian equipment, and had no way of knowing if a patient was receiving correct treatment.

The doctors were ready to do anything to protect their secret.

After explaining the icons and other nuances of the printouts and images to the doctors, Lana left the images and printouts with the doctors. Lana then told both doctors that the therapists were dangerous, and that Lana would follow up the assessment in writing.

Radiation therapists are trained and have certification on theory and the equipment. Lana was appalled that the VA hospital in Long Beach would retain therapists who proved not to be competent, endangering the patients. A certain amount of on the job training was to be expected, but not having to encounter unethical mistreatment of patients and covering up of this mistreatment.

Lana followed up on her promise to send the doctors her assessment of the abuse of patients and unsafe treatment being conducted by the therapists by sending an email to the doctors at the end of the day.

Lana was feeling like she was spitting into the wind. These doctors were not listening to her. The doctors wanted the whole drama of Varian to go away, and somehow hide their inadequacy.

There was another reason for Azawi to downplay the Varian incident: The Long Beach VA Hospital was not accredited by the American College of Radiology, and Azawi wanted this designation. Azawi would do anything to hide the Varian Incident from the American College of Radiology.

The ACR officials visited the hospital early in 2009 (just before Azawi was reinstated) and a CAP (Corrective Action Plan) was to be implemented. The CAP had to be submitted in order for the ACR to "believe" these corrections were being implemented. The corrections and procedures were never implemented. Dr. Azawi was creating a Corrective Action Plan, submitting it to the ACR, and ignoring the directives and procedures mandated by the ACR with respect to the VA Hospital at Long Beach. Procedures such as chart rounds and new patient conferences were never held. Azawi considered these an imposition of their time, and who was going to report them? The goal was to get the accreditation, even if the doctors lied to get it.

Thursday, July 2, 2009

An email was received from Dr. Azawi to Lana. Dr. Azawi stated she did not feel there was any mistreatment of patients. A return email from Lana to Dr. Azawi asked Dr. Azawi what she considered mistreatment, how she wanted Lana to prove it; the doctors saw the charts and film on the previous day so what more did they need?

Later that afternoon, Lana was back in the offices of Dr. Azawi and Dr. Williams. More printouts were shown.

Dr. Williams asked that Lana write down what was wrong with each incident as though he could not interpret the physical information in front of him. Dr. Williams said he did not see anything wrong

with the films, as he was looking at them. Lana pointed out the Time Line option and the disposed film to see the mistakes to which she was referring. Williams was lost.

The consensus between both Dr. Azawi and Dr. Williams was that "as long as the correct body part was treated" there was not a problem. Dosage, depth of radiation, and parameters did not matter to the doctors; just hit the correct organ, anywhere.

The doctors said the film did not look like mistreatment to them. Lana pointed out to the doctors exactly where the treatment was to be placed and the fact that the wrong body part was being treated. Their response was, "Did the therapists treat a knee instead of a lung?"

Azawi and Williams were told that patients were remaining on the treatment table for upwards of an hour just to take films because the therapists could not align the patient correctly. The therapists' inability to perform their jobs affected the patients. The patients waited much longer and missed treatments due to the schedules of their drivers, and medications wore off which caused patients to be in terrible pain or very nauseated because therapists were inept. Patients complained and other employees in the department were asking why it was taking so long to treat the patients but none of this was a concern to the physicians.

It was becoming more obvious that the doctors were not going to correct the therapists. These were not errors; this was blatant lack of concern, and no culpability. This was a perfect storm for Veterans to be tortured, and killed, in a hospital.

Monday, July 6, 2009

Both Dr. Azawi and Gail Francis were on vacation and Lana figured there would be some peace in the unit.

Dr. Williams contacted Lana and asked her to write down why the therapists were dangerous, sloppy, and untrustworthy.

Dr. Williams wanted the report and asked that Lana bring her personnel file with her as she presented the report. Lana had 20 minutes to do this, so Lana wrote out the report by hand in a hurried fashion. There was no reason for Dr. Williams to ask for Lana's personnel file, and Lana smelled a rat. When Lana asked for an explanation, Dr. Williams replied that he was following an order from Dr. Azawi.

That reply caused a great deal of anxiety for Lana; Azawi was on vacation, and she was dictating messages to Williams, remotely, in order to harass Lana.

Monday, July 13, 2009

It was Lana's job to analyze the raw data, film and printouts, to show the degree of variation of treatment to a specific treatment area. The variables include the height of the table, latitudinal and longitudinal position of the table, and dosage amount. These reports needed to be reviewed with the therapists for corrective training. These reports were to be signed by the therapist after the review. Azawi put a stop to the reviews.

Again, there are 4 variables with respect to targeting the transmission of radiation:
1. *Height of the table- regulates how "deep" the penetration*
2. *Latitudinal position- back and forth position*
3. *Longitudinal position- side to side positioning*
4. *Dosage- the strength of the dose*

Gail and Doug did not count on the Varian people to be able to detect a millimeter of variance, and they knew that Lana would be putting them "under the microscope" from then on because the Varian report proved their lack of care for the patients.

Lana prepared the Varian Report to present to Gail and Doug. Before the presentation to the therapists, Lana spoke with Dr. Azawi.

Azawi informed her that she was in the process of performing this duty as the Chief Radiation Therapist, and since Lana expected an outburst from Gail Francis, Lana asked for the support of Dr. Azawi. Dr. Azawi stated she would support Lana.

Lana called in Gail Francis and Doug Hollins to present them with their individual variance reports. As expected, Gail Francis wrote on her report and stated she did nothing wrong on each incident, got angry, and stormed out of the office. Lana called her back into the office because the review was not complete. Gail returned but with a very bad attitude.

Gail wrote a note on a piece of paper, showed it to Doug, then tore up the note and put the note into the trash. After the review, Lana dug out the note and pieced it together. The note read "after Lana is gone, you [Doug] will have a fulltime job."

Instances occurred over the next few days which gave Lana an uneasy feeling. The guidelines for accreditation from the ACR, which Lana was asked to create, were submitted to different areas of the department. One area which got attention was that of a dress code in the department. Inappropriate attire was being worn, and the women who did so wore the attire in a flirty and distracting manner. The department became "Club Med" as either Club Mediterranean or Club Medical.

J.B. Simms

<u>Wednesday, July 15, 2009</u>

Lana was feeling the heat. The atmosphere in the radiation department was hostile to say the least. People were meeting in offices behind closed doors. Therapists were meeting with nurses, office workers, and doctors. Therapists were being rude, passing notes, and being insubordinate.

Lana was feeling a bit suspicious, so on this morning, Lana figured she had nothing to lose and confronted Dr. Azawi.

Lana said, "Are you trying to get rid of me?"

There was no immediate reply from Azawi. Azawi then said "no."

Lana asked another question, "Are you planning disciplinary action against me?"

Azawi's face was getting red. Azawi answered "No, why would you think that?"

"Sources are telling me that something is going on, and you removed my authority for no reason."

"Who are the sources?"

"It does not matter." Lana walked away.

The source to which Lana was referring was an observation: Lana was referring to the secret meetings she witnessed, and the hostility.

Evidently someone was discussing Lana's departure with Lana's subordinate, Gail Francis.

This denial by Azawi was not much of a comfort since Azawi did not want Lana critiquing the therapist's work, which was Lana's job. If no one critiques the job of the therapists, no one will know the truth of what is happening to the patients.

Gail Francis was seen talking to Dr. Azawi after lunch. Forty-eight minutes later, at 1:48pm, Lana received an email from Dr. Azawi which was another shocker: Azawi ordered Lana to discontinue Variance Reports.

The Variance Reports were records of the performance of the therapists and showed how close the therapists come to the exact spot that the radiation was supposed to be administered.

If Lana was prohibited from submitting a critique of the reports from the therapists, and neither Dr. Azawi nor Dr. Williams could read the reports, how did the doctors plan on finding out if the therapists were competent their job? Did the doctors care if the therapists to their jobs correctly?

The therapists had no oversight, and the doctors could not read the reports.

If a patient talked to the doctor, and the family was present, the doctor would tell the patient anything the patient needed to hear to stop the patient from stop asking questions.

The patient and the family could not read the therapist's report, and neither could the doctors.

Lana communicated with Human Resources concerning guidelines, Team Agreement/Responsibility, and the dress code. Gail Francis and Doug Hollins did not like the team agreement because they stated they did not want to be responsible for the other's mistakes. Human Resources wanted the dress code issue removed.

Lana had a discussion with Herb Moisa, the Assistant Chief to Human Resources. Lana told Herb about the mistreatment of the patients. Herb asked if others in the community would see it in the same way. Lana told him "yes." Lana knew that Herb could not be trusted, after he "lost" the documentation presented to Szabo by the four persons attacking Azawi's lack of professionalism.

Lana told Herb that the therapists lacked accountability, blaming each other for mistakes, and that Dr. Azawi would not fire the therapists which she agreed to earlier. Retraining was not an issue; these were unscrupulous persons being not qualified to perform their jobs.

Herb suggested to Lana that she keep showing the error to the physicians. Lana told Herb that the physicians kept approving images which should not have been approved, and if it came to a legal issue with a patient, it would be problematic for the hospital.

Herb mentioned that Azawi and Williams, the physicians, were concerned that Lana was overstepping her authority. Lana's authority was dictated by her job description and the authority to supervise the therapists.

The doctors did not like the fact that Lana knew the doctors were approving misdeeds performed by the therapists, and injuring patients, and the doctors wrote untrue facts about treatment. This odd statement made by Herb Moisa made Lana see that Azawi and Williams had been talking to someone in the Human Resources office about Lana.

Lana knew something was going on. Lana had heard that Dr. Azawi "ran off" one Chief Therapist by humiliation.

Another left because of harassment, and another had to be carried out because the behavior of Dr. Azawi caused the Chief Therapist to bang his head against a wall in frustration. They were hiding their misdeeds, Lana knew of their incompetence, patients were being injured, and wounds to patients were called "side effects."

Tuesday, July 21, 2009

Lana had done everything she needed to do to protect the patients, who were Veterans who had protected the citizens of the United States. She showed the charts and film to the physicians and explained to the physicians that the therapist's charts were not matching. The doctors, specifically Azawi, were reminded that the report submitted by Varian cited the two therapists for making the error in treatment. Why were the doctors not getting it?

Later in the afternoon, Lana was called into the conference room by Dr. Azawi and Dr. Williams. Nothing productive every came from these meetings., but Lana knew she had to go.

Lana had been asked to bring the personnel files of the two therapists, Gail Francis and Doug Hollins. Lana was hoping that the therapists were finally going to be fired.

As Lana was seated at the conference table, Lana was given a two page "Fact Finding Letter" in response to the "Varian Incident" and the unsafe radiation the therapists were accused of administering.

Afterward, Lana was given a Letter of Reprimand for conduct, signed by Dr. Azawi. Lana wondered what else could they do? Do these doctors have any accountability?

The doctors then ordered Lana to treat patients in the treatment area during the mornings and "retrain the therapists" at other times. Retrain the therapists?

These therapists were supposed to follow a precise plan to make certain they did not harm the patients. The doctors were supposed to review the films before the patient was treated. Many times, the doctors were not available. The procedure was in place, but the doctors did not follow any procedure.

After the Varian Incident, Lana was told not to review any more film or charts from the therapists, and to stop the Variance Reports which showed the "variation" of treatment from the exact place radiation was to be administered. Now Lana is charged with training people who will not abide by rules. The doctors had no rules, either.

There was no evidence of a reprimand of the therapists. Lana was reprimanded for showing the doctors mistreatment of patients, and the persons responsible for the mistreatment were now able to harass Lana.

Lana was never consulted about any investigation being conducted by any "fact finder" delegated by Human Resources. If Lana had been consulted by Human Resources, they would have known the truth. Lana did not know what the physicians said to Human Resources to generate this reprimand.

Lana was totally blindsided by this. She asked Dr. Azawi for details about the Fact-Finding Letter and the reprimand. Dr. Azawi did not respond. Lana told Dr. Azawi the reprimand was unfair.

Azawi would not tell Lana who instigated any investigation of Lana. The only thing that had gone wrong was the fact that the patient, a Veteran, was given improper treatment, the therapists tried to hide their incompetence, Lana found it and reported it.

A short time later, after Lana had a quick session with Gail and Doug, Gail was called into the office of Dr. Azawi with Dr. Williams being present.

Afterward, Dr. Williams was seen walking down the hallway through the control area, and he spoke with Gail and Doug. They all began to laugh. Doug approached Lana and loudly announced that Lana was now part of the treatment team. They all laughed. That was Doug's dig at Lana, and the physicians would no longer listen to Lana, who was still the Chief Radiation Therapist.

The physicians and the therapists were on the same page; they covered each other's immoral behavior, allowing patients to be harmed because of limited knowledge and/or concern.

The alliance between the doctors and the therapists allowed them to hide everything, especially from the regulators.

Lana immediately filed an Informal Grievance which was to be reviewed by Dr. Azawi. This grievance was denied. Lana's next step was to file a Formal Grievance which would be reviewed by the director of the VA hospital, Isabel Duff. Lana thought the director of the hospital would listen.

Thursday, July 23, 2009

Lana continued to send emails to the physicians about the incompetence of the therapists. The setup procedure was not being followed, and all the corrections and reporting was falling upon deaf ears. New patient procedures were being ignored. Neither of the physicians responded to any emails. The doctors could not read the reports and would simply tell the patient and their family that there was no problem with or during the procedure.

There were problems, and wounding of the patients, but it was referred to as a side effect or part of the sickness.

It was now a joke with the therapists, and the goal was to let Lana be another casualty of Azawi. Insubordination was rampant, with lack of accountability and consequences.

Later in the day, Lana was called into Dr. Azawi's office to receive an additional letter to summarize the discussion of the Letter of Reprimand. More empty words and denials were received.

Friday, July 24, 2009

More emails were sent to the physicians concerning careless setups and bad filming of patients. No response was received from the physicians.

Lana had enough; she went to the Human Resources and had an extended meeting with Mary Beth McCartan, Chief of Human

Resources, and Esther Pittman who was an Employee Specialist, regarding the improper presentation of the Letter of Reprimand and the continual patient treatment/care problems referred to in the Fact-Finding letter.

After hearing from Lana, Ms. McCartan told Lana that a meeting with the director, Isabel Duff, would be scheduled so Lana could inform the Director of the critical nature of the patient care problem.

That was a nice gesture by Ms. McCartan, but that meeting never happened. McCartan became a part of the cover-up.

Monday, August 3, 2009

Lana asked for an extension to file the grievance because no documents had been received from the Human Resources department concerning the reprimand and Fact-Finding Letter.

The cover-up was in full swing. No one other than the Varian people were to ever find out what happened, and that regardless of Lana's reports, her reports would be ignored by the doctors, allowing the therapists to keep their jobs.

Friday, August 7, 2009

Lana had filed the Informal Grievance with Dr. Azawi after receiving the Letter of Reprimand; a copy of which was received by Dr. Williams. A response to the Letter of Reprimand was also included.

More insubordination and violation of procedures, including a few mind games, continued. Lana was informed by Gail that she was going to be away from work during the following week. Lana did not know this was planned. Gail informed Lana that permission was obtained from Dr. Azawi. This was a violation of procedure, but it was a game to get Lana rattled. It was later learned that the story given to Dr. Azawi by Gail, that she was looking for a house for her grandparents, was contradicted by another story which Gail told others, which was that she was looking for a house of her own to live in Corona.

Lies and more lies. Gail, the technician, had become very chummy with the doctor. This is not supposed to happen. Gail was not to get permission for time off by bypassing her boss, who was Lana.

Thursday, August 13, 2009

Lana received one of those "we need to meet" emails from Azawi. Lana stopped her work and went into the conference room as requested.

Azawi and Dr. Williams were sitting at the table. Dr. Azawi asked Lana if Lana had any more to add to the Informal Grievance.

Lana said, "No." Seeing no reaction, Lana turned and walked out.

Leaving Azawi with her mouth open gave Lana a bit of joy, but Lana knew it would be short-lived.

Wednesday, August 19, 2009

Lana received notice that Dr. Azawi wanted to meet with Lana in the conference room that day. The meeting in the conference room resulted in Lana's Informal Grievance being denied by Dr. Azawi.

At 3:32pm, Lana sent an email to Herb Moisa, the assistant HR director. Lana stated she wanted to file Formal Administrative Grievance and requested to be told the way to file. Lana then filed the Formal Grievance.

Lana trusted the people in Human Resources to follow rules and regulations. She found out that the office of Human Resources had their own secrets to protect, and they were not intent to protect Lana.

Tuesday, August 28, 2009

A directive came down from Dr. Azawi; she wanted Gail to work on an outcome study. The department did not have the personnel resources for Gail to do this. Later, Lana directed Gail to enter her workload which had not been entered correctly in three months. Lana gave the list to Gail. Gail responded, "Why don't you do them? You looked them up."

Dr. Azawi had discredited, demeaned, and disallowed all of Lana's authority. The therapists knew this and felt they could do whatever they wanted without repercussion or consequence.

If Lana attempted to correct the therapists, the therapists would go immediately to Dr. Azawi, who would publicly take the side of the therapist against Lana. This encouraged insubordination and continued the attempt to make Lana leave. Lana was tougher than they thought.

Lana was trying to make sure the Veterans, the patients, were receiving the proper treatment. The doctors and therapists continued hiding injuries incurred by the patients.

Wednesday, September 2, 2009

The time was 8:10am; A patient was waiting for radiation treatment.

Gail was late warming up the treatment machine, and the patient had to wait 30 minutes for Gail to have the machine operational. Any report of this would be laughable to Azawi since Lana was not being taken seriously. Making a cancer patient, a veteran, be treated so insensitively, was inhumane.

Dr. Azawi and Dr. Williams had been making statements that they wanted to have a meeting with the therapists and Lana, together, to discuss errors. Were the physicians going to admit to "errors" when they cover up errors? Lana sent Dr. Azawi an email and ask Azawi to define "mistreatment". No answer was received. Lana smelled the rat again.

The physicians wanted to bypass Lana and embolden the therapists by talking directly to the therapists. Lana recommended that the physicians discuss the treatment issues with Lana, who was the supervisor, and Lana would discuss or send directives to the therapists. Dr. Azawi refused. Lana managed to delay the meeting.

September 3, 2009

Dr. Azawi emailed Lana asking for another meeting with therapists. An emergency patient had to be treated so the meeting was put off again. Dr. Azawi asked Lana, in an email, if Lana was refusing to have the meeting, and Lana told Azawi "no, there was no intent to delay any meeting."

Lana wanted to meet privately with the physicians because she was the supervisor of the therapists

Tuesday, September 8, 2009

There was no way to get around having the "meeting" this day.

Dr. Azawi sent an email to Lana, giving Lana 10-15 minutes to attend the meeting. Unknown to Lana, Dr. Azawi had been communicating with the therapists, circumventing Lana, breaking the chain of command, and told the therapists to "come prepared; we are going to level the playing field."

Lana sent an email back to the physicians and told the physicians that they did not follow the chain of command. Dr. Azawi replied, and stated she disagreed with the theory of chain of command.

Dr. Azawi started the meeting by saying it was a "Fact Finding" meeting. Gail and Doug started talking and said Lana was "untruthful, that Lana has lied about them using the wrong chart for a new patient setup, and that maybe 20 years ago they did things differently."

The Varian Report did not lie.

Lana asked Gail if she (Gail) did anything wrong. Gail replied, "No."

During the entire meeting, Dr. Azawi and Dr. Williams did not attempt to bring order to the melee or keep Gail and Doug from making wild accusations. Instead, the physicians seem to revel in Lana having to respond to accusations from her subordinates in front of her superiors. The meeting was called not to discuss errors made by the therapists, but to demean and humiliate Lana in front of and by the subordinates.

Lana told the physicians again that this "meeting" was a sham, was inappropriate, and should be handled through the chain of command. It was clear that Dr. Azawi had been meeting privately with the therapists, Lana's subordinates, but was not willing or allowing Lana to state facts at the meeting. It was an ambush and the physicians sat back and watched.

Gail told Dr. Azawi and Dr. Williams that the radiation therapists trusted Lana until the Varian incident. After the Varian incident no one trusted Lana. Gail accused Lana of setting up the incident (which was impossible to do).

Lana pointed out to the doctors and the therapists that shifts (in positioning) in the setup of the patients had not recorded by the therapists. If a shift of the patient is made after setup, it must be recorded. On one occasion a breast patient had a vertical raise of .5 centimeters (over one and a quarter inches). Lana came back and did a setup with a difference of .1 millimeter, a microscopic amount.

Doug Hollins' contract was to expire at the end of September (22 days) and the only way for Doug to keep his assignment was to make Lana quit.

Lana called the therapists liars. Azawi glowed with delight.

The fact that the therapists, Gail and Doug, set up a patient using the wrong chart did not get the attention of Azawi. Azawi did not care; Azawi's demeanor never changed. "This is not on the job training" Lana said, "and the therapists should have learned these things already."

The therapists wanted Lana to do the setups and let the therapists sit back and take notes.

This was the day which Lana was supposed to receive word on the filing of the Formal Grievance. No response had been received from Human Resources.

According to the Formal Grievance Policy, Lana should have received notification from someone within 10 days of filing the grievance, but she had heard nothing. With the difficulties in the department and the continued abuse of patients, plus sloppy record-keeping, Lana was looking for someone to act and correct the situation. Lack of response and concern by Human Resources made this a devastating time for Lana.

Lana, and others knew that the VA Hospital Human Resources Department had violated the Grievance Policy. Lana was the only one to face the devil.

<u>Wednesday, September 9, 2009</u>

Lana was getting nowhere with Dr. Azawi, and her second in command, Dr. Williams. It seemed everyone had forgotten that Azawi had been demoted by Dr. Szabo for creating a problem in the department, but "somehow" got her job back. Szabo had no love lost for Azawi, so Lana planned to take her case to Szabo.

Lana attended a supervisors meeting and spoke with Dr. Szabo. Lana reminded Dr. Szabo that the deadline for the response to her formal grievance had passed. Lana asked Dr. Szabo to call her to discuss this matter.

Dr. Szabo left the country without calling Lana.

Why was everyone covering for the physicians? It wasn't always that way. There was a time when Dr. Szabo would stand up to Dr. Azawi. The Director, Isabel Duff, backed up Dr. Szabo to demote Azawi. What had changed? The Veterans were being injured by lazy and incompetent therapists, and the physicians did not care as long as their lack of knowledge was kept a secret.

Monday, September 14, 2009

On this date, Dr. Azawi and Dr. Williams tried another blindside meeting with Lana, giving Lana 10-15 minutes notice. This was another two against one situation.

Lana was being pelted with questions about the treatment area and why she (Lana) was not on the treatment machine. Lana told the physicians that there are four therapists; Lana is a Chief, and a supervisor.

Lana felt as though she were in the Twilight Zone, with the physicians appearing through fish-eye lenses asking the same questions over and over, trying to break her. They wanted her gone; they wanted her to quit so they could hide their ignorance and incompetence. They also wanted to hide the fact that they were injuring patients.

Wednesday, September 16, 2009

After the horror-show meeting on September 14, Lana took the next two days off. Was Lana paranoid? Was she simply a complainer?

Work in the department was anguishing. The therapists were colluding with the doctors because neither knew their jobs, but they made it their job to make Lana look crazy only to protect themselves. Lana was in a prison and no one was listening, or was scared to help. Lana was alone. Everyone either was scared or simply lied on reports to cover the doctors.

On this day, Lana sent an email to Dr. Azawi, telling her that since she (Azawi) had eliminated the Variance Reports (which was like a report card for the therapists) there was no way to determine if a therapist was doing the procedure correctly. The physicians did not care, and Dr. Williams did exactly what Azawi told him to do.

Monday, September 21, 2009

Dr. Azawi sent Lana an email, asking Lana to look into getting a pay grade increase for Gail Francis. "Azawi wanted to do what? This was the same Gail Francis who lied about the Varian incident." What an insult to Lana. This was just another ploy of Azawi to try to rattle Lana.

Friday, September 25, 2009

If there were ever a hint that Lana needed to be wary of Azawi, this day would prove Lana had the right to be suspicious. The plan was to put Lana's life at risk. They were trying to kill her.

Azawi Risks Lana's Life

While going through the charts, Dr. Azawi asked Lana if she (Azawi) could place a note on a treatment chart noting that a patient was HIV positive. Lana told Azawi that placing an overt note of HIV infection had not been allowed for years, to prevent patient discrimination. Lana asked Azawi to identify the HIV positive patient. When Azawi mentioned the name of the patient, Lana was shocked and scared. Lana had treated that patient.

Lana never knew the patient was HIV positive; no one told her, and Lana was not given the opportunity to use more protection. Why was that a secret?

Azawi had instituted a closed-door policy with respect to Lana having information about patients. Azawi told the nurses not to divulge information to Lana concerning the patients.

This patient had gone through the simulation procedure three times; once because of a CT malfunction, and twice because of therapist incompetence. Lana was present with the patient once during the CT malfunction. There was a Quality Assessment form to complete, plus policies and procedures in place to communicate about patient having infections and other medical problems. This documentation passed through the nurse prior to simulation, but the information was not passed along to Lana. Pikulsky had the documentation.

Was Lana the only one in danger? Donna did not like to follow these procedures, saying the procedures were picky and unnecessary, and Donna did not tell Lana that her patient was HIV positive.

J.B. Simms

After Chart Rounds, Lana asked all radiation therapists if they knew that one of the patients was HIV positive. One therapist said no; the other two said they were told by the nurse when the patient started treatment. The two radiation therapists who were told of the patient being HIV positive were the same two who Dr. Azawi was protecting, Gail Francis and Doug Hollins. Dennis, the other technician, did not know.

That violation is termed "Selective Notification".

The patient had a bloody tracheotomy that was not plugged, plus the patient had a productive cough. Doug went to Azawi to express concern over wet gauze which was needed to be placed around the bloody trachea for treatment. Neither Gail nor Doug mentioned the HIV infection status with Dennis or Lana.

Lana was livid, and scared. She went back to Dr. Azawi and informed Azawi that she knew she (Lana) and one therapist were not told about the patients' infection. Lana told Azawi that the nurse, Donna, had only informed Gail and Doug, but did not follow the protocol to share infection information on all patients. Azawi would not look Lana in the face; Azawi kept looking down at her desk and said nothing.

Dr. Azawi had consulted with the patient on July 20, 2009 and the HIV positive status was noted in the consultation notes. There were other notations by other providers which revealed the patient's infectious status. Lana was not privy to Azawi's notes.

If a person thought Lana was simply complaining and whining, that suspicion had been disproved. Why would Azawi not want Donna to share information which was life threatening, to Lana?

On October 5, 2009, Lana sent an email to Dr. Azawi, Dr. Williams, and Donna Pikulsky, notifying them of the breach of policy, and the selective notification of patient information. Lana attached hospital policy to the email. Violating policy meant nothing to people who had a lot to hide.

Dr. Azawi not only wanted Lana gone so Azawi's unprofessional and dangerous behavior would be hidden, but Azawi put Lana in a situation which could have killed Lana.

The cover up of Dr. Azawi's behavior, and the performance of the therapists, was wearing on Lana.

After reviewing emails between Lana and Dr. Azawi from September 16 to September 30, it was evident to me that Dr. Azawi was eliminating standard parts of the mid-year evaluation of the therapists to make them look competent and make Lana look like a micro-manager.

Azawi sent Lana another email and asked Lana for an update on the mid-year evaluations for the therapists. Lana responded, stating:

"The therapist's evaluations are based on Competencies. Since you told me to stop doing Variance Reports, I have no way to evaluate them based on the Critical Elements and other items of the Competencies. How do you want me to evaluate them in this case. Thanks, Lana."

Azawi's response was to have Lana forward the list of competencies to Azawi. Then, on September 30, Azawi sent an email to Lana stating:

"The variance report is not a medical center requirement and I prefer you not to use it. Employee evaluation is done based on your observation as a supervisor throughout the year."

Was Azawi crazy? Lana is a supervisor. Lana is not in the treatment room all day to observe all the therapists.

There was no way Lana could "observe" all the procedures. Reports are objective. Observations are not always objective.

Lana had supervisory work to do. Lana had meetings to attend. Lana had reports to write. Azawi was thinking up anything to diminish the authority of Lana and attempt to make the mid-year evaluation a subjective document to show bias against the therapists.

Lana knew that the Variance Reports was objective. It reported errors which burn patients. Azawi did not want the facts.

Lana's only remedy was to contact Human Resources, and Mary Beth McCartan. Lana already had a Formal Grievance filed so Mary Beth would not be surprised to receive communication from Lana.

Lana sent Mary Beth a note/email asking how to handle Azawi's directives. Ms. McCartan stated on October 2:

"Your employees should each have a performance plan. The Performance Plan outlines the critical elements and the performance standards expected to be met to perform the critical elements at the fully successful level. You need to rate the employees against each of these. Anything that the employee MUST perform should be deemed a Critical Element."

Evidently, Azawi was violating hospital policy, and no one was going to make her accountable.

An odd thing happened on the day before Ms. McCartan sent the email stating that critical elements should be included in the assessment of the therapists.

The Freckle Incident
Thursday October 1, 2009

Dennis and Doug were off from work, so Lana had to come out and work on the treatment machine. Dr. Azawi decided to come into the treatment room and see how patients were being "treated," and that was a bit suspicious.

Gail was working that day, so Lana went into the treatment room with Gail. Lana knew that Gail's attitude since the Varian incident was terrible and Gail was rude, insulting, and insubordinate. Lana was not looking forward to this, but she would suck it up and get through it.

"Tattoos" had been placed on the patient during simulation to help the therapists locate the area of the treatment area. After helping the patient onto the treatment table, the patient was "aligned" so treatment could begin. The patient was a bit anxious and moved off the marks, and a readjustment had to be made.

Dr. Azawi entered the room and walked to the side of the table where Gail was working while Gail was getting the patient back on the marks. Gail was charged with aligning the patient on the tattoos. When Gail announced that she had aligned the patient, Lana noticed that the patient monitors revealed that the patient was off the mark on both axes, longitudinal and vertical. Azawi was watching but was saying nothing.

Lana asked Gail if she was on the mark of the tattoo. Gail said "yes." Lana knew this could not be true, but if Gail were off the mark, would she even care?

Lana walked around the table to check the alignment and found that Gail had lined the patient up on a freckle instead of the tattoo. A freckle?

Lana pulled out a penlight to make sure. Gail used a freckle instead of the tattoo and was ready to give the patient radiation. It was an inconvenience for Lana to be in the treatment room, but if Lana had not been there, the patient, a Veteran, would have been injured.

The freckle was 1.7 centimeters off vertically and 1.3 centimeters longitudinally. Lana circled the tattoo, putting a star-burst around the tattoo for Gail's benefit. Gail went to the opposite side of the table, away from Lana. Azawi witnessed the entire event and said nothing.

After leaving the treatment room, Lana, Azawi, and Gail went to the control area to deliver the treatment. Lana told Dr. Azawi that it was a good thing that Azawi was there to see how Gail treated the patients and had no concern for accuracy, which injures patients. Lana thought that Azawi would then believe that Gail lied about the Varian matter, is incompetent, and should be fired.

Lana asked Azawi if she saw what Gail had done. Azawi said, *"Saw what?"* Lana reminded Azawi that Gail had lined the patient up using a freckle, knew the adjustments were off, and was ready to radiate the patient in a very harmful manner. Azawi's reply was, *"It wasn't that far off."*

Lana was horrified at what Azawi said. "Not that far off?" Azawi had just proved she was not qualified to supervise or be the Chief Oncologist. Somehow, Azawi kept her job, and Lana had no idea how she kept from being found out. Lining up on a freckle was something a student might do. Gail Francis was not a student. Gail was a licensed radiation therapist with a degree in radiation therapy and licensed by ARRT (American Registry of Radiologic Technologists) and was not supposed to make errors like that. That behavior was that of a therapist who was careless and had wanton disregard for the welfare of the patient, the Veteran.

Friday, October 2, 2009

Lana filed a Formal Grievance on this day. She had experienced being unknowingly exposed to HIV because of an overt act of vengeance by Dr. Azawi.

This had exposed the incompetency of an employee only to see Azawi cover for the employee (the freckle incident), be isolated from necessary information, been demeaned and ridiculed in front of subordinates, and put her life in jeopardy. Lana was tired of it.

At 4:00pm, Dr. Azawi called Lana into the Conference Room under the guise that she and Dr. Williams wanted to talk to Lana. Before the "meeting" began, Lana mentioned the issue with Gail Francis and that Gail used a freckle as orientation to treat a patient.

Azawi's response, again, was, "It wasn't that far off."

Lana reminded Azawi that the patient had moved, and they were re-aligning the patient. Gail was using a freckle as a landmark instead of the tattoo, which was why Lana was off by .5 centimeters. If Lana had not seen the error, the patient would have been terribly injured.

Lana told both Dr. Azawi and Dr. Williams exactly how far off from the treatment area the radiation was going to be given. Azawi was not concerned. The lack of understanding of accuracy and how it is achieved by therapists was shocking, and their reaction to the incident proved the incompetence of the physicians.

The physicians accepted this lack of skill from therapists and would not allow Lana to make the therapists accountable and correct them. Lana "was the supervisor," but the physicians took away her authority as a ploy to force Lana to resign.

October 5, 2009

Dr. Azawi was at it again; dismissing policies which made people accountable.

The Chief of Staff, Dr. Szabo, must have feared this woman. What kind of leverage did she have over Szabo and Duff, the hospital administrator?

This morning Dr. Azawi sent out an email stating she would not allow "competencies" for yearly evaluations, although it was the policy of the Department of Molecular Medicine and the Veterans Administration to do so.

This meant that Lana was not to make an objective judgment about the competency of the persons she was supervising, which was the job of a supervisor. Lana knew the job better than the subordinates, which authorized her to "grade" them.

Azawi wanted to take away any way to determine who is better than the other, or who needed correction. Azawi wanted Lana simply to observe the therapists and do and say nothing.

Later in the day, an email was sent to Mary Beth McCartan (HR), notifying her that the therapists had signed off on their competency reports (which Azawi would not allow), and Azawi was also eliminating the Variance Reports, which was the objective barometer of competency.

Violating policy did not concern Azawi. No one was going to enforce policy on Azawi while Azawi was in the department, regardless of whether she was the Chief Oncologist.

Lana took the time to send an email to Azawi, Williams, and Donna Pikulsky concerning the violation of policy and the deadly health risk which jeopardized the lives of the therapist, namely "selective notification". These people knew an HIV positive patient was being treated, and these people decided to advise only two therapists of the infection and did not advise any other therapists. This was part of the hidden policy exhibited by Azawi in which she mandated communication and sharing of information was suspended for Azawi to have more control. Azawi did not want everyone to know everything, and that was the way it was to be.

Lana and Dennis very easily could have contracted HIV. Azawi, Williams, and Pikulsky made sure that possibility existed.

Lana found out that Cancer Committee meetings were being held and she had not been notified of the meetings. It was later determined that the notification of the meetings was being emailed by Donna Pikulsky's husband. Lana was conveniently left off the list, although Lana was the Chief Radiation Therapist. That was no coincidence.

Lana was wanting to have her meeting with Isabel Duff, the Director.

This request had been before Human Resources for some time now and the grievance had been filed.

Azawi was consistent; she was being shockingly irrational. Evidently Gail Francis, was talking privately to Azawi about getting the pay raise. A pay raise for Gail? No document was more damaging than the Varian report, and Gail was supposed to have been fired. Azawi had sent the email to Lana ordering Lana to give Gail Francis a pay raise. Azawi went to the extent of dictating to Lana what to write on the form.

During the next two weeks after October 9, 2009, Lana learned that Dr. Schuldheis would be the grievance examiner for her Formal Grievance. Mary Beth McCartan, the Human Resources Chief, told Lana to bring up the patient abuse issue to the examiner. Lana did not know who to trust. Human Resources seemed to throw her a few crumbs to pacify her, but nothing was done about Azawi.

Lana asked for a more experienced mediator. Lana was feeling bad; the grievance was probably going to be dismissed and nothing was going to happen.

Lana was getting desperate. Patients were being injured, then their wounds were treated afterward. Azawi would not allow therapists to be graded on performance. Azawi was dismissing VA regulations, violating "selective notification" policy, creating subterfuge in the department, and no one was brave enough to hold her accountable.

Tuesday, October 27, 2009

Lana had experienced enough mistreatment of patients and she could not stop it.

On October 27, 2009, Lana filed for Whistleblower Protection and violation of Prohibited Personnel Practices with the Office of Special Counsel. This governmental office, the Office of Special Counsel, was set up with four divisions, two of which involved the matters to which Lana would be reporting.

Lana was being targeted for retribution for reporting the Varian Incident and reporting violations committed by Dr. Azawi. Azawi stripped Lana of all supervisory power over her subordinates and humiliated her in their presence. Lana thought someone would see the violations, the patients being injured, and the administration turning a blind eye.

Lana was looking for someone to save the patients, and for someone to have the courage to make these people accountable. Lana was looking for someone to trust. Lana did not know she was about to be violated again by those she thought she could trust. More people had more to hide.

Chapter Six:

Filing Complaints to Protect Veterans

Lana had received Fully Successful performance evaluations prior to the events which led to her filing of grievances in 2009. It was quite odd that Azawi would give another Fully Successful performance evaluation and not mention the fact that Azawi was referring Lana to a counselor.

If Azawi thought Lana needed a counselor, would Azawi think that any person needing a counselor would have a problem treating patients? This was a blatant contradiction; the reason Azawi did not document the counselor referral was because Azawi and her cover-up was the reason for Lana's distress, and Lana's distress did not have a negative influence upon the care Lana was giving to the Veterans. In fact, the abuse and the cover-up perpetrated by Azawi and her legions made Lana more aware of lack of care for the Veterans. Lana saw it all, and no one could keep up with her. Lana had to protect the Veterans from the therapists, and Azawi.

After the Varian Incident, the months of vicious harassment of Lana continued, including all persons emboldened by Azawi. Lana became more proactive in her attempt to protect herself and the Veterans from these people.

October 1, 2009

Azawi was very creative in her harassment. On this day, Azawi would stoop to a level only Machiavelli could appreciate; Azawi sent an email to Lana, telling Lana to endorse Gail Francis for an increase in pay, from a GS-7 to a GS-8.

Gail Francis, getting an increase in pay grade? Gail Francis had to have had very damaging information about Azawi for Azawi to, not only direct Lana to endorse Gail for the promotion, but in doing so, Azawi was violating protocol.

Azawi was not supposed to be involving herself in a personnel issue in which Lana was the supervisor.

This promotion was to be only at the discretion of Lana. This was just another way to attack Lana's authority and sow discord in the department.

Lana refused to endorse any advancement for Gail Francis. When Dr. Azawi realized that Lana was not going to endorse the increase for Gail Francis from a GS-7 to a GS-8, Dr. Azawi dictated precisely what Lana was to write for justification and how competent Ms. Francis was in performance of her duties. Azawi sent this dictation to Lana in an email and directed Lana to sign and submit the endorsement which included false information.

Lana was directed to write this for Dr. Azawi because of the limited language skills of Dr. Azawi. Dr. Azawi attended medical school in Iraq, and regularly had persons in the department write emails and other communication for her.

Dr. Azawi was violating protocol by being involved in the personnel matter of increasing the pay grade of Gail Francis. This matter was supposed to be initiated by the direct supervisor, which was Lana. Lana was not in agreement with the pay increase due to the performance and conduct of Gail Francis, but there was nothing Lana could do but follow Dr. Azawi's orders. Lana was not putting her name on the submission. Lana completed the documents for Gail Francis' Grade Increase and delivered the documents to Azawi. Azawi would have to sign for the pay increase. Lana knew that if her name was on the referral for increase in pay, this would be interpreted that Lana condoned Gail Francis' conduct. That was a trap into which Lana would not fall.

Lana did not bring up the pay raise matter for the next few weeks, until Lana was advised that Gail Francis had filed and EEO (Equal Employment Opportunity) complaint against Lana for delaying her Grade Increase, which Azawi supposedly submitted. Gail was loving the drama.

Many issues kept Lana's head spinning; one of which was Azawi was sending emails to Lana insisting that Lana fill out the paperwork for Gail Francis to get an increase in pay grade, which Azawi knew would irritate Lana. Gail Francis had proved to be non-compliant, insubordinate, not conscientious, dishonest, and was supposed to be fired at the end of June 2009 because she lied about moving the table on which a patient was lying during treatment, creating the Varian Incident.

On the following day (October 2, 2009), Lana filed a Formal Complaint with Human Resources. Azawi was destroying the department in ways which were worse than when she was demoted. by Szabo a year earlier. These people were afraid of Azawi, and Azawi was afraid of Gail Francis. What was wrong with this picture?

October 22, 2009

Lana wanted to talk to a friend. Lana met outside the building with the Chief Safety officer, Lynette Fox. Lana was a bit concerned talking to Lynette in the office so outdoors seemed a bit more private. Lana dropped the bomb of filing the action with the OSC (Office of Special Counsel) with respect to Azawi violating Prohibited Personnel Practices (PPP). Lynette praised Lana for filing the action. Lana was filing it later in the week.

Lana had known Lynette for quite some time, and Lynette knew about the Varian Incident in her capacity as the chief safety officer. Lynette also knew the history of Azawi with others. The meeting was intended to advise Lynette that Lana was taking the next step to have the authorities know what was being hidden, and how these secrets affect patient care. Lynette and Cindy were two of the few persons Lana could trust.

As Lana and Lynette were talking, Donna Pikulsky, the head nurse and ally of Dr. Azawi, walked outside to see the two ladies talking. It would not seem unusual to see a Chief Safety Officer and a Chief Radiation Therapist having a chat, but since the Varian incident 4 months prior, and the denial by Dr. Azawi of human error by Gail Francis and Doug Hollins, Lana had become the enemy of the department. Lynette was receptive to Lana's concern.

Monday October 26, 2009

Azawi was getting nervous; Lana could talk circles around Azawi on technical issues, but Lana was no match for Azawi's demeanor. On this date, Azawi made a request for an experienced mediator from the ORM (Office of Resolution Management) to be assigned resolution of the Formal Complaint.

Tuesday October 27, 2009

On October 27, 2009, Lana filed the complaint with the Office of Special Counsel of the Office of Veteran Affairs. The nature of the complaint was a PPP claim, Prohibited Personnel Practices, which cited Azawi and the hospital for a variety of offenses, including ignoring the chain of command, attacking and harassing Lana after the exposure to HIV by inept physicians during the Varian Incident, observing that the HR department was allowing Azawi to commit these acts, and more.

After filing out the action report with the Office of Special Counsel, Lana thought someone would see what was happening to the patients, veterans, and swoop down to take away Dr. Azawi and the other culprits. As with all government work, things do not move quickly, although there could be a mandate to investigate a filed report.

Lana contacted Lynette Fox, and they meet again. Lana told Lynette that the OSC paperwork had been sent.

The VA departments could be represented as a "finger-painting" of supervisors, and some authority overlaps. Lana knew that Azawi's mandate of eliminating the Variance Reports, which was the report that held the therapist accountable and showed the accuracy of treatment, put Veterans in danger, and eliminated accountability for the therapists. Lana did not hold back in announcing her shock that Azawi would eliminate these reports, and she told as many people she could find to stop this reign of terror.

Wednesday November 4, 2009

Lana had been in touch with Leo Moons, head of Quality Improvement and Education Safety Coordinator. On this date, Leo sent an email to Lana, and attached to the email was a copy of the QI (Quality Improvement) Manual, where Lana could find that Variance Reports were mandatory.

Lana sent the email and the attachment to Mary Beth McCartan in HR. Lana's best wish would be for the ACR were nearby to see Azawi at work.

J.B. Simms

<u>Monday November 16, 2009</u>

Lana finally received a Formal Grievance hearing on November 16, 2009 with Human Resources at Long Beach VA Hospital. Prior to the meeting, Lana had a meeting with Mary Beth McCartan, Chief of Human Resources, and Esther Pittman, Employee Specialist regarding the improper presentation of the Letter of Reprimand and the patient care problems covered up in the "Fact Finding Letter".

During this meeting, Lana began receiving changing promises from Mary Beth McCartan and Herb Moisa. Months later, Ms. McCartan told Lana the delayed response would probably allow Lana to receive a favorable finding. Answers to other questions on the status of the response to the Formal Grievance were "it is imminent", "on Duff's desk", "in process", and other diversionary responses.

Again, the meeting was on November 16, 2009. Lana did not receive the response to the Formal Grievance until the Spring of 2011 (over 15 months the grievance was filed). The significance of this delay will be explained later.

Ten months after the meeting, Lana was ordered by her doctor to take a Leave of Absence because of abuse induced stress; Lana would be absent from September 15, 2010 until December 15, 2010. By the time Lana had left (September 15, 2010) she had not seen any response to her Formal Grievance, which had been filed eleven months earlier, on October 2, 2009.

Within days after Lana returned on December 15, 2010, Lana tracked down Ms. McCartan. Ms. McCartan said after seeing Lana, "We had the response on the Formal Grievance ready, but you were on FMLA (disability leave from September 15, 2010- December 15, 2010 as a result of developing PTSD due to work conditions)". Lana told Ms. McCartan, "I am here now" but Ms. McCartan postponed revealing the results of the Formal Grievance until months later, in violation of policies in the VA Employee Manual.

McCartan never called or emailed Lana during the time Lana was on leave.

J.B. Simms

Friday December 4, 2009

Lana was growing weary of Gail Francis' complaining that she was not getting her pay raise, so Lana met with Susan DeMasters, manager of EEO/ADR concerning the complaint. How could Gail Francis go over the head of Lana to try to get a raise.?

On December 4, 2009, the issues were presented to Ms. DeMasters. Lana advised McMasters of the issues of Gail Francis not being worthy of a pay raise, and that she should have been fired. Lana also told McMasters that Azawi was the person who generated the request, Azawi wrote it, and this violated protocol. After the meeting, Lana thought matter was cleared.

During this time, Gail Francis refused to sign her evaluation, and ran to the Human Resources department for support. Lana continued to refuse to endorse the pay grade increase for Ms. Francis, and the response from Herb Moisa was that it "is a management decision to promote based on performance in light of standards". These new "standards" were in-house standards of covering for each other.

The involvement of Azawi with Gail's pay increase was not the only questionable behavior exhibited by Dr. Azawi. On the morning of December 10, 2009, Dr. Azawi tried to convince Lana to bill a procedure which was improper although Lana told Azawi the submission would not be correct.

Dr. Azawi demeaned and berated Lana about her refusal to agree to the demand by Azawi. Lana knew the submission would be considered fraud.

The behavior of nurse Donna Pikulsky had created many problems, and she acted with impunity as she violated policy: (1) destroying new forms used for writing steroid taper instructions for patients; previously, notes had been scribbled on scraps of paper or paper towels (2) simulation instructions with skeletal figures to expedite patient simulations without physician approval, and (3) ignoring a spreadsheets requested by Dr. Williams in September 2008 to track patient progress of tests and procedures. Ms. Pikulsky's response for not using the spreadsheet was "I am not a data manager".

In December 2009, Lana had requested mediation with Dr. Azawi which was to address Lana's Functional Statement; Lana's job description. Since Dr. Azawi had eliminated using Variance Reports as a tool to grade the therapists, and the fact that Dr. Azawi had curtailed Lana's review and reporting of errors made by therapists, Lana did not know what her job entailed. All she knew was that her job, based upon Azawi's dictates, was to ignore the therapists' mistakes and ignore the fact that the physicians could not interpret film and data taken from IMRT.

On January 4, 2010, the first mediation took place. The persons in the room were Lana, Dr. Azawi, Dr. Williams, and nurse Donna Pikulsky. The meeting was a "free for all"'; yelling, standing and yelling, refusing to answer questions and the meeting was a failure.

Another meeting was held on January 12, 2010 in which Lana was pointing out treatment errors to Dr. Azawi and Dr. Williams. Lana was accompanied by Dr. Frank, another doctor in the department. Dr. Williams was being asked questions by the mediator, Dr. Frank, who was a staff physician. Dr. Williams responded by saying, "Do I need my libel attorney?" The meeting was so volatile that it had to be suspended. Lana was gaining sympathy from the mediator, which angered Azawi and Williams, who had no valid responses for the demotion of Lana and circumventing Lana to communicate with the therapists.

Dr. Frank told Lana a few times after the meeting that he had never heard anyone spoken to the way the physicians did to Lana.

After the first mediation on January 4, 2010, Dr. Azawi decided to hassle Lana by insisting that Lana tell Dr. Azawi everywhere Lana went, how long she would be gone and what Lana was doing. Since Lana was being bombarded by Dr. Azawi, Lana gave Dr. Azawi computer permission to access her Outlook calendar for reference. Lana also had a pager which Dr. Azawi could call, but never would. According to Lana, Dr. Azawi preferred an accusatory method of determining Lana's whereabouts.

The reply for Lana's Formal Grievance expired on February 1, 2010. This expiration, and violation of VA policy, came and went without any notice or comment from the administration.

The first eight and a half months of 2010 had similar events but with increased frequency and aggression on the part of Dr. Azawi and Dr. Williams.

Lana sent an email to Ms. Pikulsky asking her to "try not to schedule 'sims' (simulations) on Friday morning" because of the changed date of Supervisor's meeting. Within 30 minutes, Dr. Azawi and Ms. Pikulsky found Lana in the control area of the treatment machine. Dr. Azawi angrily accused Lana, in front of her subordinates, of telling Ms. Pikulsky not to schedule any simulations on Friday "mornings". That was the way the accusations from Dr. Azawi and Dr. Williams were presented. The ineffective sessions in the conference room continued, the physicians stated they had no time to discuss patient care issues, nor the fact that therapists were not following procedures.

The following two mediations, one with Dr. Azawi alone and one with both physicians, on January 12, 2010 and March 5, 2010 were both ended by the mediator.

Meetings had to take place, regardless of the tension and unsettled complaints. Lana attended a meeting with Dr. Williams on February 2, 2010, and when Lana began taking notes, Dr. Williams forbade Lana from doing so. Williams took his notes at his pleasure.

Shortly after commencing, the mediation attempts were labeled a failure due to lack of cooperation by Dr. Azawi. However, Lana presented Dr. Azawi's manipulated version of standard operating procedures which allowed Dr. Azawi to violate VA policies and hide patient abuse and mistreatment.

During a mediation session on March 5, Dr. Azawi was asked, by the mediator, for the reason for her actions. Dr. Azawi answered, "Because I can". That ended the mediation.

Lana had heard nothing from HR on her Formal Complaint. On February 9, Lana sent an email to Herb Moisa, telling Herb that it had been 78 days since the grievance had been filed. There was no response from Herb, but a day later Lana received an email from Mary Beth McCartan; she stated workload was reason for delay of response.

By 2010, Lana knew that "Because I can" was the law of the land, as did everyone else in the department, and others took up that mantra. Here is what did not make sense:

1. Dr. Azawi had been dismissed as the Chief Oncologist for the same behavior she was currently exhibiting, (berating staff members, not following procedures, not being accountable for her lack of knowledge) but now no one was listening to the complaints about her.

2. Human Resources knew of Azawi's behavior and did nothing. Dr. Szabo, along with Herb Moisa, who had lost a two-inch-high stack of evidence against Dr. Azawi which caused her demotion in June 2008, was now ignoring evidence of abuse and neglect by Dr. Azawi.

3. Azawi had sued Szabo for making derogatory comments and was awarded $50,000, so now Szabo was scared of Azawi, or something Azawi knew.

4. The Varian Incident was dismissed by Dr. Azawi as misreading the report rather than the human error, but initially when Lana brought the film and records of the Varian Incident to Azawi, Azawi's response was "good catch" and to fire the therapists.

5. Azawi misrepresented the procedures being conducted in the department to the American College of Radiology in order to obtain accreditation. No one reported her for this, although Human Resources and the EEO (Equal Opportunity Office) assigned to the hospital had been informed of Azawi's deceit.

It was like a David Copperfield magic act; a den of thieves, a chief thief, people lied for each other, no one really trusted one another, and the thought was if one person got caught or "went down", then everyone would go down. This took CYA to a whole new level.

For example, on January 5, 2010, Dr. Azawi sent an email to Lana at 2:50pm. Dr. Azawi wanted the names of the patients who had been mistreated over the past two weeks, and wanted the information in 40 minutes with no concern for any task Lana was performing. Lana sent the email to Susan DeMasters at EEO, stating that this request was not agreed upon at the last meeting. DeMaster's response was:

"... I am working on the agreement right now...I think it best if you do what she wants right now... can you do it in 30 minutes?"

On the following day, (January 6, 2010) Lana emailed the list of five (5) different patients who had been abused within the last two weeks. Five patients had been abused in a two-week period? If my math is correct, that is 130 people a year. Nobody cared.

What was Dr. Azawi going to do with the files of the abused patients? Why did she need the files? Two days after sending the list of injured patients, Lana notified Szabo of Azawi's behavior, and Lana asked for a meeting with Azawi. Azawi's reply was that she would not meet with Lana alone.

Whatever Szabo said to Azawi about her Iraqi heritage in 2009 gave Azawi free reign and Azawi cared nothing for the Veteran patients.

After Azawi's mantra of authority, "Because I Can," the spring of 2010 continued as "business as usual."

As Lana entered the conference room, it was apparent to Lana that the meeting would be just the three of them. Dr. Azawi lit into Lana with petty fault-finding accusations about an incident which had occurred a month prior to the meeting. Dr. Williams followed suit. Lana asked if she could record the meeting and document the vitriolic attitude of the doctors. The doctors refused to be recorded or allow Lana to take notes. Things were out of hand. This was another ambush. Lana walked out.

During the month of February 2010, Lana continued to contact Human Resources in an attempt to determine the resolution to her Formal Grievance. On February 9, 2010, Lana sent an email to Herb Moisa, the assistant director of Human Resources. Lana stated to Herb that. the time for a response to the Formal Grievance had expired. It had been 78 days since Lana filed the Formal Grievance. Lana was under the impression that the grievance expired after 70 days, which is a long time.

On the same day, Lana received an email from Ms. McCartan, head of Human Resources. Ms. McCartan stated to Lana that the delay was a result of a heavy workload at the Human Resources office. The truth was they were "waiting out" Lana to see if she would crack, and leave, like the other two chief therapists. Lana was not about to bang her head against the wall.

Over two months later, Lana had yet to receive any notice of a hearing on her Formal Grievance. On April 13, 2010, Lana sent an email to Human Resources asking about the status of her grievance. The following day, Lana received an email stating that the response to the Formal Grievance would be completed by the end of the week.

It had been over 100 days since the filing of the grievance. Lana knew that the battle just took on another front; not only could Human Resources not enforce violations of staff and employees, they could not even monitor themselves.

On April 16, 2010, Lana sent an email to Dr. Szabo, advising him that a patient named Frank had to be transferred to another unit because the improper radiation treatment caused an "oozing neck wound." Lana was hoping for sympathy for the Veteran.

This became another of many emails to Szabo in which the response was "I will look into it" or no reply was received at all.

This was not the same Dr. Szabo who, when he received emails from Lana concerning Azawi's behavior, he replied, "Things will change." Was it pressure? Was it leverage? Was it blackmail? Did Szabo have skeletons which Azawi was aware?

During the Spring of 2010, Lana began communicating with fellow Chief Therapists from different hospitals. Lana was also communicating with Wendy Kemp; whose title was Administrative Officer. Wendy's work address was: National Radiation Oncology Program, Office of Patient Care Services, VA Medical Center, 1201 Broad Rock Blvd., Richmond, VA 23249. Ms. Kemp reported directly to Michael Hagan, the Chief Radiation Oncologist for the VA, whose office was in Richmond, Virginia.

By the end of April 2010 emails were flying between the Chief Radiation Therapists all over the United States.

The tone of the emails between the Chief Radiation Therapists was of supportive of one another and attempted to create a way to communicate and show others the problems which could cause a department to be "shut-down," as was the case in Philadelphia. Patti Hall, the Chief Therapist in Tampa, Florida, stated in an email on May 12, 2010 to Lana that Wendy Kemp was going to be setting up a National Radiation Oncology Web Share site for shared information such as:

1. Functional statements (job descriptions)
2. Scope of practices SOP (Standard Operating Procedures)
3. Policies

This seemed to be a good idea to Lana, and Lana was one of the first persons asked to be involved.

This idea was shared with Dr. Hagan on May 13, 2010 via email from Patti Hall in Tampa.

Two days earlier (May 10, 2010), Lana sent Lucinda Swan, the office manager at the Long Beach VA, a list of the questions being submitted by the Office of Inspector General.

May 13, 2010

Although Dr. Azawi did everything she could to demean Lana in front of her subordinates, micromanage to the point of harassment, and remove Lana's authority, Lana retained the respect of her peers. This was evident when on May 13, 2010 Lana sent the following email to Dr. Azawi and Dr. Szabo:

"I have been asked to be a member of the Chief Therapist Work Group. Other members are from Jackson, MS; Boston, MA; St. Louis, MO; and Tampa, FL. A VANTS has been set up for 5/19/2010 to include these initial items: ACR Checklist to benefit those who have yet to be reviewed. Staffing Standardizations Coding Guidelines To be or not to be... Under Diagnosis Imaging Services"

Azawi certainly would not want Lana involved with a work group which involved the ACR. That would expose Azawi.

A subsequent email copy was sent from Lana to Dr. Azawi and Dr. Szabo which was a letter from Wendy Kemp. Ms. Kemp advised that she was working on the Radiation Oncology intranet website and hoped to have it up by the end of August. Ms. Kemp was to be the contact person on this matter.

Lana was a very important person in the nationwide Radiation Oncology community with the VA. Those persons outside the hospital sang her praises; persons at the Long Beach VA who were allies of Lana were afraid to stand up publicly for Lana because it could mean their job. Lana knew that she was like a leper at the Long Beach VA hospital.

Chapter Seven:

NY Times, OIG, and ACR

Fewer than two weeks after date of the Varian Incident (June 17, 2009) a New York Times writer named Walt Bogdanich began writing articles about the dangers of improper radiation treatment at various hospitals, including the VA Hospital at East Orange, NJ and the one at Philadelphia, PA. This series was entitled "Radiation Boom".

(http://topics.nytimes.com/top/news/us/series/radiation_boom/index.htm l?8qa.)

One article, dated, June 29, 2009, revealed that an outrageously incompetent doctor, Dr. Gary D. Kao, admitted mishandling radioactive seed implants, admitting he "could have done better". Mr. Bogdanich further wrote that in 57 cases, Dr. Kao's unit delivered too little radiation to the prostate, and in 35 other cases the unit overdosed other parts of the body.

Oddly enough, this was within days of the Varian Incident at the Long Beach VA Hospital.

Mr. Bogdanich, along with contributing writer Kristina Rebelo and others, published a piece on January 26, 2010 in the NY Times as a part of a series of articles concerning injuries suffered by patients at the VA Hospital in East Orange, NJ.

These articles prompted the US Congress to mandate that the VA Office of Inspector General (OIG) make onsite inspections of over 20 VA Hospital radiation oncology departments. The inspections were to verify the training of physicians in the highly complex planning and treatment of IMRT.

In the case of the Long Beach VA Hospital, the OIG report published March 10, 2011, the "mandated inspection," never addressed these issues. It was only after Lana filed the Hotline report, at the request of the OIG inspectors, that patient injuries were addressed. The report was published March 9, 2011.

A copy of the OIG report of the Long Beach VA Hospital at the link below, or read the report in the appendix.

http://www.va.gov/oig/54/reports/VAOIG-10-03861-119.pdf

It was quite interesting that during the time of the Varian Incident and the 6 months afterward, there was scant mention of the articles written by Bogdanich and Rebelo among the administration and the chief of radiology within the hundreds of printed emails I viewed from the VA Radiation Department.

Since these emails were used as one of the sources for this writing, a person would think that the NYT articles written by Mr. Bogdanich would have garnered more attention at the local VA Hospital, especially in the radiation department. It was not known if the articles caused much anxiety to the administration. There was no reaction, which is consistent with the attitude or denial exhibited by the administration at the Long Beach VA Hospital during that time.

The administration at the VA never mentioned the news articles to the staff.

Evidently the articles in the NY Times and the upcoming scrutiny by the OIG did not concern the persons in charge of the Radiation Therapy department at the Long Beach, VA, namely Dr. Azawi.

Life continued as usual for Dr. Azawi and her "management style"; dysfunctional, abusive to employees and patients, dictatorial, unaccountable, and lethal.

In late 2012, after I had reviewed the binders of Lana's emails, it occurred to me that if the American College of Radiology gave accreditation to the Long Beach VA Hospital in September 2009, they must have had no knowledge of the Varian Incident, nor the results of the two OIG publications, both published in March 2011.

If the OIG found troubling matters because of a VA hospital inspection, the accreditation agency for the Radiation Oncology Department, the ACR, never knew. The news of the inspections was in the NY Times, and was mandated by Congress. Someone at the ACR should have known the OIG was inspecting the Radiation Oncology Department of at least 30 VA hospitals.

The shocking conclusions were these:

The OIG had inspected the radiation oncology department of over 30 VA hospitals, and the OIG never forwarded any results to the agency which gives accreditation to those departments.

The ACR did not know that the OIG was inspecting the radiation oncology departments of the more than 30 VA hospitals, even after NY Times articles brought attention to improper care.

It would not be until February 2013 that the ACR would be exposed, and Lana Miller Boyer exposing the Long Beach VA Hospital to the ACR in June 2013.

J.B. Simms

Chapter Eight:

Doctor Denials and Fraud Conspiracy

Lana had filed the Formal Grievance with the Long Beach VA Hospital in hopes to gain an audience with the director of the hospital, Isabel Duff. The EEO action was separate from the Formal Grievance because the Formal Grievance was being handled by Human Resources at the Long Beach VA Hospital (McCartan and Moisa); the EEO (DeMasters) was to address violations of federal law.

There was a lot of activity during the spring of 2010, not to mention that the mediation between Lana and the Azawi/Williams team in the spring of 2010, while ongoing, was a complete waste of time. The responses which Lana received from Dr. Azawi and Dr. Williams during mediation were unbearable to hear. The physicians refused to discuss why the therapists were problematic. The physicians stated to the mediator that they knew everything about the technical aspect of radiation. The truth was the doctors were lying to the mediator. There was no way Lana could put the doctors to a test in front of the mediator.

Dr. Azawi's reaction to being exposed was to write up a different job description for Lana, taking Lana from a position to be able to examine the work of the doctors, and try to intimidate Lana into signing it. Dr. Azawi tried at least 3 times to change Lana's job description, but Lana refused each time.

Since the initial episode in March 2008, when Dr. Azawi related to nurse Pikulsky that Lana should be removed, Lana sought help and counsel from those in authority who could and should stop this unprofessional conduct, and intimidation by Azawi. Lana was trying to find someone in the hospital who would enforce a level of civility which would insure that standards of care be followed as was written in the VA handbook, and that the Veterans would stop being injured.

Stress was being felt by everyone in the department, and it affected the job performance of everyone, not to mention patient care and safety.

Lana talked with Dr. Szabo, the Chief of Staff, as well as communicated via e- mail concerning events which occurred between staff meetings. One patient threatened to contact his congressman. Dr. Szabo would write notes and say he would talk to the physicians. That never happened. Dr. Szabo became scared of his own shadow.

Walt Bogdanich, Kristina Rebelo, were effective

They had gotten the attention of Congress and the House Energy and Commerce Committee, where hearings were held as stated before. This activity generated quite a buzz, and within a few months, mid 2010, a select number of VA hospital radiation oncology department around the US would begin being inspected.

The NY Times series of articles had done the trick. Everyone in the department was getting a bit nervous. During the spring of 2010, rumor was that the OIG was going to inspect the Radiation Oncology Department at the Long Beach VA. Even though the department had obtained accreditation less than a year before, Lana knew that Dr. Azawi had eliminated many of the regulations set forth by the American College of Radiology, and that the OIG should catch the violations and recommend that Isabel Duff dismiss Dr. Azawi. That would end the problem of Azawi. That sounded simple.

When the Long Beach VA Hospital was notified that the Office of Inspector General (OIG) was starting an inspection of all Radiation Therapy departments, which was mandated by the House Committee, the physicians were not overly concerned until a list of hospitals to be examined by the OIG was issued.

On May 11, 2010, it was official; the Office of Inspector General was coming to visit the VA hospitals Radiation Oncology departments. Wendy Kemp, the Administration Officer reporting directly to Michael P. Hagan sent out emails advising which departments would be visited, beginning in the few weeks.

In preparation for the site visits, Wendy's office requested the following information:

"Physician Peer Review"

MD: IMRT specific training (case numbers and sites: pelvis, head and neck, thoracic)"

There were more requests, such as certification from dosimetrist and others, but this looked like the OIG was going to check out the certification of Azawi and Williams.

On the heels of Wendy Kemp's email, Dr. Hagan sent out an email to Wendy, which was forwarded to the Radiation Department in Long Beach. Dr. Hagan emphasized that the OIG would be concentrating their efforts on IMRT processes, and this is "largely in response to the NYT articles." The three areas to be focused upon would be:

1. Physician Peer Review
2. Machine Quality Assessment
3. Patient treatment

Dr. Hagan wanted the information to his office within 2 weeks so there would be no surprises.

This was good news. This was great news. Lana thought this visit from the OIG might rid the VA of doctors Azawi and Williams and the patients would not be injured anymore.

Azawi's Attempt to Secure Counterfeit Certification

If there was any confusion or need for interpretation about the first paragraph of the email from Wendy Kemp, that confusion ended when, on June 15, 2010, Lana walked past Dr. Azawi as she was talking to a resident, Dr. Schiffner, and Lana heard Azawi ask Schiffner if he thought "she could obtain a certificate of training from UCI for IMRT." Dr. Schiffner's response to Dr. Azawi was that he did not think Dr. Azawi could get a certificate, which would have been a fake certificate.

Lana sent an email to Lucinda Swan (Cindy) to confirm she heard the conversation.

Why was Azawi worried about getting a certificate of training for IMRT? She had been giving prescriptions for IMRT radiation for years and had not been able to present any certification.

Dr. Azawi and Dr. Williams had not been able to read the results of the treatment to determine abuse and were not concerned. None of the hospital administrators (Norby or Duff) had any certification from Azawi, but they allowed Azawi to continue in the Radiation Department.

How did Azawi think she was going to get away with giving prescriptions for a discipline which she was not certified? Azawi simply signed off on the suggestions of the physicist and dosimetrist. Azawi had no idea what she was doing to or for the patients.

Lana did not know who was going to be the "point man" at the Long Beach VA and furnish these required documents to Wendy.

What would happen when the OIG found out that the doctors Azawi and Williams were not certified, and the Chief of Staff (Szabo) and the administrator (Duff), along with HR (McCartan) allowed this illegal violation?

The harassment and lack of professionalism continued as the VA Hospital readied themselves for the big OIG inspection.

Lana told Azawi that she had met with the therapists during a meal and there were issues which Lana wanted to present to the physicians. Azawi wanted the meeting, a "supervisor" meeting, to be attended by the therapists. Lana wanted to meet privately with the physicians; Azawi refused. The meeting never happened. Azawi wanted the therapist there to back her up. Azawi was no match for Lana's direct honesty.

A few weeks earlier, Lana, who was appointed to be on the national Board of the Chief Radiation Therapists, sent an email to Robert Williams, the Chief Radiation Therapist in VA hospital located in St. Louis, MO.

Within the email, Lana presented many questions, which Robert replied in red within Lana's email; questions concerning specific ACR guidelines which were to which Azawi was to comply.

One of the questions was:
"Have you ever been barred from any department meetings that discuss patient treatments, chemo, etc.?"

The answer from Robert Williams was "no" and he gave a personal aside about being asked to attend multiple meetings.

A person would think that since the OIG was scheduled to appear at the Long Beach VA Hospital, no incidents of safety violation need to take place. An incident did occur.

Patient Fell Off the Gurney

On May 26, 2010, a quadriplegic patient fell off the treatment table while the therapists were inflating the air transfer mattress. The table was about three and a half feet (3.5 feet) off the floor. The air mattress had air in it and the patient was buckled to the mattress. There was also a pillow under this head, so his head did not make direct contact with the floor. The doctors checked the patient, and the patient was lifted from the floor to a low gurney and transported to the ER.

The attending therapist (Gail Francis) was on the side where the patient fell but she did not try to block the patient's fall. Instead, she leaned down to turn off the blower for the air the mattress.

This gave Dr. Azawi another chance to go after Lana even though Lana was not in the area. Dr. Azawi fired back an email to Lana after being notified, stating:

"Our priority should (be)and it IS our patients [sic]." Especially after the fall of Mr. (deleted), which was horrible and never happened before. The therapist need hands on supervision."

Who the hell did Azawi think she was talking to?

It was evident to Lana that Dr. Azawi had to get someone to type the email for her, even though it was a poorly constructed email. Secondly, stating that the therapist, who was Gail Francis, needed "hands on supervision" was a joke. Gail Francis was the person who, with Hollis, created the Varian Incident.

Dr. Azawi agreed to fire Gail at that time, then recanted, and began covering for all Gail's mistakes. Dr. Azawi would not allow Gail's reviews to have a Variance Report which showed her incompetence. Gail was having closed door sessions with Dr. Azawi. This is the same Gail who became insubordinate and disrespectful, with the endorsement of Dr. Azawi. Dr. Azawi wanted Lana to closely supervise this incompetent and uncaring therapist?

Azawi blaming Gail Francis for any act of professional failure was of no concern to Gail. Gail and Azawi had a pact; Azawi could say anything about Gail, and Gail knew that there would be no repercussions. This was a game, a charade, just to get Lana's intuitive nature and her intelligence out of the department.

Lana was being gas-lighted.

It did not take long for Dr. Azawi to go viral with blaming Lana for the patient falling off the gurney.

At 3:06pm on June 2, Lana sent an email to Susan DeMasters, the EEO official. The email from Lana began:

"Well, seems Dr. Azawi is working behind the scenes again to cause me grief. She contacted HR to try to remove me as Supervisor again. They referred her to our Business Manager. All of this because Gail allowed a patient to fall off the table. When she saw the patient (quadriplegic) slipping off the table instead of stopping the patient from sliding, she leaned down to turn off the blower for the air mattress. Now Azawi is trying to blame me because I was not supervising the transfer from table to gurney. The therapists have been doing this since April with this patient with no problem."

This was not paranoia. This was real. The accusations/emails began coming from Azawi. Azawi sent out emails insisting that corrective action be made, and the appropriate person notified.

The Incident Report which Azawi said she never received had been emailed to her, but that was not the first time Azawi ignored emails and claimed she never saw them.

Lana went on to tell Azawi in a subsequent email,

"The cause was bad judgment on the part of the therapist not the therapist inability to operate equipment. Stopping the patient from falling off the table is the priority- not turning off the air. This has been discussed with the therapists."

Lana further told Azawi that disciplinary action did need to be taken, but due to difficulties in the past (the attempt to fire Gail Francis and Azawi changing her mind and protecting her) Lana reluctantly chose to notify Azawi, even though Lana had the authority to go directly to HR herself. If Azawi had followed through by agreeing with Lana to fire Gail and Doug for the Varian Incident, this patient would not have fallen off the table.

J.B. Simms

Rational thought did not exist. Azawi wanted Lana fired because one therapist, one who could not be trusted, allowed an accident to happen with a patient and it was the fault of the supervisor? Lana filed an incident report with Lynnette Fox, the Senior Safety Officer, just to cover herself.

What was the real connection between Ms. Azawi and Ms. Francis?

The radiation department was gearing up for the visit from OIG. In the meantime, Lana was exchanging many emails with Chief Therapists from VA hospitals across the United States. The emails involved streamlining the radiation procedure as well as having some sort of uniformity in procedures. Lana knew that Azawi was not going to like rules and procedures.

From May through August 2010, there had been many patients experiencing questionable side effects and some with obvious burns. Some patients had to receive a series of hyperbaric oxygen treatment to be healed of their injuries, which were the result of radiation technician indifference.

Everything was out of control in the department. The physicians spent more time badgering Lana, trying to make her quit than they were knowing that the patients were being injured.

During this time, Dr. Azawi asked Lana why so many patients were having repeated simulations. Simulation is the procedure prior to treatment, and scans are done at that time to generate a product from which to compare the film in treatment, making certain that the dose of radiation goes to the right place.

Two patients were coming for repeat simulation on the same day. One of Dr. Azawi's patients was scheduled for re-simulation, so Lana walked over to Dr. Azawi's office to determine why this person, a Veteran, was going through this procedure again. Lana found Dr. Azawi outside the office door talking with Dr. Williams and research assistant Mina Behdad. Lana approached the group and asked why the patient was being re-simulated, which was the directive from Dr. Azawi. Dr. Azawi turned toward Lana, and spoke in an elevated tone, very loudly at the top of her voice, and said:

"I don't have to tell you anything." Lana left.

Other times Dr. Azawi and Dr. Williams, insisting a patient begin treatment, would leave the hospital before film was ready to be approved by the doctors. A doctor must approve film before treatment, but Dr. Azawi would leave on a regular basis before approving film, and the patient could not be treated. This behavior by Dr. Azawi was cruel to the patient. These patients had cancer, and some endured a mammoth effort to come get treatment while Dr. Azawi left work early. Dr. Azawi and Dr. Williams would take leave without telling others in the department, except the nurse, Ms. Pikulsky, who used it as a game.

Lana asked Ms. Pikulsky where the doctors had gone, Ms. Pikulsky would say that she did not know and then later let it slip that she knew all along. It was power.

There was an occasion when Dr. Azawi blatantly lied, stating she was not taking leave, and departing from the hospital.

It was necessary to know if the physicians were going to be on leave since it affected patient care and getting patients started on their treatments. This became a big problem at the end of July 2010.

There were eleven (11) patients waiting for the physicians to do their part of the plan and were stalled in getting their treatments which was apparently of no concern to Dr. Azawi and Dr. Williams.

Lana emailed Dr. Szabo, the Chief of Staff, about the problems of the patients waiting for treatment, some more than 30 days. Azawi and Williams would come and go as they pleased with no thought of patient care. Dr. Szabo replied to Lana's email, stating he had talked to Dr. Williams, not Dr. Azawi, about completing treatments. Lana replied to Dr. Szabo, informing him she feared retaliation. Dr. Szabo's reply was, "Calm down. Nothing would happen."

Lana refused to literally bang her head against a wall out of frustration with Azawi, Williams, and their enablers, Duff and Szabo. The Veterans deserved to be defended.

Chapter Nine:

More Patient Incidents, and the OIG

In July 2010 there continued to be minimal communication regarding patients between the physicians and nurses with the therapists, notably Lana. Since they kept information from Lana about an HIV positive patient, exposing Lana to a life-threatening situation, why should they tell her anything else?

It had been a year since the American College of Radiation gave accreditation to the Long Beach VA Hospital. The accreditation was a sham. Dr. Azawi made false statements of intent on the Corrective Action Program (CAP) in order to obtain accreditation and had been violating the standards and procedures. Lana hoped (and prayed) that the OIG would see what was happening and recommend that the hospital remove Azawi.

A Chief Radiation Therapist from another VA hospital suggested to Lana that she contact Wendy Kemp, and see if Wendy could convince Dr. Hagan to inspect the hospital to witness that Dr. Azawi was not performing the procedures necessary for accreditation, and that Azawi was not certified. Lana contacted Wendy Kemp, requesting she contact the ACR with respect the non-compliance, and ask the ACR to make an unannounced visit. Wendy stated she would discuss the suggestion with Dr. Hagan.

Lana also asked for the help of Susan DeMasters, the EEO (Equal Employment Office) Manager, to set up a meeting with Ms. Duff and Dr. Szabo because of the horrendous state of the department. Ms. DeMasters did not reply to that request.

Lana stayed in contact with Wendy Kemp. Dr. Hagan had investigated (supposedly) the action plans submitted to the ACR by Dr. Azawi and Dr. Williams after the accreditation was denied and was going to wait until the OIG findings before making his first move.

Issues other than patient safety and patient care continued to be a problem with respect to Dr. Azawi.

An email was received from Wendy Kemp on June 11, 2010, 5:07pm. It was addressed to all doctors and chief therapists in the Long Beach VA Radiation Oncology Department. Wendy's email revealed that the OIG was going to inspect the department, there was going to be Peer Review for all doctors, and the OIG would want to see all IMRT certifications for doctors and therapists.

Lana knew Azawi was not only not certified, she could not read the film and charts. If Azawi had obtained the counterfeit certificate, she would not be able to withstand technical questions from any inspector, doctor, or therapist. Lana, and others, were thinking Azawi, and Williams, and maybe Duff, would be gone soon.

A week later, Azawi fired out an email concerning curtailing overtime. The issue of overtime was the fault of Azawi; the scheduling and rescheduling of therapy given to patients was based upon the availability of the physicians, Azawi and Williams. After the patient had been to simulation, and had been placed on the treatment table, the films from simulation and treatment must have been approved by the physicians. Azawi was leaving the department, not telling persons she was leaving, and therapists had to remain until a physician returned. This was Azawi's theater.

Cindy Swan had heard Azawi ranting about the overtime issue. Cindy sent Lana an email as a precaution and stated that Azawi was trying to create insubordination.

On July 20, 2010, an exchange of emails, beginning with one sent from Dr. Azawi to Lana, and the comment of one of the office personnel, confirmed that Lana was not living in a bubble, and that others observed the behavior of the physicians.

One of the therapists, Dennis, had a shoulder injury and was limited with respect to his ability to perform certain tasks. Normally, issues concerning therapists are taken up by the Chief Therapist, but Dr. Azawi was taking any opportunity she could to overstep her bounds, interfere with Lana's job, and demean her to her subordinates.

Lana had a discussion with Dennis with respect to his options of taking leave, retirement, etc., and it was not an issue of concern for Dr. Azawi, but she made it so.

J.B. Simms

At 2:58pm, July 20, Dr. Azawi sent Lana an email asking for written information about Lana's conversations with Dennis about his options with respect to his absence from work. Dr. Azawi stated in her email that she wanted information about Lana's conversation of his retirement, her suggestions to him, samples of his work performance, and if Lana had given Dennis any direction with respect to his options.

Lana replied that this issue had been addressed in some meeting 5 days earlier. The reply to Lana from Dr. Azawi was she wanted Lana to write down her concerns about Dennis:

"and what you have been instructing him to do about his shoulder and retirement. I need this to be completed by COB [close of business] 7/23/10."

Lana was being subjected to more petty intrusions into her work, and Dr. Azawi was simply harassing Lana. Lana sent a copy of the email to Esther Pittman (Human Resources) and Lucinda Swan (Office Manager). Lucinda Swan's reply, July 20, 2010 at 4:40pm, was as follows:

"You need to give her an accounting. State Your being instructed by Esther and cc Esther on your response. Azawi is making you look line [sic] insubordination. She is really harassing you, but there is no option to address her behavior anymore."

Lana's response was, *"That gives me such comfort."*

Here was the proof: Lana was not making up stories, nor being paranoid. Cindy Swan, as the Business Manager, could see what was happening and how Lana was trying to save more persons from being injured, and how the administration attempted to discredit Lana and make her claims appear invalid.

Another way nurse Pikulsky would work in concert with Dr. Azawi to discredit Lana was to go directly to Dr. Azawi with any issue concerning the therapist, bypassing Lana.

This occurred on July 30, 2010 when Pikulsky and Mina were checking to see when Gail Francis was arriving at work. Pikulsky went into Azawi's office to report her findings without notifying Lana. Lana confronted Pikulsky with her act of subterfuge, and Pikulsky had no comment. Lana related this incident to Dr. Szabo, Lucinda Swan, and Susan DeMasters (EEO Manager) via email.

If there was ever any question that Dr. Szabo, the Chief of Staff, was not aware that the guidelines of ACR accreditation were being ignored and/or eliminated, the email sent from Lana to Dr. Szabo on July 23, 2010 would eliminate all speculation. The following is the text of the email sent to Dr. Szabo from Lana, of which a copy was sent to Cindy Swan, the office manager:

July 23, 2010
1:52PM
To: Sandor Szabo
From: Lana Miller CC: Lucinda Swan Dr Szabo-
Here are some questions I posed to a member of our National Chief Therapist Work Group. This discussion was requirement(s) for American College of Radiology accreditation we already had but some departments had not. Dr. Azawi will not allow these requirements although ACR was given policies showing that we were/would be in compliance. Please disregard the first question/response since it pertains to a particular form that was attached above. The response and forms attached are from the VA in St. Louis. We have similar patient loads but we do a broader range of procedures.
I appreciate your time in reading this. Thanks,
Lana

Lana had been telling people that Dr. Azawi had been eliminating ACR regulations since she returned as the Chief Oncologist in February 2009. The Long Beach VA had failed accreditation numerous times under Azawi. The Corrective Action Policy, or CAP, submitted by Dr. Azawi was approved by the ACR later in the year, but the ACR never investigated compliance by the hospital after Dr. Azawi sent in the bogus CAP. The ACR also did not know that the doctors were not certified in IMRT.

One of the problems was that Dr. Szabo, the Chief of Staff, was being told by the Chief Radiation Therapist, Lana, that Dr. Azawi submitted false information to the ACR in order to gain accreditation. Another problem was that Dr. Szabo should have passed this information on to the hospital director, Isabel Duff, and Duff should have fired Dr. Azawi.

Why was Azawi a golden calf?

J.B. Simms

Azawi's anxiety was evident to everyone. A patient was burned on July 28, and at 2:57pm Lana advised the EEO official, DeMasters, of the incident, of which Azawi was fully aware.

Lana was afraid that Azawi would conceal the issues in the department from the OIG. Everyone knew the issues of Azawi's absence, the fact she was not certified in IMRT, her suspension, the mystery behind her reinstatement, the Varian Incident, the Freckle Incident, and the attacks against Lana for "knowing more than Azawi." The OIG would direct their attention to the doctors; Lana was feeling that everything was going to be hidden.

Lana knew that the head of the Radiology Department for the entire VA, Dr. Hagan, was going to be involved and Lana continued communication with Wendy Kemp, the assistant to Mr. Hagan. Lana knew that Dr. Azawi was violating the procedures set forth by the American College of Radiology and was looking for a way to involve the ACR in the OIG investigation. Hoping that Dr. Hagan would do the right thing and involve the ACR with the OIG, Lana received the following email from Wendy:

August 5, 2010 9:40am

"Lana, [I]Spoke briefly w/Dr. Hagan this AM over the phone about your situation. He recommended that you sit tight, and if something is not right as far as: Physician Peer Review, Machine Specifics QA [Quality Assessment], Patient Specific QA, and the patient list your facility (IMRT) or general XBRT) sent to the IG, the OIG should pick up on it. He also said they should request to interview you as Chief Therapist[s], on that your door to alert them to any patient issues. Please continue to document your concerns for lack of patient safety (specifics if possible) to substantiate any of these issues.
If for some reason you are not allowed to speak with and of the OIG team members at any point during their visit, get the team leader's name and I will send them a message.
I don't know when they plan to visit your facility. Keep your ears to the ground."

Somehow, someone got to the OIG and told them of the problems, and the OIG would talk directly to Lana. Lana could not believe it.

Lana thought she had the attention of Dr. Hagan, and maybe he would bring in the ACR, remove the accreditation of the hospital, have the physicians and bad staff members replaced, then things would work to treat the patients effectively.

Lana replied, *"What about contacting ACR?"*

Lana's excitement was deflated when on the following day, (August 6) a patient was set up for treatment, and neither Azawi nor Williams were in the hospital to approve the film for treatment. Lana was getting ready to treat a cancer patient at the end of the day. The patient was having films made before treatment as was the usual course of action. The therapists tried to find Dr. Azawi and Dr. Williams. Neither could be found, and the patient could not receive treatment because a physician was not present to approve film from the treatment area. This was not unusual.

At 4:50 pm, Lana sent Dr. Azawi an email telling her that treatment could not be given since neither physician were available and neither physician bothered to tell anyone they were leaving the hospital. Dr. Azawi became upset that the patient was not treated, but there was no way he could be treated if there was no physician available. The doctors simply left, with no regard for the Veteran patients.

Lana reported this incident to the EEO Manager, Susan DeMasters, and Wendy Kemp. In an email sent on the afternoon of August 9, Lana asked for a meeting with Dr. Szabo and Ms. Duff, the director of the VA Hospital. Lana stated, with respect to Szabo and Duff:

"...[I]f they know and are not willing to do what it takes, that will let me know which direction to go. I want to allow them the ability to fix this and not just talk."

Lana also sent an email to the Human Resources department, specifically Esther Pittman and the head of the department, Mary Beth McCartan. Lana stated that Dr. Azawi was trying to bring a charge against the therapists, including Lana, of refusing to treat a patient and "Refusal to Follow a Direct Order". Therapists were not allowed to treat Veteran patients on the first day of treatment without physician approval of initial films. Lana further stated that Dr. Azawi had upset everyone with her rant.

Lana knew, that, somehow, Azawi had a hold on the hospital. If Azawi was to be held accountable for anything, who was she going to throw under the bus?

Replacing a physician who had no certificate of any kind which showed she had no training on radiation technology, did not seem to be difficult.

Lana had kept close ties with Wendy Kemp, Dr. Hagan's assistant. Wendy was coordinating the group of Chief Radiation Therapists as an educational forum, and Lana was a key member of the group. Lana expressed her fear that the OIG would come and go, and listen only to Azawi.

Wendy knew what the OIG would be looking for, and Wendy's message to Lana was evidenced in this email received by Lana, from Wendy Kemp:

Wendy Kemp to Lana Miller Boyer:

August 8,
2010
9:40a
Hagan said, "SIT TIGHT". OIG to talk to you; report all issues

Did Hagan and/or Kemp contact the OIG? Lana was encouraged, but scared. Would the OIG listen to her? How was Lana going to approach the OIG?

Less than a month before the arrival of the OIG, the following event occurred:

Wendy was advised of the incident of August 6 (doctors missing for treatment) on August 9, 2010 via email, as was DeMasters. Lana asked DeMasters for a meeting with Isabel Duff (Administrator) and Szabo (Chief of Staff). HR was also advised. The patients were being abandoned.

Wendy replied in an email to Lana:

August 10, 2010 8:32am
"I don't think contacting ACR will serve any purpose for now as they have already accredited your facility for 3 years, and the only thing they would probably do is contact our office as we hold the contract. OIG is the best oversight for any potential wrong doing. You may also be able to report patient safety issues to your Patient Safety Officer, who could initiate a Root Cause Analysis, or our Medical Center Director, who could initiate an Administrative Investigative Board-problem with both of these reviews would be appointment of a team that has no clue about the radiation field. And, if I were you, I would see where my grievance stands and ask them to expedite for a review."

Wendy was protecting Dr. Hagan and did not want the ACR to find out that the Long Beach Veterans Hospital falsified the accreditation application.

The grievance which Lana filed in the fall of the previous year had not been heard. It had been almost a year.

The OIG is coming; the OIG is coming. Lana was wondering if this would make Dr. Azawi act in a more professional manner.

Evidently, Dr. Azawi did not care. What hold did Dr. Azawi have over this department, or the hospital administration? What secrets did she know?

Lana's emotions were being pulled back and forth; either being hopeful or being discouraged. This was evident when Lana received an email on August 11, 2010 from Douglas Henao, an officer of the OIG, whose office was in Los Angeles. Henao emailed Lana directly at 2:00 pm, stating that he and Kathi Shimoda would be the OIG officers visiting the Long Beach Facility.

Lana was elated. Lana emailed Cindy Swan, who sent a return email to Lana. at 4:24pm, shared in Lana's excitement, said, *"Don't tell Azawi."*

Azawi Refuses to Treat a Patient
August 13, 2010

An emergency patient was brought into the Radiation Department. Dr. Azawi sent him to the chemotherapy section because she stated he could not be treated in the radiation department because he could not lie flat for the CT scan.

Dr. Azawi did not know that a patient need not lie flat; the patient needed to be stabilized. Lana had carefully treated patients who were a condition that they could not lie flat.

At 5:08pm, Lana emailed Cindy Swan, telling her that Azawi did not know that a patient did not need to lie flat.:

"This aberrant behavior by Dr. Azawi, injuring patients who were Veterans, needed to end. These veterans were less than lab rats to Dr. Azawi; they were an inconvenience. Their pain was being caused by therapists, Dr. Azawi knew it, and Azawi would not allow any corrective measures."

Lana was being isolated, not only because she knew too much, but nothing could be hidden from her. Lana's problem was going to be finding someone who could and would stop the people from injuring the Veterans. It was evident that these people were hiding documents, hiding files, disregarding procedures, and acting as though they had the knowledge and expertise to perform a duty. These people had no conscience. They were injuring people.

Their attitude was that these people have cancer and are going to die anyway; give them a pain pill. Tell the patients that their injuries and abuse is a side effect of treatment. The truth was no one cared enough to hold anyone accountable, except Lana, and some very scared people.

Lana had reported the abuse to the Office of Special Counsel on October 27, 2009. The main job of this office was to intervene when a federal employee is "whistle-blowing" or reporting what is termed Prohibited Personnel Practices, which was part of the complaint filed by Lana. By mid-2010, Lana had heard nothing from the Office of Special Counsel.

Who is so scary that no one wants to confront them? Lana did not know, but it became apparent that Lana was as smart and insightful as any of them, and these people were in for the fight of their lives to protect the lives of persons who offered the ultimate sacrifice, to die for their country.

More issues arose daily.

Lana pointed out issues and she was ignored:
1. The consent form was missing essential wording about tattoos.
2. Patient pain was not being documented in the charts.
3. Vague side effects were listed.
4. Patients were not being seen weekly as required.
5. Details were being omitted from documents.
6. Patients were being treated at the convenience of the physicians or not at all.
7. Physicians refused to answer questions.
8. The front area, including nurse Pikulsky refused to provide required documents.
9. Forms relating needed information on patient history and condition were being destroyed.
10. Notes were being made on paper towels because the nurse did not like using a form.
11. Supporting documents for billing were absent.

These issues existed because Dr. Azawi claimed the department was too small to adhere to ACR regulations, regardless of the harm she was allowing to be caused to the veterans. Azawi had sent an email to Lana, telling Lana that this hospital was not Cedar Sinai Hospital, and she did not need these regulations. The OIG needed to know this.

Lana made Wendy Kemp aware of these issues. Wendy knew that Azawi would be an embarrassment to the entire VA if she was not stopped. Wendy passed these concerns on to Dr. Hagan.

Violation of the CAP (Corrective Action Plan) which Azawi submitted to the American College of Radiology, did not concern of Azawi., nor did the effect of negligence upon patient care. The doctors would not answer questions on patient care, treatment issues, standard protocols.

Donna Pikulsky, the nurse, encouraged by the physicians, spent her time refusing to answer questions about patients, blocked procedures, and was rude to patients. Ms. Pikulsky would "make rounds" in the department and report back to Dr. Azawi what she observed in the technical area, where she was not assigned, or needed, and even admitted being directed by Dr. Azawi to do so.

On August 17, 2010, Lana was asked to take photographs of a patient's head and neck area. The patient had suffered terrible radiation burns due to poor therapist care. With the concentrated quantity of patients who had suffered needless injuries (which doctors called side effects), others treated for emergency purposes, and patient abandonment (doctors leaving without advising anyone, leaving patients to miss treatment), this patient came in, and became another one harmed. It could have been prevented. All the unnecessary patient problems could have been prevented if Lana had been allowed to make the therapist follow procedures, or be permitted to openly discuss patient issues with the physicians. Instead, the nurse, Ms. Pikulsky, used her time to block any attempt to confer with the physicians.

The injuries were shocking. Photographs of one Veteran, wounded in the Long Beach VA Radiation Department are shown on the following two pages. Veterans wounded in the Radiation Department were sent to the Emergency Room, or the Wound Center, for rehabilitation treatment. Falsified records relating to the nature of the wound would exonerate the doctors.

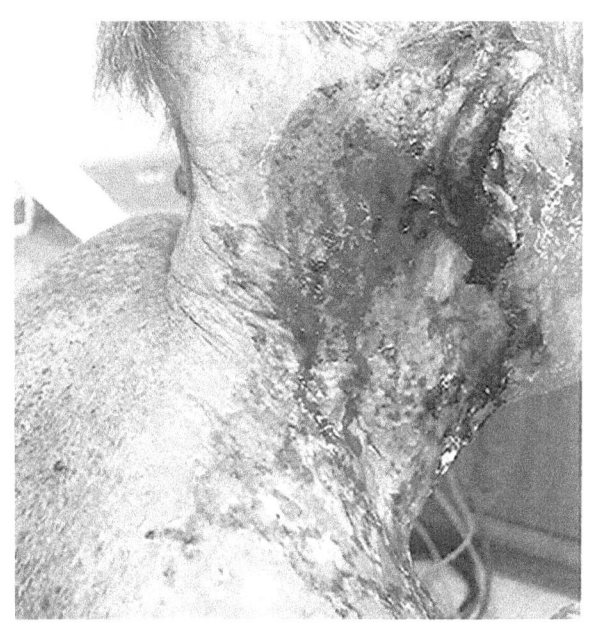

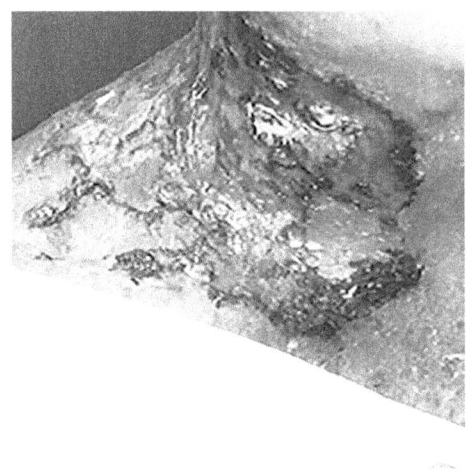

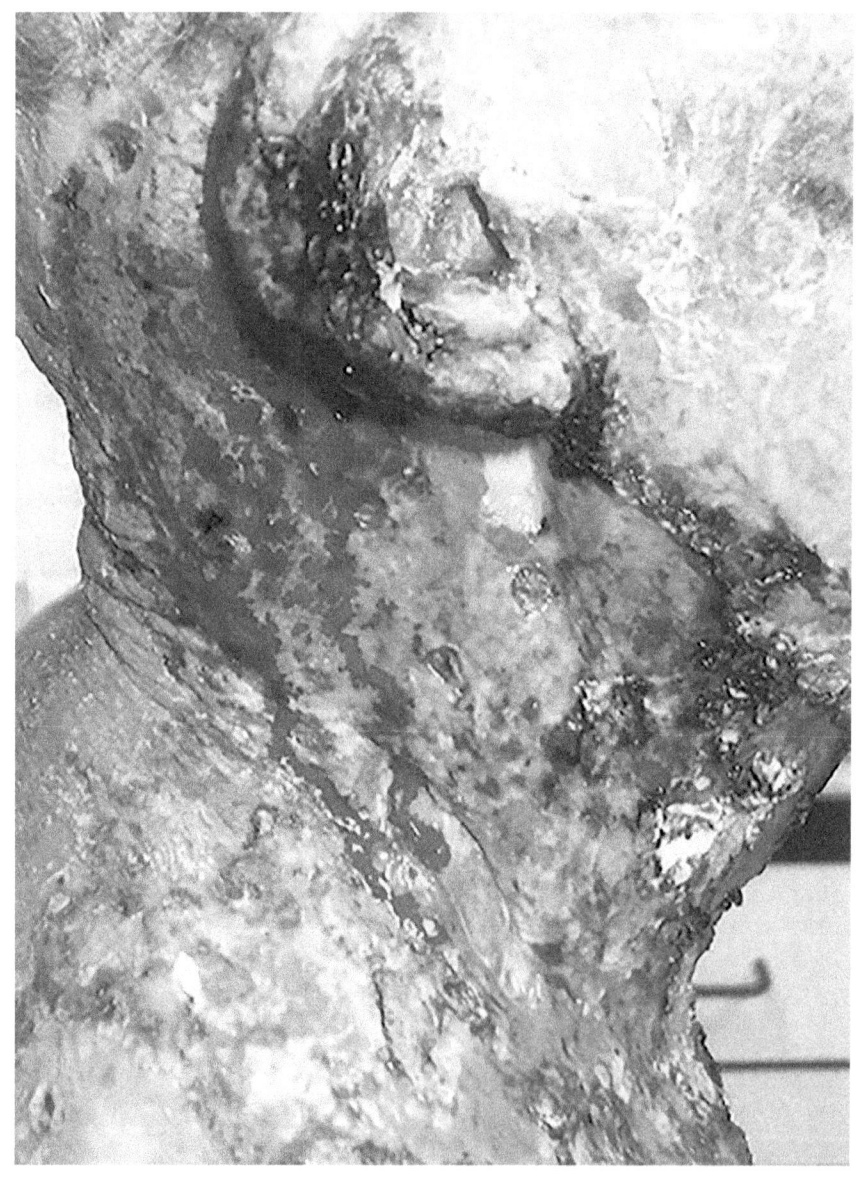

Lana sent the photos to Wendy Kemp. Wendy's response was

"Lana, in my opinion, this doesn't look good for the patient. At least he was given a break in treatment. I will share all with Dr. Hagan tomorrow."

Lana suggested that Wendy contact the Wound Care Nurse, read the notes of August 16, 2010, and see what excuse was given for the injuries.

Lana also told Wendy about two more prostate patients having to receive hyperbaric oxygen treatment due to damage from radiation. Again, the therapists were injuring the patients.

Patients had suffered needless side effects; some needing emergency treatment. Patient abandonment was not being addressed. A patient who had such a serious skin reaction could have been prevented by Dr. Azawi. Lana was devastated, stressed, and felt totally helpless. All the unnecessary patient problems could have been prevented if Lana had been allowed to make the therapists follow procedures or be permitted to openly discuss patient issues with the physicians. The supervisor of the physicians, Szabo, feared the physicians, specifically Azawi.

Wendy Kemp and Lana continued communicating, with Lana hoping that Dr. Hagan would be proactive with respect to correcting the abuse of the Veterans. Wendy suggested that Dr. Hagan review the Corrective Action Plan which was submitted to the ACR for the Long Beach VA Hospital to become accredited, and maybe follow up on the plan.

Lana was visibly shaken, on many different levels. She immediately made an appointment with Dr. Suzie Schuder. Lana's PTSD, Post Traumatic Stress Disorder, because of witnessing the doctors neglect patients and not allowing Lana to do her job to help the patients, resulted in Lana being ordered by Dr. Schuder to leave work for 90 days.

Lana knew the OIG was coming in a few weeks, and needed to have things ready (records available, etc. Lana would not be able to leave until September 15. Everyone was aware that the OIG was coming in to check out the Radiation Therapy Department. Lana was hopeful someone would have a conscience and rid the department of the persons harming the Veterans.

J.B. Simms

Some people knew that Lana was on a single person crusade, and she was receiving shielded encouragement from others because the "others" were afraid of losing their jobs.

Lana's continued to get Wendy's attention, in this email to Wendy:

August 31, 2010 128pm

"The physicians do not follow the requirements of ACR. There have been no Chart Rounds in months, they refuse do to M&M's [Morbidity and Mortality Conference], the physicians review each other's work-nothing there. There are no New Patient meetings, just a mini Tumor board with the Chemo docs. Whatever was put into place at time of survey was quickly reversed by Dr. Azawi 2 months later when she was returned as Chief after being demoted for 8 months. Dr. Azawi believes we are too small to follow any standards since we are not Sloan Kettering or MD Anderson. In addition, she does not understand much of what goes on."

That was hard to ignore. The OIG was coming.

Chapter Ten:

OIG Visits and Hagan's Betrayal

Wednesday, September 1, 2010- the OIG arrived.

With all the advance notice, the physicians did not have things ready for the OIG investigators. The Chief of Staff was hot and sent the physicians and e- mail and copied Lana.

The result of the inspection was as follows:

1. Physics was ok.
2. Peer review was not current
3. Chart Rounds only had a sign in sheet with the last 4 listed (only to get temporary credit). They did not ask for documentation of current chart rounds.
4. The New Patient Meeting, as identified by the doctors, was a list of patients. There had been no meetings, as designated by the ACR (Azawi violated that regulation).

An OIG "inspector" approached Lana and asked how the hospital in Long Beach got accredited by the ACR. Lana told the OIG that they had set up everything required and initiated meetings, then when Dr. Azawi was brought back as Chief, on the month after the survey, she reversed everything and refused to do what was required since, according to Dr. Azawi, the department was "too small" to do it.

The inspectors went to Dr. Azawi concerning the deficiency in patient records. Dr. Azawi pointed the finger at Lana, and directed the questions of malfeasance toward the prospective scapegoat: Lana. Azawi directed all perceived incidents of poor recordkeeping and other indiscretions upon Lana. (Evidently Azawi had cleaned up the stack of patient records which were piled up behind her desk, and not reviewed).

That was not a smart move for Dr. Azawi; trying to put the blame on Lana.

Lana gave the OIG investigators an earful of improper patient care, hostile work environment, falsified ACR accreditation, and lack of professional knowledge on the part of the physicians

Lana was asked (by the OIG) to submit files on patients who had suffered from inappropriate care. Lana furnished the files, and the OIG took the files.

Azawi thought she could make Lana look bad in front of the OIG in an attempt to make herself look good. That plan backfired on Azawi. It did not take the OIG long to figure out that Lana was the "go to" person in the department. Wendy and Dr. Hagan had been communicating with the OIG about Lana, and the OIG appeared to be listening. Lana had been validated by Wendy and Dr. Hagan, so the OIG knew Lana would be the person to find in the department.

Lana shared the history of Azawi with the inspectors. Azawi had created a hostile workplace, which was evidenced by her demotion. The OIG should have had a clue when Azawi could not discuss patient history, and the OIG went to Lana to get the histories on the ten patients. Lana thought the OIG would listen.

Lana was told by one of the inspectors from the OIG that if she felt that strongly about the patient treatment and abuse, as well as the hostile work environment, Lana should file a Hotline report to the OIG, which was confidential; no one would know (by penalty of law) that a Hotline complaint had been received, or who submitted the report.

Lana immediately filed the report with the OIG hotline. Lana outlined the following issues:

1. *Inappropriate care Lack of competence of radiation oncologists*
2. *Lack of communication with facility leadership about adverse events*
3. *Hostile work environment*

Lana could not wait to send Wendy the results of the inspection, and emailed Wendy the next morning. Wendy replied, stating:

Thursday, October 2, 2009
To: Lana Miller From: Wendy Kemp

"OMG! Well that's what needed to happen. I have advised the National Director that he will probably receive a call and /or unfavorable report for this visit. OIG said they would call us when they stumbled across something. You're a good, strong person to take a stand for what is right! Hang in there-this will probably set things straight. Thanks for reporting back to me."

J.B. Simms

The email received from Wendy validated Lana in the eyes of Wendy, Dr. Hagan, and anyone in the VA hospital system. Lana was telling the truth, and they were simply waiting for the OIG report to come out, which would take months.

Wendy and Dr. Hagan had gotten the attention of the OIG. They came directly to Lana. Hagan had to have believed Lana to allow Wendy to communicate with the OIG, and for Hagan to do the same.

Lana was hoping that the Dr. Hagan, would contact ACR and inspect the department again. Wendy said she would see what Dr. Hagan suggested before suggesting that Lana contact the ACR herself.

A few days later, Lana contacted Wendy, asking what the reaction Dr. Hagan had been to the initial OIG visit, and the falsified American College of Radiation Corrective Action Plan submitted by Azawi in an attempt to obtain accreditation. Wendy replied that Dr. Hagan had reviewed the Correction Action Plan which was submitted before the accreditation on September 9, 2009.

Wendy also stated that their office was preparing to send a memo to the VISN (Veterans Integrated Service Network) Director to obtain a report (evidence) that the Corrective Action Plan had been performed as stated. That, according to Wendy, was the "angle" she would pursue first. It was to catch someone lying. No one thought the VISN director would be part of the cover-up. That was a false assumption.

Lana replied to Wendy that Dr. Azawi did, in fact, discontinue the procedures mandated by the ACR.

The current VISN Director, Ronald Norby, left as the Director of the same hospital under suspicion of misappropriating funds among, other things. Lana further stated that the only thing that would be effective would be a surprise visit from the ACR. Norby had other acts he committed to while he was the hospital administrator and covering for Azawi would not be a surprise. Norby wanted no spotlight on himself.

Wendy had been supportive of Lana, but Wendy's reply to Lana's request for a surprise visit seemed a bit defensive. Wendy stated in an email on September 9, 2010 at 12:41pm, that for any ACR survey visit other than a renewal, the facility must pay $9,000.

J.B. Simms

Wendy began spelling out the process for accreditation and corrective action plans. Here is the list of provisions in a nutshell:

1. *The facilities and VISN's were asked to develop internal processes and procedures to monitor progress toward resolution of outstanding items.*
2. *Dr. Hagan, as the National Director, will monitor the completion of the Correction Action Plan.*
3. *Upon completion of the final item, the Radiation Oncology Service Chief will certify to the National Director for Radiation Oncology (Hagan) that the plan had been accomplished.*

Wendy also stated that although the Long Beach VA submitted the CAP to the ACR (supposedly), her office never received a copy through the VISN as required, nor the two CAP's (Corrected Action Plan) submitted by Dr. Azawi. Time was being established to monitor the completion of each corrective action. A letter was being sent by Dr. Hagan to state this, and that the Network, VISN, was accountable.

Wendy ended the email stating,

"Let's give the process time to work and do it the right way."

"Do it the right way? What was the "right way" to do this? Lana trusted Wendy.

The accreditation had been conveyed on September 9, 2009 (fewer than 2 months after the Varian Incident) a year before, and no one had checked on anything even though Lana had been reporting the deficiencies for many months. Plus, Wendy had not received the Corrective Action Plan from Azawi, as mandated.

Dr. Schuder told Lana that the stress had caused Lana to suffer additional PTSD because of the emotional and psychological battle against the doctors and the hospital administration in her attempt to protect the Veterans.

Lana's world would be on hold until the OIG submitted their report, which could take 6 months. Dr. Schuder came to rescue, telling Lana that she needed to be away from work for at least 90 days. Dr. Schuder wanted Lana away from the VA hospital immediately. The Veterans were at the mercy of Azawi and her disciples.

The OIG was gone. The VA Long Beach was anticipating Dr. Hagan visiting the hospital in December 2010, just 3 months away. Lana knew that the OIG would be giving Dr. Hagan information about the inspection. Wendy told Lana that Dr. Hagan would visit after the OIG had left. The problem was that Lana was going to be on leave when Dr. Hagan came to visit in mid-December.

Another issue was the Hotline Report. Lana did not know how that was going to be handled. The OIG asked for ten files of improper care, which Lana gave them. Lana mentioned these files in her Hotline Report.

September 14, 2010 was a busy day. The following emails were sent: 10:15am:

Lana Boyer emailed Lucinda Swan, Gail Frances, and others, notifying them that Dr. Schuder had mandated that Lana be away from work for 90 days.

2:25pm:
Szabo emailed Lana Boyer- Szabo stated he thought PTSD was not work- related illness.

2:54pm:
Azawi emailed Lana Boyer-"Heard you to be out 6 weeks. Need a report in by cob today at 3pm. Have 6 minutes"

4:38pm:
Lana Boyer emailed Azawi- Boyer to be on FMLA for 6 weeks.

Lana left that day. She was fearful for the Veterans as patients, but she was hopeful she was stopping the suffering, regardless how long it took, and it had to stop.

Lana's time away from the hospital was not without anxiety. She found out that the Hotline Report she filed generated enough interest for the OIG to visit the Long Beach VA Hospital, but, the visit would be November 15 and 16, which was during the time Lana was on medical leave. Lana knew the doctors and the administration would be filling the heads of the OIG with justifications and rationalizations. The hope was that the OIG would find that the ACR accreditation was a sham, and heads would roll.

Lana wanted to be at the hospital to defend herself. She knew what might happen when she was not there.

Another surprise was the visit of Dr. Hagan. Dr. Hagan visited the VA Hospital in Long Beach, CA on December 9 and 10, 2010. His report would be submitted within the month. Lana was on medical leave during his visit.

Lana was not at the hospital when Hagan arrived. Azawi and the others had Hagan all to themselves.

December 15, 2010

Lana returned to work on December 15, 2010. No sooner had Lana arrived, and sat in her office, Lana received an email from Azawi, stating that a meeting was to be held. This meeting was to be held within two hours of Lana's return.

At the meeting, Lana learned that Azawi was changing the job description and performance standards of the staff in the Radiation Oncology department.

Azawi used a familiar refrain when asked who in HR authorized this. Azawi stated, "I don't have to tell you anything."

Nothing had changed.

Dr. Hagan had made his visit on December 9 and 10, 2010, and submitted his report. There were three different reports:
1. A draft guidelines report- 12/10/2010 9 pages
2. A final Guideline report- VHA-PCS Issue Brief (first five of 10 pages available
3. Action Plan for National Chief, Radiation Therapy Report

Within the report, Dr. Hagan stated that more employees were needed in the Radiation Department, and part time employees made full time.

As Lana was reading the Final Guideline Report (only the first 5 pages were available), the following entry was found on page 5:

> "Chief Therapist is likely not conversant in IMRT treatment delivery. Therapists are required to maintain written records of measurements which are electronically recorded. Some concerns relative to movement of the treatment couch appear to originate from concepts which do not apply to IMRT treatment delivery."

Hagan wrote this? Wendy Kemp knew Hagan wrote this? Lana was on a consultant committee for IMRT delivery, which Wendy coordinated. Hagan knew that Lana was one of the most proficient and most knowledgeable persons in the VA system in the field of IMRT. The Varian technicians, specifically Geraldine Lauzon, who consulted with Lana on technical matters involving the Varian machine. No one in the Long Beach VA was more conversant in the delivery and interpretation of IMRT than Lana Miller Boyer.

Lana was white hot. The OIG had just left doing their inspection and cited the doctors for not having their reports done. The OIG knew that Lana was more conversant in the technology because Lana was the person on point when the OIG needed reports and consultation.

Lana had told Wendy Kemp about the stack of reports sitting behind the desk of Azawi. Dr. Hagan tried to blame the Chief Therapist for being "non-conversant in IMRT treatment delivery." Neither the Varian inspectors nor the OIG came to that conclusion, and that was only because Lana was at the hospital to talk to them.

The only reason that Dr. Hagan would make a comment about Lana being incompetent was because 1) Lana was not physically there to defend herself or discuss procedure with Hagan (and have a witness), and (2) Azawi used Lana as the scapegoat for anything Azawi did not understand.

Dr. Hagan did not address the issue that neither Azawi nor Williams, the two oncologists, were certified in the discipline (Varian) used to treat the cancer patients. The doctors took the advice of the physicist and dosimetrist, allowed the therapists to use the correct parameters, but the doctors did not know how to read the reports.

How can the uninformed doctors interpret and explain the procedure and the reading of the results to a patient and their family by a doctor who is not certified in the discipline?

Lana sent an email to Wendy Kemp, asking why Dr. Hagan would turn on Lana. If Lana's reports to Dr. Hagan were not credible, Dr. Hagan would not have traveled to the VA Hospital at Long Beach. Lana told Wendy that she had been betrayed. Wendy's tone was not supportive.

Lana was alone again and was seeing the VA administrators covering for each other. Even though the doctors and administrators were busy covering for each other, the abuse and wounding of Veterans did not stop.

The Hagan visit had mixed results, and Hagan made it known to Lana that he could not be trusted, and that Hagan was part of the corruption. In his report, dated December 14, 2000, Hagan reported to the administration than a person in the department had been communicating with the OIG, and Lana was known to be the only one to have done that. The administration was not pleased, but the rank and file were proud of Lana.

The OIG had shared Lana's confidential information to Hagan. Lana's confidentiality had been violated. This was a crime. The OIG knew that they did not want the public to know what was happening to the Veterans, so the OIG conspired with Hagan to communicate the Hotline filing to threaten Lana.

Lana made a phone call and talked to Hagan. Lana was upset about being cast as the problem. Lana asked Dr. Hagan how he could write such a falsified report. Hagan told Lana, "I wrote what they told me to write." Hagan became a part of the corruption which was evident when Hagan submitted his report of his December visit.

Draft of Hagan Final Report:

Beginning on the next page, you will find the copy of the final report from Dr. Hagan. Reading this report, after reading the emails which Lana had given me, and listening to the witnesses, I could see that Lana had been betrayed. This challenged the integrity of Wendy Kemp and Dr. Hagan. Not only was she betrayed by those at the VA hospital in Long Beach, she was betrayed by Wendy Kemp and Dr. Hagan. Kemp and Hagan depended upon Lana's expertise to lend credibility to the program, and Lana's peers exhibited the utmost confidence and trust in her.

J.B. Simms

VHA- PCS ISSUE BRIEF

Issue Title: Radiation Oncology Evaluation, Long Beach Healthcare System

Date of Report: December 14, 2010

Background: In response to an allegation from an employee of the VA Long Beach Healthcare System (VALBHS), VA-OIG investigated radiation oncology operations at VALBHS (11/15-16/2010). The investigation raised several operational concerns, which were detailed in the 11/18/2010 IB prepared for VISN22 leadership (attached as Incl 2).

As a result, Director VALBHS requested a review of radiation oncology operations by the National Director, Radiation Oncology Program (NDRO).

Radiation Oncology at VALBHS is fully accredited by the American College of Radiology (ACR), which on 9/9/2009 awarded three-year accreditation on the basis of an acceptable corrective action plan (CAP). The CAP included 15 items submitted to the ACR on 6/29/2009, supplemented by an additional 5 items submitted 8/26/2009.

Radiation Oncology VALBHS operates as a part of the Diagnostic Molecular Medicine Healthcare Group, which provides administrative control.

Problem: Issues raised in the 2009 ACR accreditation survey continue to be apparent to the investigators from the VA-OIG.

Results of Site Visit by the NDRO:

1. **Most significant finding.** Multiple mandatory quality assurance procedures have not been performed by the medical physicist. A list of these is attached. Issue was noted both by the 2009 ACR survey and the VA-OIG inspection.

   Cause. Medical Physics staffing is grossly inadequate.

   Root cause. The radiation oncology unit has no inherent administrative support. Several decisions related to the contract for medical physics services have been uninformed, placing patient care at risk for errors in radiation treatment delivery.

   Recommendations.

   - Do not initiate the planned program in stereotactic radiation therapy.
   - Immediately increase medical physics FTE from 0.5 to 2.0 by increasing the contract hours for the incumbent physicist from 20 to 40 per week, while amending the contract to provide a junior physicist.
   - Add 1.0 FTE Administrative Officer (example PD is attached).

- Add 1.0 FTE clerical assistant.

2. **Related findings.** The Varian Trilogy LINAC is not routinely utilized secondary to inadequate staffing of radiation therapy technicians (RTT). Issue was noted by the 2009 ACR survey. Confining all treatments to a single LINAC severely limits the use of image-guided radiotherapy (IGRT).

    Root cause. Lack of inherent administrative support.

    Recommendation. Hire immediately two additional RTT. Although each LINAC is equipped to perform IGRT, treatment of 25 patients on a single unit compresses these complex IMRT/IGRT treatments unnecessarily. Spreading these treatments to two fully-staffed LINACs will reduce the chance for radiation delivery errors and allow routine use of the coned-beam CT capability of both machines.

    Additional findings and recommendations: Attached as Incl 1.

Contact for further information: Michael Hagan, National Director of Radiation Oncology; (804)675-6270; michael.hagan@va.gov; Wendy Kemp, Administrative Officer, NDOR; (804)675-6270; wendy.kemp@va.gov.

Incl 1

Additional findings of site visit by NDOR, 12/9/2010

Staffing:

Medical Physicist. Medical physics operations are being performed by 0.5 FTE contractor. Appropriate medical physics staffing for this operation should be 2.0 FTE As a result of this shortfall physics operations must be triaged to keep the clinic operating. Thus, several routine quality assurance procedures are not performed; physics peer review does not occur; and the 0.5FTE contractor is on site a substantially greater time than that for which he is paid.

Radiation Therapists. The service operates two state-of-the-art Varian LINACS and a Toshiba simulator. Routine use of this equipment requires a minimum of 6 therapists. Currently, two therapists are available for duty.

Administrative Officer. The service must have a dedicated administrative officer. As a result of this staffing shortfall, no coherent business plan exists and several of the major administrative functions do not occur.

A list of the administrative functions is attached, as is an appropriate PD.

Clerical Assistant. The radiation oncology service requires a clerical assistant. Duties of this position include, but are not limited to the following:

- Management of patient correspondence, which is required to insure timely follow-up and on-time consult appearances.
- Management of correspondence with outside physicians and hospitals, which is required to insure safe patient treatment and coordinated follow-up care.
- In addition, clinic files, which constitute the principal medical record of radiation therapy treatment delivery, must be kept current and complete.

Staffing Responsibilities:

Medical Physicist. The medical physicist must have technical supervisory control of the dosimetry and therapy staff.

Consult Procedures:

The service operates a weekly planning conference to coordinate the care of new consults. Medical Oncology routinely attends to coordinate combined modality patients. In addition, service physicians attend the weekly thoracic and GU conferences and the weekly tumor board. The latter operates in a patient management format.

As a desired future goal, patients with cancers of the head and neck should be managed with a weekly ENT conference as well.

J.B. Simms

Treatment Planning:

Clinic operations. Secondary to the staffing shortfalls listed above time from consult to treatment is typically three weeks, which is not acceptable. Increased planning and therapy staff should drop this period to less than two weeks and permit "same-day" starts when required.

Several operations in IMRT treatment planning must be improved. These include the calculation techniques for IMRT plans; use of individualized DVH planning guidelines; validation of deliverable IMRT plans; care in the use of bolus during IMRT.

Physics operations.

1. Treatment planning and patient specific QA
    a. Observation:
        i. The same individual who creates an IMRT plan also performs QA for that plan. The whole idea of double check is for another person to review plan created by somebody else.
        ii. Criteria or tolerance level for IMRT QA is not well established. By observing 10 charts, I noticed 3%, 4% and 5% criteria were used to judge the quality of the plan.
        iii. Only RTOG guidelines are being used for IMRT planning.
        iv. Some of the IMRT plans are being normalized to increase isodose coverage. While this increases dose coverage to target, it can lead to unnecessary dose to normal tissue. This normalizing technique is useful for 3D treatment planning. For IMRT, it is better to let the optimizer achieve the objectives.
        v. Monitor Unit calculation second check is being done using two differ in-house built software. One from previous contractor and one from the current contractor. The previous physicist's software is password protected and the password is not available to the current physicist. This doubles the effort to maintain the software.

    b. Recommendations:
        i. More IMRT training would be useful for planners.
        ii. Develop policy for tolerance level used for judging IMRT QA plans. Normally, such tolerance is documented in the IMRT commissioning report. Because the IMRT commissioning report is not available, a document must be created to include tolerance level and action plan when criteria are not met.
        iii. In addition to using RTOG guideline for IMRT treatment planning, it is recommended that the service created its own IMRT treatment planning guideline.
        iv. The LBVAMC medical physics has recommended the purchase of the Rad Calc software for monitor unit double check for the two machines.

2. Imaging Guided Radiation Therapy (IGRT)
    a. Observation:
        i. No written guideline for patient daily set up shift. Such guideline would include shift scheme for each body site.
        ii. Daily patient OBI shifts are being documented unnecessary. These daily shift are available online as part of the patient treatment records in the record and verify system.
        iii. Cone Beam Computed Tomography (CBCT) is not being used for treating certain cases such as patient with lunch cancer.
    b. Recommendation:
        i. Develop IGRT guideline which would include patient daily shift policy for each body site. This shift policy must be approved by physicians.
        ii. Resources used to document daily OBI shifted can be directed toward performing daily QA.
        iii. Use of CBCT for certain patients daily setup. Because therapists are under staffed, it is recommended that CBCT is performed for lung patient only.

Patient management during treatment:

Chief therapist is likely not conversant in IMRT treatment delivery. Therapists are required to maintain written records of measurements which are electronically recorded. Some concerns relative to movement of the treatment couch appear to originate from concepts which do not apply to IMRT treatment delivery.

The service must define and then operate a program for the daily verification of IMRT localizations. Patient shifts of greater than 5mm should require physician evaluation.

The service nurse does an excellent job of managing on-treatment visits. Breaks in treatment can be reduced through improved treatment planning

Patient follow-up:

The service needs to define its follow-up policies with tumor specific guides.

Documentation:

Several policies and procedures documents are quite out-dated. The incomplete nature and general paucity of these documents reflects the absence of an administrator.

Notice, above on page 5, under Patient Management during treatment, where it states, " Chief therapist is likely not conversant in IMRT treatment delivery..."

Lana was the chief reference in the procedure, as acknowledged by her peers in the VA system. How could Dr. Hagan write such a lie, implying that Lana was not conversant in the IMRT procedure. If Lana was not conversant, why was this not mentioned by the Varian inspectors?

Hagan: "I Wrote What They Told Me to Write."

Hagan knew Lana was more knowledgeable in IMRT than was anyone in the hospital. How could Dr. Hagan allow someone like Azawi, who he knew was disreputable (through the information sent to his communication with his assistant, Wendy Kemp) to manipulate him? Was Hagan afraid the VA hospital was going to be embarrassed because the doctors were injuring the Veterans?

Hagan's report, was 5 pages in length (the printing on the bottom stated the report was ten (10) pages and I only saw five (5) pages. While the plan did circumvent a major problem by not mentioning the inadequacy of the doctors and their lack of certification.

Hagan Recommends Shutting Down Department

Hagan told Lana that he met with Isabel Duff for 45 minutes, and advised her to shut down the Radiation Oncology department. Duff refused.

None of that was in the report. Hagan knew Lana was correct in her assertions, but Hagan lacked the integrity to follow his moral compass.

Number Thirteen (13) recommended:

"...[A]dditional IMRT training for planners, Per Dr. Azawi..."

Azawi had to have charts and film explained to her. She pulled the wool over the eyes of Hagan, or Hagan was under pressure to do as he was told so as not to embarrass the hospital.

The Action Plan was a much of a white-wash as was the report by Hagan, and he let Isabel Duff call the shots to hide the corruption. Hagan said he wanted the department shut down. What did Duff have on Hagan?

It appeared the conspiracy to cover-up the condition of the Radiation Oncology Department had reached a higher level.

Chapter Eleven:

2011-Patient Abuse and Cover-Up

The year of 2010 became 2011. It had been over 90 days since the OIG of the Veterans Administration has made their visit in September 2010, and no report.

Lana was hoping she will be able to help the Veterans. The OIG report will be coming out soon. The OSC should be deciding on her Whistleblower complaint and the PPP (Prohibited Personnel Practices) claim. Hopefully the ACR will come in and take the accreditation from the department.

Hagan knew there were problems; he tried to get the department shut down.

On January 4, 2011, Lana received an email from the OSC (Office of Special Counsel) which read as follow:

From: Maria Davis
Sent: Monday, January 4, 2011,
10:45a To: Lana Miller

Subject: OSC Complaint Ms. Miller,

I am currently reviewing your allegation of retaliation for whistle- blowing. I am seeking clarification of some information included in your complaint.
I found included in the material attached to your file that you contacted Acting Director Isabel Duff in June, 2008 to complain about Dr. Azawi. You state that you told Duff that you planned to go to the IG to report Dr. Azawi's conduct unless she did something about it. As a result, Dr. Azawi was removed as the Chief of Radiation. Do you know if Dr. Azawi ever knew that you went to Duff or that you had planned/threatened to report him to the IG? Please explain.
Thank you for your time and attention to this matter. Maria Davis

After the OIG (September 2010, and November 2010) and Dr. Hagan (December 2010) had been in the hospital, everyone was on edge, and people were scared to associate with Lana. The attitude of Dr. Azawi and Dr. Williams was combative.

Dr. Hagan had given directives to hire more physicists and more radiation therapists, but since Dr. Azawi was controlling the department, the directives of Dr. Hagan were ignored.

Wounding of A Patient's Shoulder

In January 2011, on a patient's first day of treatment, the contract therapist named Amber Gabbard saw that a patient's shoulder was in the treatment field (the shoulder was "in the way"). Ms. Gabbard called Dr. Williams and the Resident, and Dr. Pinn-Bingham to look and make a change but they did not think it was a problem. The therapists were speechless but could not demand that the physician change it, so a note was recorded in the patient's treatment record, noting that the physician saw that the patient's shoulders were in the treatment field and the physicians told the therapist to treat the patient anyway. After two weeks of treatment, the patient complained that his shoulders and skin hurt. He had a skin reaction on his shoulders, just as the therapist expected. Lana explained that this could have been prevented as most patient problems but Dr. Azawi and Williams did not want patient problems discussed; discussions which would allow problems to be corrected prior to causing harm to the patient.

Although the ACR protocol, to which Azawi signed-off, the Corrective Action Policy (CAP) was to have New Patient Meetings. Dr. Azawi eliminated the New Patient meetings or other discussions regarding patient conditions near the time for simulation or treatment. These meetings exposed Azawi as having insufficient knowledge of IMRT. Sharing information about the patient was important because there were many people involved in the treatment.

Eliminating New Patient meetings violated the procedures of the American College of Radiology. Even though, after many denials of accreditation, the coveted accreditation was conferred in September 2009, less than two months after the Varian Incident.

The Long Beach VA Hospital succeeded in quashing the Varian Report which would have brought scrutiny upon the department. The ACR would never have granted accreditation if they knew of the Varian Incident, because no one from the ACR ever interviewed Lana.

J.B. Simms

On January 21, 2011, a Quality Management meeting was held. A discussion was held concerning deficiencies in the department, the OIG inspection, and other matters which had caused stress for Lana.

During the meeting, Dr. Williams leaned over to Lana and said:

"We wouldn't be in this mess if it weren't for you."

Michael Conconi, the Lab Manager, was sitting on the opposite side of Lana and heard Williams' remark. Sometime after the meeting, Dr. Williams stopped Lana in the hallway and accused her of calling the OIG and causing all the problems.

Dr. Williams was becoming aggressive. This was not his style.

Later in the afternoon, Lana sent an email to Dr. Azawi: Lana to Dr. Azawi,

January 21, 2011
4:31pm:

"I think it would be beneficial for us to have a productive conversation. Can we set up a time next week to meet...you and me? How about Monday morning? Tuesday afternoon?"

This email was sent to Azawi on a Friday afternoon. Azawi had all weekend to make the arrangements for the meeting.

Azawi did not reply to the email until January 24. Azawi stated:

January 24, 2011
3:27pm
"I am not sure what you want to talk about. We are having all those meeting(s) you can bring issues in? ...But I can offer you 10 minutes tomorrow with Dr. Williams presence [sic] so he will know first hands what is going on."

Azawi needed Williams to buffer the problem and with both Williams and Azawi in the meeting, Azawi would become more empowered.

Lana replied:

J.B. Simms

January 24, 2011
3:33pm

"This does not involve Dr. Williams. As stated below, I would like to have a productive conversation with you regarding the best way we can work together. Probably allowing 30 minutes- calm, open discussion... you and me. What time would be good for you?"

Lana knew that her appointment with Dr. Schuder, her psychiatrist, was later that day and that Azawi's response would not be received before then.

Lana knew that everyone was aware that the OIG had approached Lana during their inspection, and that they requested the names of ten patients having received mistreatment be submitted to the OIG. The problems involving the doctors and staff members were becoming unbearable.

Lana sent an email to the Chief of Staff, Dr. Szabo, with the subject being a "Formal Request", asking Dr. Szabo to stop the retaliation, attempts at intimidation, and humiliation by Dr. Azawi and Dr. Williams. Azawi, Williams, and others, would not stop until someone made them stop. They were not to be accountable.

Szabo did not reply to this email.

Lana had continued to keep Wendy Kemp advised of the behavior of the doctors, and the fact that the directives handed down by her boss, Dr. Hagan, were being ignored.

As usual, Lana left around 4:00pm to go to her doctor, Dr. Schuder, for continued sessions and treatment for the PTSD suffered at the hands of the hospital officials.

Lana stayed in touch with Vivian Wells, the "investigator" at the Office of Special Counsel, who had been assigned to handle the PPP claim submitted by Lana.

Before Lana left for her appointment with Dr. Schuder, Lana sent a copy of her year-end evaluation, evidence of hostility as result of being on leave for 3 months, as well as the invitations to the conference rooms for "discussions."

True to form, Azawi fired off a harassing email to Lana at 8:35am the following day:

"What time did you leave yesterday"

Azawi knew the answer to the question. Lana had a letter from her psychiatrist, Dr. Schuder, noting that Lana had a standing appointment at 4:00pm every Monday. Azawi was sending the email to imply that Lana was skipping out, and that Azawi would use her absence to indict her.

Fewer than 30 minutes later, Lana replied:

"I left at 4:00pm for my weekly Drs appointment. Every Monday."

An appointment with Dr. Azawi occurred as planned on January 25.

The following morning, Lana felt a need to follow up on the meeting. Lana did not like confrontations. As intelligent and strong a woman as Lana appeared, she was vulnerable to personal attacks. Lana looked for the best in people. She gave you the benefit of the doubt. She was too nice for her own good.

Below is Lana's email to Azawi:

January 26, 2011 8:52am
Dr. Azawi,
Thank you for taking the time yesterday to discuss some issues at hand together. As I expressed yesterday, I am here to help accomplish what you want-a smooth running department. I am here to support you and to do whatever task is best for the department. There are times when I can shift priorities in order to complete critical projects with you and for you. ... If we know what each other's thoughts are on tasks, we can more easily work in the same direction...Looking forward to more productive discussions and direction.

Lana

Lana felt good about sending the email. It is hard to believe that Lana was such a good person that she could reach out to a person who caused her so much pain, and want to be her friend. Lana knew that the Veterans were to be the focus, and Lana unselfishly sacrificed her sense of self for the betterment of the care of the Veterans.

Azawi responded a bit over an hour later, stating:

"Thank you for your enthusiasm....
I would appreciate your offer to clear the action required. I understand this is a clerical work and when we have clerk back to work you will not need to do it. However, please prioritize your routine work with the understanding not to fall behind on your routine duties..."

Lana sent back an email telling Azawi that she (Lana) would be more than happy to help with anything that did not jeopardize immediate needs.

Lana had many stresses or balls in the air. She had weathered storms created by the hospital and the doctors, and was alive, barely.

Some of the issues she handled were:

1. Having been unfairly reprimanded for the Varian Incident when the administration initially agreed to fire the perpetrators.
2. Having filed an informal grievance, only to have it denied.
3. Having filed a complaint with the Office of Special Council, only to have the investigation and findings delayed.
4. Having filed a Formal Grievance with the hospital administrator, only to be ignored and to be made to field delays, excuses, and lies from the Human Resources department.
5. Having to witness the harm being perpetrated against Veterans because of poor technique and depraved indifference, and lack of accountability, of the therapists who were given the freedom of no accountability by Dr. Azawi.
6. Having the authority of her position stripped from her, enabling the lower level therapists to escape review of their professional performance.
7. Having been betrayed by the Office of Inspector General, who, by divulging the origin of a "Hotline" complaint to Dr. Hagan, violated the most sacred of trusts from any agency promising anonymity to escape reprisals.
8. Having been betrayed by Wendy Kemp and Dr. Hagan, who encouraged Lana to fight to expose the fraud in Azawi's accreditation and her lack of knowledge.

Experiencing only a few of these would cause most persons to fail to function.

Lana was still trying to get her Formal Grievance heard by the Director, Isabel Duff. The grievance had been filed over a year prior. The head of Human Resources, Mary Beth McCartan, and her assistant, Herb Moisa, perpetuated continuances which kept Lana from sitting with the Director. The mistreatment of the Veterans at the hands of the therapists, the cover-up, and the retaliation against Lana did not appear to be a priority to Isabel Duff.

J.B. Simms

Isabel Duff could keep the position of Director through the Human Resources department, and Mary Beth McCartan. Both Duff and McCartan had been placed into their respective positions by the former Director, Ronald Norby, who resigned his Director position under a cloud of fiscal suspicion. Duff lacked the prerequisite credentials for the director job, but Norby's influence made the difference.

Azawi implied to Lana was that there probably were clerical chores which needed to be addressed, chores which had been ignored or were a result of laziness by the minions of Azawi. Azawi wanted Lana, a Chief Radiation Technician, one of the brightest ever to work at the VA, to help with clerical work. Lana did not see it as demeaning; Lana was the ultimate team player, but those around her knew Azawi had a different motive.

This became evident as the tone from Azawi changed from the conciliatory supervisor to the manipulative doctor who was setting Lana up to fail.

Sent: Friday, January 28,
2011 From: Azawi, Samar
To: Miller, Lana (Long Beach
Cc: Williams, Richard C (Long
Beach) Subject: Clinic
Schedule
Hi Lana,
You [sic] clinic schedule will be on either trilogy or ix from 10-12am 5 days a week treating with therapists and 1-3pm treating with therapist.
This is being planned to improve patients [sic] treatment operation. This is my instruction to you and I expect you to start implementing this from today on.
If there is any major conflict with patients [sic] treatments let me know. Samar Azawi, M.D.

Lana was the Chief Radiation Therapist. Her job involved many different functions. Azawi wanted Lana to participate in the treatment of patients, which was the job of the therapist who she supervised. This took time away from her other duties, which would cause Lana to be criticized for the getting behind on her reports and other matters. Lana was falling into the trap being laid by Azawi.

Azawi had stopped Lana from reporting mistakes being made by the therapists, referred to as variances. Variances were deviations from the proper procedure or administration of the dosages of radiation. Many of the variances refer to the variances of position of the table upon which the patient is lying, whether the table is too high, low, or laterally out of position.

January 28, 2011

Since Lana's job had been changed, and Azawi had basically demoted Lana to treating patients instead of performing her supervisory duties; this was to be interpreted as a "prohibited personnel practice," a PPP. Lana had reported these same types of practices to Vivian Wells of the Office of Special Counsel in October 2009 and sent an email to Ms. Wells on February 1, 2010 because of Azawi changing Lana's job description and duties again.

Lana knew that Dr. Hagan had directed the hospital to increase the number of therapists because of several issues he wanted corrected:

1. The hospital did not want to pay overtime.
2. The wait time for patients to receive treatment would be excessive.

Azawi never increased the number of therapists and caused a problem when some therapists were out for a variety of reasons.

Lana had to send an email to Azawi and Williams on February 8, 2010 because Gail Francis was off that day, Amber was leaving early, and two therapists were needed on each machine. That was going to put the department behind schedule for treating the patients. Moving patients on the schedule could be possible but there were limitations.

Doctors in the radiation oncology department had to sign off on film approvals before the Veteran patients could be treated. The inability of the therapists to find the doctors was becoming a problem, again.

Lana had to cover herself, so she sent the following email to the doctors:

J.B. Simms

Date: Thursday, February 10, 2011
8:53am To: Samar Azawi, Richard
G. Williams Subject: On Board
Imaging, CBCT
From: Lana Miller Importance:
high
The therapists have brought to my attention regarding the inability to contact you in the department for your ordered CBCT's and OBI's requiring Dr approval prior to treatment. Please give me the procedure to follow when you are not available to approve these ordered tasks. Thanks,
Lana Miller
Chief Therapist- Radiation Therapy VA Long Beach Healthcare System

The truth was that the doctors made their own schedules, left when they wished to leave, with no regard to scheduled patients. Forms would be filled out later. Authorizations would be back dated. Many forms and reports the doctors were supposed to complete would be piled up behind the doctor's desk. The OIG found this to be true when they visited the Long Beach VA on September 1, 2010, and Azawi tried to blame the record keeping issue on Lana. It was not the fault of Lana. Lana was hoping that the OIG report would get rid of Azawi and Williams.

An ROC (Report of Contact) was written by Lana concerning an event which occurred later in the morning of February 10, 2011. The other persons listed, as having been involved, were: Samar Azawi, MD, Donna Pikulsky, RN, William Parton, and Patient x.

Below is the text of the Report of Contact, submitted by Lana Miller Boyer, with respect to the February 10, 20111 event:

"Late morning, the radiation therapist, Gail and Amber, found out that Mr. Parton (Head and Neck IMRT patient) would be late for his 11a.m. appointment. Donna told them she wanted to see the patient first then Dr. Azawi for his weekly visit (OTV).
We later found out he was still in chemo receiving a treatment. Not knowing when he would arrive in our department, and send Donna and Dr. Azawi insisted on seeing the patient first, the therapists and I discussed treatment time options-(1) treat patient at 1:00pm and allow the patient to eat and complete chemo and Dr/Rn visit, or (2) wait for patient to arrive in department, be seen by Dr. Azawi and Donna, and wait around to get access to patient for treatment. With too many unknowns, it was determined to allow patient to eat then return to department at 1pm.

J.B. Simms

Amber and Gail left for lunch an [sic] I was getting ready to leave since I had a QM (Quality Management) meeting at 1:00pm in our conference room. (The day before I had to go without lunch due to a meeting in my office from 12:00-1:00pm with Dr. Moran.) I received a phone call from Dr. Azawi (you could hear Donna very clearly in the background) telling me I had to treat the patient right then. I was not given an opportunity to inform her of the therapists [sic] situation or mine.

She then said, "If you do no treat the patient right now, he is going up to the 11th floor to complain." I asked her if the patient had said that. She repeated the same threat to me. (Donna was still speaking loudly in the background.) I told Dr. Azawi if she wanted the patient treated right then I would go ahead [and treat the patient].

I was in shock but not surprised at the tactics. Donna wheeled the patient to the treatment area and left him. About that time, Dennis came around the corner (he eats in the department at lunch) to help. As the patient removed his shirt, I told him if he had any problems we would certainly address them. He was really confused, and said 'What 11th floor?' He did not know there was a floor like that or what it was. Mr. Parton, our patient, is the meekest patient and would not even know how to make a threat like threat like that. If you meet him you will understand.

Mr. Parton said on 2-9-2009 he had gone for lab work at 11:30a.m. and had to wait for treatment until 4:30p.m. (5 hours). I asked him if he did not receive a treatment in our department until 4:30p.m. and he said no. He had been treated on time that day then went to his other appointments in other areas of the hospital.

Dennis and I came out of the room and there was Donna frantically turning the corner to our area.

[I]told her that I did not appreciate (her) using a patient to threaten me. She claimed no knowledge of the event. I reminded her she could be heard very clearly near Dr. Azawi on the phone call. She was frantic and upset because chemo needed the patient back in chemo for some magnesium. (Don't know if Cheryl(?) was rushed to get the patient down to the department before lunch for Dr. Azawi and Donna or what happened [t]o cause the missed meds prior to leaving chemo).

I offered to take patient down from the table to go back to chemo then she acted like it was not so important.

J.B. Simms

The patient was finished in our area around 12:40p.m. at which time Donna came to pick him in the wheelchair. She began saying Mr. Parton had not been treated until 4:30 yesterday and was apologizing to him. He tried to explain but she (Donna) continued insisting he had been in our department until 4:30p.m. for treatment.

I interjected that was not true, and Mr. Parton clarified the situation. She (Donna) was trying to stir up the problem she was not even familiar with.

Because of the threats by Dr. Azawi and issues not understood by Donna, I was too upset to go to the QM meeting since I would have to deal with Dr. Azawi and Donna at the meeting.

I have been accused of many things in this department, intimidated, harassed, bullied, lied about, but it is totally unconscionable to use a patient to threaten anyone and use that patient for their own agenda.

Lana Miller
Chief Radiation
Therapist Dept of
Radiation Therapy
LBVA

Dr. Hagan knew about the problems of the record keeping, because his report in December revealed he must have had advance information about the OIG report.

The harassment of Lana was increasing.

Below is an email dated February 18, 2011 from Azawi:

Date: Tuesday, March 01, 2011
8:19 am
From: Samar Azawi To: Lana Miller Subject: Leave
Lana
Yesterday I came looking for you about 3:45pm and the therapist said you had left for the day. Can you please explain?

I do not see a leave request entered in the computer.
Also, on 2/23/11 you cam[e] late about 10 minutes. You saw me in George's office. Also the day after that you came late too. I did not see a leave request entered in the computer. Please reply and explain by COB (close of business) today."

Azawi followed up with an email at 8:31am, telling Lana that she (Azawi) needed to know when Lana left.

At 8:25am the following morning, Lana sent Azawi a email reminding Azawi that Lana had a standing appointment every Monday with her psychiatrist, Dr. Schuder:

March 2, 2011 8:25am
From: Lana Boyer To: Dr. Azawi
"Do you want me to find you in the mornings when I arrive? I will be happy to. Also, if you are not here or unavailable when I arrive what would you like me to do? ...Thanks for asking."

Lana knew this was not going to be the last of it.

Azawi was not a computer oriented person. She refused to use the computer for many updated procedures of review, but Azawi had taken the time to go on a computer and check to see if Lana was not available for periods of time ranging from 10-15 minutes.

Azawi was doing this so there would be a paper trail of alleged insubordination, which would be the attempt to discredit Lana and validate Azawi. Up to the point of Lana going on leave for PTSD, there was harassment, but this was becoming ridiculous.

On March 1, 2011, another incident of harassment occurred which Azawi thought would give her another weapon.

Dr. Azawi issued an order on March 1, 2011 that Lana could not use the back door except for emergencies since she had reported a theft to Dr. Williams. Supplies had been missing from the department and it appeared as though the escape was made from the back door. Azawi was going to restrict Lana from using the back door for anything other than an emergency. That door had been used by everyone in the department, and Azawi was going to exclude Lana from use of that exit. One day, Lana, out of habit, departed the area via the back door.

The email which Azawi sent Lana on March 1 reiterated that new order. Lana fired back in an email to Azawi:

"You are correct on the back door. Without thinking and out of habit I went out the back door when I left- so was my husband was watching for me come out the main door. That is the only time I have used that door since our discussion.

I was not aware of notifying Dr. Williams in your absence if I leave the dept but will do so in the future. That has occurred maybe 2 times since our discussion otherwise I have followed your wishes.

Although you are aware of my standing appointment, do you still want me to tell you when I leave?"

Lana was not being sarcastic, but it could be interpreted as such. Lana would do anything for peace, to the point of humiliating herself.

This had to be so frustrating to Lana's husband, Jeff. Lana was being victimized daily, and Jeff had to listen to the stories, and deal with the emotional swings Lana was experiencing.

March 3, 2011
On March 3, 2011 "EF" approached Lana and told her that Azawi had driven a new therapist, Monica, to tears, and Monica did not want to come back. This is the same behavior exhibited by Azawi in 2008.

Azawi ordered Lana to train the contract therapists for simulation, (although the contract therapists were not hired for that purpose) within a week and later included a threat to Lana that if the contract therapists did not comply, she would replace them.

Lana knew that a therapist could not be trained to conduct simulation within a week. Neither of the therapists had performed a simulation in over 9 years and had never operated a CT.

Dr. Azawi and Dr. Williams did all they could to aggravate Lana. They both made it clear, mainly by dictates from Azawi, what Lana was doing each day. The doctors did not like the response Lana gave of the list of numerous tasks Lana performed. The doctors insisted that Lana provide a detailed list of who, what, and how long it took, and the charts checked.

It never stopped.

J.B. Simms

Chapter Twelve:

Two OIG Reports- More Cover-Up

After Lana filed her report with the OSC on October 27, 2009, Lana was convinced by the OIG inspectors to file the OIG Hotline complaint during the OIG visit September 1, 2010. The September visit by the OIG was a planned visit, but the November visit by the OIG was a result of Lana's Hotline complaint.

In March 2011, the OIG reports of both the regular visit (September) and the Hotline complaint visit (November), were published.

On March 9, 2011, the highly anticipated OIG report of the November 2010 visit to the Long Beach VA Hospital was published. This report was a result of the Hotline submission (which was supposed to be confidential) which Lana submitted at the request of OIG inspectors. The OIG inspectors wanted at least ten (10) patients who had received improper care. Lana submitted the names and reports to the inspectors, and the following was their report.

A full copy of the report can be found in the appendix,

and at: http://www.va.gov/oig/54/reports/VAOIG-10-03861-119.pdf

A copy of the review is follows. My review of the report was conducted, and my commentary of the report is underlined and in italics.

J.B. Simms

Review of Department of Veterans Affairs,
OIG Report Number 10-03861-119
Alleged Poor Quality of Care in Radiation
Therapy VA Long Beach Healthcare System
Long Beach,
California Report
Dated March 9, 2011
http://www.va.gov/oig/54/reports/VAOIG-10-03861-119.pdf

This report is the product of reviewing the investigative report submitted by the OIG, attached to the Department of Veterans Affairs. The onsite investigation of the VA Long Beach Health Care System began September 1, 2010. The investigation was to address four (4) alleged harmful practices/observations having been reported by an employee of this facility.

The allegations as listed by the OIG were in the Executive Summary

were: Inappropriate care

Lack of competence of radiation oncologists

Lack of communication with facility leadership about adverse

events Hostile work environment

We substantiated the allegation of poor care for 1 of the 10 patients reported and identified deficiencies in medical record documentation for 9 of the 10 patients. We also substantiated that facility leaders were not aware of adverse patient outcomes in RT and found that action was not taken to correct deficiencies identified in peer reviews.

We did not substantiate the allegation that radiation oncologists lacked competence.

Purpose

The VA Office of Inspector General (OIG) Office of Healthcare Inspections conducted an inspection to determine the validity of allegations regarding poor quality of care in radiation therapy at the VA Long Beach Healthcare System (the facility) in Long Beach, CA.

Background

The OIG Hotline Division received allegations that the facility's Radiation Therapy Service provided inappropriate radiation therapy (RT) care to 10 patients. Allegations included:

Inappropriate care

Lack of competence of radiation oncologists Lack of communication with facility leadership about adverse events Hostile work environment

Scope and Methodology

We conducted a telephone interview with the complainant to clarify the allegations prior to a site visit November 15–16, 2010. We interviewed managers and employees and reviewed pertinent VHA policies and procedures, facility documents, credentialing and privileging (C&P) information, and medical records. We did not address the allegation of a hostile work environment in this report.

We conducted the inspection in accordance with Quality Standards for Inspection and Evaluation published by the Council of the Inspectors General on Integrity and Efficiency.

Inspection Results

Issue 1: Quality of Care and Competence

We substantiated the allegation of inappropriate RT care for 1 of the 10 subject patients. We also found deficiencies in the documentation of treatment for 9 of the 10 patients.

We did not substantiate the allegation that radiation oncologists lacked competence. The C&P folders and profiles of the radiation oncologists complied with VHA policy. In addition, peer reviews for ongoing professional practice evaluations were appropriately documented.

Executive Summary

The report substantiated "poor care for 1 of the 10 patients reported and identified deficiencies in medical record documentation for 9 of the 10 patients.

Allow me to interpret the contradictions and the attempt to hide culpability of the Long Beach VA Hospital:

Inappropriate Care

First, you cannot substantiate any fact based upon missing information. No conclusion can be drawn because of missing data or missing records. A record of care of any patient, or plan for future care, could not be determined by the medical records because, as the report stated, there were deficiencies (missing information) in 90 percent of the medical files. This is inappropriate care.

The conclusion presented in the OIG report, that facility leaders were not aware of adverse outcomes, is faulty. Facility leaders such as the Chief of Radiation Therapy and the Chief of Staff were notified on a regular basis by email and in person by the Chief of Radiation Technology. Copies of the correspondence were available to the OIG.

The statement made that action was not taken to correct deficiencies in peer reviews was made in the same sentence as the statement that facility leaders were not aware of adverse outcomes.

How do you correct something of which you are not aware? This contradiction reveals false statements made by hospital officials to the OIG investigators, and a troubling fact is the OIG investigators not only did not see the contradiction, the investigators printed the contradiction in their report, which revealed the lack of competence of the OIG investigators.

Deficiencies in peer reviews are to be considered and corrected to insure proper care of patients as well as insuring competent personnel are staffed. Why would there be no action taken to correct deficiencies?

Lack of Competence

The OIG stated on Page 2 of the report that they did not substantiate the allegation that radiation oncologists (doctors) were incompetent.

The complainant clearly stated that the doctors were not familiar with the IMRT film to the point that they did not know the dangers of misapplication of radiation, nor did the doctors know the definitions of icons on the film. The lack of knowledge with respect to how to interpret the film is lack of competence. The attitude of the doctors, more specifically Dr. Azawi, was that the treatment was "close enough" (an exact quote), negating the pain, discomfort and ineffective treatment prescribed by the doctors.

Nowhere in the report does it reveal any evidence of training received by the doctors in the curriculum of IMRT technology. Only the Chief Radiation Therapist has this knowledge, and the doctors would not defer to a person more knowledgeable in the treatment of the patients or the administration of the radiation.

Neither Radiation Oncologist was certified by the American College of Radiology. The Chief Radiation Technologist overheard the Chief Radiation Oncologist (the doctor in charge of the Radiation Unit) ask a Resident if the Resident could obtain a fraudulent certificate for her, the doctor, in anticipation of the OIG visit.

No Certification of Physician Was Requested

In paragraph 2, it was stated that "...peer review encompasses the ongoing evaluation of professional practice." This quote was said to have come from the VHA Directive 2010-025

If no corrections were made to correct deficiencies in peer reviews, there was no way to prove competence on the part of the oncologists.

While it had been documented that the Chief Radiation Therapist had to explain reports and icons to the doctors because the doctors were not competent to read and interpret the results, and that the doctors dismissed inaccurate radiation treatment (beyond the bounds of safety) as "close enough", this behavior can easily be defined by one or a combination of the following: ignorance, indifference, and lack of competence on the part of the radiation oncologists, and inappropriate care.

Adverse patient outcomes were reported many times to the doctors, and at one time the Chief of Radiation Therapy agreed to terminate the employment of two therapists who were found to have been untruthful when their faulty treatment was discovered. This was referred to as the Varian Incident, which occurred June 17, 2009. This same Chief of Radiation Oncology did an about face after agreeing to terminate the employees, made the issue public (which violated HR regulations, and was a personnel matter and was to be privately handled), allowing the offending therapists to remain employed, thus undermining the authority of the Chief Therapist who discovered, reported, and tried to correct the issues.

Noted in the first paragraph of this section, the word "We" is used to identify someone, or anyone, affiliated with the OIG. It is stated in this paragraph that the complainant along with others were interviewed. There is no record of the list of those interviewed. Also, the "We" supposedly reviewed VHA policy.

J.B. Simms

Failure to Address Hostile Work Environment

OIG failed to address the real the genesis of patient care: the hostile work environment.

The last sentence of this first paragraph is troubling. The sentence reads, "We did not address the allegation of a hostile work environment in this report." Why? It was documented that Dr. Azawi was relieved of her duties as the Chief of the Radiation Therapy on June 6, 2008 because of her hostile actions toward many people, which contributed to poor patient care.

Dr. Azawi regained that position some 7 months later February 17, 2009.

The complainant submitted the complaint to the Office of Special Counsel on October 27, 2009. Dr. Azawi was Chief of Radiation Therapy at the time of this investigation and report, and was in this position when the complainant contacted the OIG.

Quality of care and inappropriate care were the reasons for the report to the Office of Special Counsel. This falls under the direct supervision of the Chief of the department under question, Radiation Therapy. If the environment is hostile, and patient care is sacrificed, or neglected, resulting in the documented injuries sustained by veterans, then it is incumbent that the genesis of the problem be addressed, which is the hostile work environment. Again, as read on Page 2 of this report, the OIG did not address the issue.

Below is a paragraph taken from the website of the Office of Special Counsel, found at https://osc.gov/pages/whatwedo.aspx

The U.S. Office of Special Counsel (OSC) is an independent federal investigative and prosecutorial agency. Our basic authorities come from four federal statutes: The Civil Service Reform Act, the Whistleblower Protection Act, the Hatch Act, and the Uniformed Services Employment & Reemployment Rights Act (USERRA).
According to the OSC Organization Chart, the Investigation and Prosecution Division of the OSC should have taken over this investigation, especially with respect to the hostile work environment. The OSC should have been communicating with the OIG with respect to this dangerous behavior of workplace hostility in a VA hospital. The regional office is listed as being in Oakland, CA.

The hostile work environment existed, resulting in the demotion of Dr. Azawi, and subsequent report filed by the complainant with the Office of Special Counsel after the return of Dr. Azawi.

No reference to any investigation having been conducted by the Office of Special Counsel is noted in the OIG report, and the OIG ignored this complaint.

The OIG report, was reviewed. An abbreviated version of the results, and comment, are italicized.

Patient Number One
"The patient was found to have received inappropriate care. Skin breakdown was reported to the doctor, and the treatment plan was modified without new scan images. The new radiation prescription (prescribed by a doctor) did not spare an unaffected gland, damage was done, and progress notes were not entered. The treatment notes lacked details about treatment dates, patient response, and radiation dose."

Conclusion:

Progress notes required during treatment were not entered, and the treatment summary lacked details about treatment dates, patient response, and radiation dose.

With this missing information, how can a patient receive subsequent treatment?

This lack of documentation by a doctor, and prescribing subsequent therapy with no reference to previous history of treatment, is malpractice.

This is inappropriate care.

Patient Number Two
A patient had received 30 treatments in an attempt to correct the side effects of different types of radiation.

Conclusion:

The OIG report stated the side effects were "anticipated".

The treatment documentation had discrepancies with respect to cumulative dose and type of treatment given.

The next sentence reads: *"However, treatment documentation had discrepancies with respect to cumulative dose and type of treatment given".*

Again, how can subsequent treatment be given when there is no documentation for previous treatment? Is the doctor guessing what might work?

This is inappropriate care.

Patient Number Three

A patient undergoes an IMRT procedure from February-April 2009. Five months later the patient begins hormone therapy, and the patient suffers from diarrhea, dysuria, and urinary frequency. Hormone therapy continues a year later. While no substantiation of improper care was found, it was found that "However, documentation had discrepancies with respect to radiation doses and dates of treatment."

Conclusion:

Treatment documentation contained discrepancies with respect to radiation doses and dates of treatment.

A patient cannot be "treated" with radiation when the wrong amount of radiation is administered. Discrepancies mean the wrong amount of radiation was given. The doctors never knew there was any discrepancy in dosage given and the amount prescribed. Doctors never reviewed the file.

This is inappropriate care.

Patient Number Four

The patient received IMRT to the head and neck area for 3 months in 2010. The patient suffered painful inflammation and ulceration of the mucus membrane of the lining of the digestive tract. The patient required blood transfusions.

The abdominal side effects were said to be anticipated as a result of IMRT to the head and neck, and chemotherapy. It is assumed the blood transfusions were also anticipated.

The report concludes, *"However, there was no required treatment summary describing the patient's response to IMRT or resolution of symptoms"*.

How can you prescribe treatment to a person when you do not know how the person responded to the last treatment, or other treatments?

Conclusion:

There was no required treatment summary describing the patient's response to IMRT or resolution of symptoms.

This is inappropriate care.

Patient Number Five
The patient was diagnosed with low grade prostate cancer. IMRT was administered under "research protocol" from July-September, 2009.

Is research protocol any different from treatment protocol?

"The patient developed urinary frequency, nocturia, dysuria, and rectal irritation".

The OIG found no inappropriate care, but "However, we found a change in the prescribed dose prior to initiation of treatment and noted the lack of documentation of this change and of the type of treatment delivered".

Conclusion:

The prescription was changed, and there was no documentation of this, nor the type of treatment delivered. How was the next technician to determine how to treat the patient?

This is inappropriate care.

Patient Number Six
A patient underwent IMRT for prostate cancer under research protocol. A skin irritation was experienced in the buttocks area, not the prostate area.

Again, no substantiation of inappropriate care was reported. What is the definition of "inappropriate?"

The report continued. *"However, the prescription was not complete, the iodose was not specified, and treatment summary was not completed until eight weeks after treatment ended".*

What are the doctors doing for eight weeks after a treatment? These treatments are discussed in staff meetings and reports must be made to be conversant with administrators.

Continuing, the next sentence reads:

"We noted that treatment progress notes written by RT residents were not co-signed by an attending physician as required by VHA policy" (VHA Handbook 1400, 1, Resident Supervision, July 25, 2007).

The doctors violated VHA policy. This was the finding of the OIG; the doctors violated policy. What sanctions were to be placed upon these doctors? When policy is violated, as reported by the OIG, a division of the VHA, what were the consequences? Does a doctor receive a reprimand? Is a doctor suspended? Fired? Does an investigation begin to determine if this is an isolated incident or a continuing lack of adherence to mandate set forth by the VHA and "research protocol"?

Conclusion:

While finding there was no inappropriate RT care, the prescription was not complete (doctor writes prescription) the iodose was not specified (doctor order) and the treatment summary was not completed until eight weeks after treatment ended. Treatment progress notes written by RT residents were not cosigned by attending physician as required by VHA policy.

(Note: This is also standard operating procedure in all residency programs and hospitals. The lack of an attending physician's co-signature indicates that the "attending" did not review the progress notes and the resident is assumed to be unsupervised. The Department of Veterans Affairs VHA HANDBOOK 1400.1 (2005) is even more specific about what is necessary for patient safety and what is required to meet educational standards for resident physicians. Clearly the attending physicians in question violated VHA policies for patient safety and residency education.)

This is inappropriate care.

Patient Number Seven
A patient underwent IMRT treatment for prostate cancer from October- December, 2009 under "research protocol". The patient was subsequently diagnosed with "radiation cystitis" which is inflammation of the bladder. The patient underwent 30 HBO (hyperbaric oxygen therapy) treatments to resolve the bladder inflammation.

J.B. Simms

Does IMRT treatment result in side effects in the bladder? Could the area to be treated not be treated accurately, which involved the bladder?

Again, the author of the OIG report stated there was no inappropriate care and that the bladder inflammation, and subsequent 30 HBO treatments were anticipated side effects.

The report continued:

"However, we noted that the radiation oncologist [doctor] changed the radiation prescription for the patient but did not document the change in the medical record".

Evidently this is contrary to protocol as stated in the ACR Practice Guideline for Radiation Oncology, Revised 2009.

When did the doctor change the prescription? Where is the documentation for the change? Why was the prescription changed? What was changed? How did the RT and Chief RT know there was a change?

If a change was made, and the patient came in for treatment, and the RT only has the medical records, the patient will continue to be treated with the therapy prescribed before the unknown change was made.

Was the doctor responsible for the bladder inflammation?

Conclusion:

The radiation oncologist (doctor) changed the radiation prescription for the patient but did not document the change in the medical record. This would allow the patient to be treated incorrectly.

This is inappropriate care.

Patient Number Eight
"A diabetic patient, having an above the knee amputation, was diagnosed with anal margin squamous cell cancer. Surgery was performed, and RT was completed in August 2009. Therapy resulted in radiation cystitis. "Residual bladder abnormalities were noted to be slowly improving as of March 2010".

No inappropriate care was found, and the bladder abnormalities sustained as a result of RT completed in August 2009 were said to be improving as of March 2010. Really?

That seems to be a long time to "continue improving".

The report continued:

"However, follow-up evaluation of the patient was not completed within the 4-6 weeks required. Discrepancies were also found in the documentation of dates and type of treatment delivered".

How often were follow-up evaluations supposed to be made, especially on a person who was basically living at the VA Hospital? Don't doctors have to do follow-up evaluations to determine whether to continue with certain therapy or make a change?

As stated above, follow-up evaluations were required within 4-6 weeks. Required by whom? What sanctioning body doles out consequences for violating the requirement?

Conclusion:

Follow-up evaluation of the patient was not completed within 4-6 weeks as required. Discrepancies were also found in the documentation of dates and type of treatment delivered.

This is inappropriate care.

Patient Number Nine
A patient having head and neck cancer received RT and chemotherapy. The patient was admitted into the long care unit from June-August, 2010.

The neck wounds worsened, but when this occurred it was not documented accurately. (Does that mean it was not documented at all?) The patient was transferred to a private facility, then back to the VA Hospital. The patient was discharged in September 2010.

The report continued:

"However, the combination (cetuximab and RT) imparted a high risk of skin complications. Facility staff reported that this case had been reviewed by an interdisciplinary team to determine the appropriateness of reporting to the U.S. Food and Drug Administration. The team concluded that reporting was not necessary for an expected reaction."

Who was supposed to be on this "interdisciplinary team?"

If the reaction was expected, what prompted the interdisciplinary team to determine if an inappropriate action was taken? Why did the team convene? Who was alleged to be investigated for disciplinary reasons?

There was found to be inadequate documentation of patient's response to treatment. And, hidden as the last sentence pertaining to Patient Number Nine, is this: "In addition, the treatment summary was missing."

Is this the reason for the conveyance of the disciplinary team, the fact that the treatment summary was missing? When did it become missing? How did any of the staff know how many times the patient had been treated? Who oversees the file? Why was the patient treatment summary removed from the file? Was it missing during the time of treatments and no one said anything?

The OIG swept this one under the rug and hoped no one would read that sentence. If the patient knew this, or the family of the patient, there would be attorneys crawling all over the place.

Conclusion:

The combination of cetuximab and RT imparted a high risk of skin complications. Facility staff reported that this case had been reviewed by an interdisciplinary team to determine the appropriateness of reporting to the US Food and Drug Administration. The team decided not to make the report.

There were found inadequate documentation of patient response to treatment, including the status of neck lesions.

In addition, the treatment summary was missing.

(Note: With that knowledge, it was incumbent upon the Radiation Oncologists to monitor the patient closely and more frequently than the weekly monitoring required by ACR. However, the patient was seen less frequently than once per week!)

This is inappropriate care.

Patient Number Ten

A patient was admitted to the VA Hospital in late July 2010 for RT. The radiation oncologist (doctor, unidentified) determined that RT could not be done because the patient was unable to lie flat. (It is uncertain if this procedure is not possible if not lying flat). Chemotherapy was initiated but discontinued as a result of patient's shortness of breath.

It is not clear if RT would have helped the patient, who expired approximately a month after this incident. The question was whether the patient would have been able to receive the RT since the patient was unable to lie flat.

Conclusion:

The OIG did not find inappropriate care because the report implied that the patient was going to die anyway, so why be conscientious with respect to treatment.

The Constant Used of The Qualifier: "However"

The word "however" is used after eight of the ten patient summaries. The author of the OIG report might unknowingly be using the word as a suffix to each individual patient summary in order to sway the reader to interpret this as a well-thought-out report. Grammatically speaking, the word is normally used to show contrast.

The irony is the report content on each patient before the word "however" is full of questionable actions and violations of ACR policies.

There is no contrast between errant behavior in any summary either before or after the word "however". There is no contrast between errant behavior, be it losing treatment documentation, or a doctor prescribing a dosage of radiation in an area and the dosage being inappropriate or not in the right location.

Communication with Facility Leadership

In the first paragraph, it was stated that the facility staff confirmed that peer reviews had been performed, but that the results had not been communicated with facility leadership.

This is not true.

The peer review of RT therapists had been communicated with Dr. Azawi on many occasions. Dr. Azawi and Dr. Szabo were well informed with the concerns of the lack of competency of specific RT personnel. The Chief RT Therapist kept records of emails and noted on a timeline of communication concerning this matter.

A new committee was said to be formed by the facility staff to address the issue of "unawareness of RT patient outcomes." This committee would not be necessary if the doctors were conscientious about patient care and followed up on making certain that competent staff were hired in the RT area. Instead, the doctors ignored the mistreatment of patients and failed to enforce the chain of command. The RT therapists did not hold the doctors accountable for their lack of concern. The Chief RT Therapist is the only person designated to review the work performed by the RT therapists, and explain the errors made to the doctors. If the doctors must have the reports explained to them, not understanding the reports as the Chief RT Therapist does, a prudent man would think the doctors would be pleased to have a person of that intellect on the staff. The problem is that the Chief RT Therapist is also aware of misdeeds performed by the doctors, which causes contention.

Here lies the problem, and here lies the genesis of the hostile workplace.

This new committee supposedly to be formed, the Radiation Therapy and Oncology Quality Management Committee, was said to focus upon issues involving patient care, but did not address the issue of the lack of knowledge of the IMRT technology. The OIG was given physical evidence of CT scan and x-rays taken during treatment, showing inadequate administration of IMRT cancer radiation treatment. The doctors were not able to discern from the x-rays that the patient was being given improper treatment, and was being injured.

This is lack of care is verified by the fact that, by the admission of OIG officials who wrote this report, nine of the ten cases investigated had deficient medical records. One file was missing the treatment plan. Others were missing documents which would have been necessary to make decisions to treat the patient properly.

If a doctor was capable and professional, a routine inspection of the file would show deficiencies. The deficiencies were on the part of the doctor because no one reported this to the Chief of Staff. Based upon the OIG report, the executive staff was not aware of the issues of deficient files and mistreatment of patients. The doctors were not going to indict themselves or each other.

J.B. Simms

Conclusions of the OIG Report: Inappropriate Care of Ten Patient/Veterans

1. If the OIG investigators stated that the radiation oncologists did not lack competence, how would they define their own findings that 90 percent of the medical records were deficient, one missing the entire treatment plan, some missing treatment dates and treatment amounts, and some with missing records of treatment injuries versus side effects? Did it ever occur to the investigators that the deficiencies in the record keeping by the radiation oncologists could be a way to keep their "lack of competence" hidden? The cavalier attitude, violating VHA policies and mandated state and federal protocols, is grounds for license revocation.

2. The reasons the patients had not reported these doctors to the medical board are (1) they trust their doctors, and (2) many are too ill to ask to review their records and would not understand the technical reports. The surprise is that 90 percent of the patients would find that their reports are incomplete and deficient, and they do not know it. The doctors know the patient will not ask for a paper copy of their medical records, nor would they ask for the electronic records, to include photographs and any radiological studies, such as types of x-rays, CT scans, or other studies.

3. There are many reasons why the doctors might not want to record incompetent, harmful treatment of patients, and dangerous activities. One reason may be the desire to obscure the lack of proficiency with more advanced technology. However, there is no accountability because the patients were not going to complain or initiate a lawsuit. The attitude was cavalier at best because the patients never knew enough to ask questions.

4. Maybe the doctors thought they would be disciplined if the administration knew they had violated protocol and were not conversant with the technology or the documentation of such. The administration did not discipline rogue doctors; the administration shielded rogue doctors from accountability.

5. The doctors knew that the patients' treatment was substandard and that the patients were sustaining injuries rather than having side effects. However, the doctors were the only ones who could tell the patient that a mistake was made and that they received radiation to the wrong area or had inadequate radiation or excessive and damaging levels of radiation.

6. The doctors withheld this information from the patients. The radiation therapists could not tell the patient that the doctor did not review the treatment film to make sure of the positioning and dosage.
7. The patient cannot file a malpractice claim unless they know that something was wrong with their treatment. Although others in the department knew the care and treatment given to the patients was inappropriate and harmful at best, they could not say anything to the patients or family members. No one in the department including the radiation therapists could tell the patients that they were subjected to injurious malpractice. The patients never knew, and the doctors and the hospital were not telling.

The second document, published March 10, 2010, is another OIG publication, oddly enough dated on the date after the OIG report of the inspection of the Long Beach VA Hospital. This report is entitled Healthcare Inspection: Radiation Safety in Veterans Health Administration Facilities. This was the report from the September 1, 2010 visit, which was scheduled as a part of the inspections of approximately 30 Radiation Departments of the VA system. Selected pages will be printed here in this chapter; the full report can be found in the Appendix. Upon reading the Conclusion, you will see that the OIG knew that Lana was telling the truth and had read the Varian report.

A synopsis of this report is copied below. A copy of this report can be found on-line at:

https://www.va.gov/oig/54/reports/VAOIG-10-02178-120.pdf

J.B. Simms

Department of Veterans Affairs
Office of Inspector General

Healthcare Inspection

Radiation Safety in
Veterans Health Administration
Facilities

Report No. 10-02178-120　　　　　　　　　　　　　　　March 10, 2011
　　　　　　　VA Office of Inspector General
　　　　　　　Washington, DC 20420

Executive Summary

As requested by the U.S. House of Representatives Committee on Veterans' Affairs, we evaluated program oversight and quality assurance (QA) processes for diagnostic and therapeutic radiation procedures at Veterans Health Administration (VHA) facilities. The review focused on four areas associated with the greatest potential for harm—radiation therapy (RT), computed tomography (CT), fluoroscopy, and nuclear medicine. We excluded brachytherapy as this has been examined in detail in a recent OIG report.

To evaluate RT care, we queried 32 VHA facilities about processes pertaining to physician peer review (PPR) and conducted onsite inspections at 26 facilities. Site visits focused on compliance with American College of Radiology QA requirements for RT. For the 41 linear accelerators at the 26 facilities we inspected, there were 1,092 treatment days during April–May 2010. We found a day for one linear accelerator on which a daily machine check was not documented. All but 1 of the 771 treatment records reviewed for patient-specific QA demonstrated full compliance. For PPR, we found that the 32 RT programs varied widely with respect to the frequency of peer reviews.

VHA has disseminated information to hospital radiology departments in an effort to reduce CT dose variability, but we found no oversight of actual doses being delivered. In our review of patients with the highest cumulative radiation doses from CT scans, we found that neither patients nor providers had data about cumulative radiation exposure available to them at the time of clinical decision making. We also found that patients were not informed that CT scans may cause cancer. To explore the issue of radiation exposures which may confer a particularly high risk of cancer, we identified patients who had undergone multiple CT scans. Based on published estimates of radiation levels associated with each type of CT study, we enumerated those patients with the greatest cumulative radiation exposure.

For nearly 2 years, VHA has been developing, but has yet to publish, guidance regarding the use of fluoroscopy. In nuclear medicine, VHA monitors data provided by all facilities and proficiency assessments are accomplished annually.

We recommended that the Under Secretary for Health: (1) clarify the current expectations for frequency of PPR in RT, (2) develop a process for monitoring delivered radiation dose to ensure that patients do not receive excessive doses from CT scans, (3) develop risk-based criteria for informed consent prior to CT scans, (4) plan for the development of a mechanism by which patients and providers have information about prior radiation exposure available to them at the time of clinical decision making, and (5) ensure that the fluoroscopy handbook is implemented.

The Under Secretary for Health agreed with our findings and recommendations. The implementation plans are acceptable, and we will follow up on the planned actions until they are completed.

Introduction

Purpose

On January 28, 2010, the U.S. House of Representatives Committee on Veterans' Affairs requested that the VA Office of Inspector General (OIG) investigate "quality assurance and program management of all nuclear medical care, patient safety, and oversight at the Department of Veterans Affairs."

This review evaluated program oversight and quality assurance (QA) processes for diagnostic and therapeutic radiation procedures at Veterans Health Administration (VHA) facilities, with a focus on areas with the greatest potential for harm to patients—computed tomography (CT), fluoroscopy, nuclear medicine, and radiation therapy (RT).

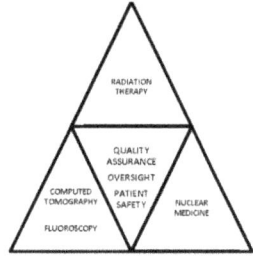

Background

Radiation has been used for more than a century to diagnose diseases and conditions, contributing greatly to advances in medical care. While any exposure to radiation entails the possibility of harm, the benefits from more accurate diagnosis are generally considered to exceed the risks inherent in radiation exposure. However, with the increased application of sophisticated technologies involving radiation, concerns have arisen about whether radiation is being used appropriately.

Many imaging procedures are employed in current medical practices, but most radiation exposure associated with diagnosis occurs with CT, fluoroscopy, and nuclear medicine studies. Because these procedures involve repeated or extended exposure to radiation, they are associated with a higher radiation dose. Although CT, fluoroscopy, and nuclear medicine studies account for only 26 percent of imaging performed annually in the U.S., together they comprise 89 percent of the total yearly exposure of patients to radiation.[1]

While the magnitude of increased cancer risk from exposure to diagnostic radiation is debated, some degree of increased risk is implicit.[2] Patient safety is optimized when clinical practice guidelines are followed, equipment is functioning properly, staff adhere to standardized procedures, shielding and engineered safety features are employed, and radiation doses are as low as reasonably achievable.[3,4]

In October 2009, officials at Cedars-Sinai Medical Center in Los Angeles notified the Food and Drug Administration (FDA) that more than 200 patients had received excessive radiation while undergoing CT perfusion scans. Because these studies require multiple scans during intravenous injection of a contrast agent, they entail substantially more radiation exposure than more typical CT scans. The FDA subsequently identified additional patients at other hospitals who were exposed to excessive levels of radiation and in February 2010 issued interim recommendations to address ongoing concerns about CT perfusion imaging.[5]

In December 2009, a VHA survey found that 12 facilities performed CT brain perfusion scans.[6] None of the 984 brain scans reported by these 12 facilities were described as exceeding the maximum recommended radiation dose. Subsequently, VHA instructed radiology service chiefs and chief technologists on calculation of CT radiation dose, methods to control dose, target dose levels, and levels that would require disclosure to the patient.

In contrast to diagnostic radiology, such as CT and fluoroscopy, which uses x-rays from outside the body, nuclear medicine makes use of radioactive materials which are ingested, inhaled, or injected into the body. The use of radioactive materials in nuclear medicine provides an assessment of metabolic function and may be diagnostic or therapeutic in nature.

According to the American Nuclear Society, an estimated 10 to 12 million diagnostic and therapeutic nuclear medicine procedures are performed each year in the U.S. In fiscal year (FY) 2008, VHA's Nuclear Medicine and Radiation Service (NMRS) program reported that VHA facilities performed 602,895 procedures. Cardiac procedures comprised about 75 percent of the workload while positron emission tomography/CT (PET/CT) studies grew at the fastest rate (an average of 25 percent in each of the previous 3 FYs).[7]

Radiation can also be used therapeutically to treat cancers and other abnormal cell growth while protecting normal cells as much as possible. In the most common form of RT, conventional or external beam RT, intense radiation from linear accelerators is directed at tumors. With intensity modulated RT (IMRT), higher doses can be delivered to abnormal tissue while reducing exposure of adjacent non-target structures.[8]

With higher doses and better targeted delivery of radiation, IMRT offers the possibility of more effective treatment with fewer side effects. However, its use also carries an increased risk of harm to patients when practice guidelines and patient safety systems are not in place or are not followed. On January 27, 2010, the New York Times reported that 36 cancer patients at the East Orange campus of the VA New Jersey Health Care System had been over-radiated and that 20 more had received inappropriately low doses of radiation.

This was the white-wash of the problem with the Radiation Department. Lana had spoken to the OIG investigators during their September 2010 visit, and it was the discussion with Lana which generated these comments.

Azawi had violated the ACR regulations by curtailing many of the corrective action plan (CAP) provisions which Azawi presented to the ACR in order for the hospital to become accredited.

Duff, DeMasters, McCartan, and Szabo knew that Azawi was violating the ACR guidelines. Since Azawi submitted the application, having a falsified action plan, with no intention of fulfilling the proposal, and the application was accepted, Azawi was the "star" and no one could touch her.

The conclusion, and the list of hospitals inspected will be listed on the following two pages.

Conclusions

We found compliance with standards of practice for machine- and patient-specific QA processes in RT. However, we found inconsistent performance of physician peer review, which could be improved by clarifying national expectations for frequency of physician peer review practices in RT.

Regarding CT scans, we found an absence of oversight to ensure that delivered doses of radiation are not excessive. We also found that patients are not routinely informed prior to imaging procedures which carry a significant risk of induced cancer. Further, we identified a need for patients and providers to have information about prior radiation exposure available to them at the time of clinical decision making.

Patient safety during fluoroscopy procedures could be enhanced system wide with expedited implementation of the VHA fluoroscopy handbook.

We found that VHA has appropriate oversight and QA activities in place to minimize radiation risks to nuclear medicine patients.

Recommendations

We recommended that the Under Secretary for Health, in conjunction with VISN and facility senior managers:

Recommendation 1: Clarify the current expectations for frequency of physician peer review practices in RT.

Recommendation 2: Develop a process for monitoring delivered radiation dose to ensure that patients do not receive excessive doses during CT procedures.

Recommendation 3: Develop criteria for patient informed consent requirements prior to CT testing.

Recommendation 4: Include in strategic planning a mechanism by which patients and providers have information about prior radiation exposure available to them at the time of clinical decision making.

Recommendation 5: Ensure that the fluoroscopy handbook is implemented.

Sites Visited for Radiation Safety Review

Name	Location	VISN
Samuel S. Stratton VA Medical Center	Albany, NY	2
James J. Peters VA Medical Center	Bronx, NY	3
VA NY Harbor Healthcare System, Brooklyn Campus	Brooklyn, NY	3
VA New Jersey Health Care System, East Orange Campus	East Orange, NJ	3
Northport VA Medical Center	Northport, NY	3
Philadelphia VA Medical Center	Philadelphia, PA	4
VA Pittsburgh Healthcare System	Pittsburg, PA	4
Washington DC VA Medical Center	Washington, DC	5
Hunter Holmes McGuire VA Medical Center	Richmond, VA	6
Durham VA Medical Center	Durham, NC	6
Atlanta VA Medical Center	Decatur, GA	7
Miami VA Healthcare System	Miami, FL	8
James A. Haley Veterans' Hospital	Tampa, FL	8
Mountain Home VA Medical Center	Mountain Home, TN	9
Memphis VA Medical Center	Memphis, TN	9
Louis Stokes VA Medical Center	Cleveland, OH	10
Dayton VA Medical Center	Dayton, OH	10
VA Ann Harbor Healthcare System	Ann Harbor, MI	11
Richard L. Roudebush VA Medical Center	Indianapolis, IN	11
Edward Hines Jr. VA Hospital	Hines, IL	12
Clement J. Zablocki VA Medical Center	Milwaukee, WI	12
St. Louis VA Medical Center	St. Louis, MO	15
Michael E. DeBakey VA Medical Center *	Houston, TX	16
VA North Texas Health Care System – Dallas VA Medical Center	Dallas, TX	17
VA Greater Los Angeles Healthcare System	Los Angeles, CA	22
VA Long Beach Healthcare System	Long Beach, CA	22
Minneapolis VA Health Care System	Minneapolis, MN	23

* pilot site

J.B. Simms

Analysis of The OIG Conclusion

In the Conclusion of the inspection of September 2010, the OIG found "compliance with standard practice" Evidently the OIG was not made privy to the Varian Incident, where the therapists "were not in compliance with standard practice" and lied about violating protocol.

With respect to the doctors, the report stated:

> *Regarding CT scans, we found an absence of oversight to ensure that delivered doses of radiation are not excessive. We also found that patients are not routinely informed prior to imaging procedures which carry a significant risk of induced cancer. Further, we identified a need for patients and providers to have information about prior radiation exposure available to them at the time of clinical decision making.*

1. Absence of oversight on the part of physicians.
2. Patients were not informed of risks of procedure
3. A need existed for patient being informed before consent
4. No evidence of certification was requested, nor was any certification presented, by Dr. Azawi nor Dr. Williams to satisfy the inspectors that the physicians were qualified to conduct IMRT treatment for any patient.

Dr. Azawi anticipated having to produce evidence of certification because she attempted to obtain a counterfeit certificate. It appears that either the OIG was not thorough in their investigation, false information was given to the OIG, or that Azawi simply dodged a bullet.

Recommendation #2 implied that there was no current process or policy in place to monitor radiation given to the patients. That recommendation was laughable. Lana Miller Boyer discovered the mistreatment of the Veteran because she was "monitoring" the two therapists. The policy was in place; it was the doctors and persons in the administration who did not know there was a policy; nor how to monitor the radiation. Lana got their attention.

Chapter Thirteen:

No Accountability for Abuse

It was the spring of 2011. The OIG reports were published. Lana was sick, heartbroken, and scared. Azawi was emboldened.

The OIG investigators convinced her to submit the Hotline report, then the OIG investigators dropped the ball; the investigation was a sham, and the OIG had given Lana's name as the person reporting to the hotline. No OIG inspector asked to see any certification of any physician.

The Office of Special had not communicated with Lana concerning her report she submitted on October 27, 2009. Mary Beth McCartan had not communicated to Lana as to when Lana would be meeting with the hospital director, Isabel Duff.

Azawi certainly did not like to be inconvenienced. First thing on the morning of Friday, March 11, 2011, Azawi sent out the following email to Dr. Eric Frank, a contract physicist:

March 11,
2011 Eric,
I am really not happy with the way the Miler treatment was arranged. George gave me a hard time about his treatment. George did not know anything. Amber did not know anything. Chart was not filled. This is not acceptable. We need to talk about this. Did you tell Lana? I do not want this to happen again. Let us meet in my office to talk about this for a few minutes
Samar Azawi, M.D.

The indignant and arrogant attitude of Dr. Azawi, noting that she is a doctor and that rules do not apply to her, was evident by an exchange (below) between Lana and Azawi. Lana sent Azawi an email, telling Azawi that Lana would be sending Azawi the policy Azawi requested Lana to write about CT to Treat Timeline. Azawi's reply:

March 14, 2011
751am
"I do not need this QA (Quality Assessment) form and I do not to use it for many reasons that I have told you before."

Lana was telling the truth, and she had the evidence. Here was the email which Azawi sent which confirmed she had no intent to use the forms which were needed for patient files. An interesting side note was the only person copied on the email was Michon Dean, a clerk who was one of the minion/disciples of Azawi.

A few moments later, Azawi sent out the following email to Lana, and copied Michon Dean:

March 14, 2011
Lana
I asked you to update the simulation policy about two weeks ago since we had the training/demo by Civco. I do not recall seeing it. I explained to you I need a detailed step by step simulation policy and procedure. I am sure you have been working on it. I am asking (you) submit b(y) COB tomorrow.
Thank you.

Was Azawi going to adhere to some policies? Maybe she would adhere to those which do not affect her scheduling and put more constraints upon her time.

Azawi fired off another email within the hour, asking for copies of communication regarding a server. Lana was getting a bit overwhelmed.

The next day, March 15, Azawi was at it again. Lana received an email from Azawi, and Azawi was asking why Lana had:

"...[a]ltered my clear instructions that were given by Michon (Dean) to you..."

The reply was that Michon had talked to the therapists herself, and Lana supplied the lists and forms.

Azawi accused Lana of lying, changing her statement, and tried to involve another therapist, Amber by name. Lana told Azawi that there was no change in the story, and reiterated the technical information necessary.

After Azawi accused Lana of lying, bringing Michon Dean into the mix relating Azawi's directives to Lana, Amber came to Lana. Amber told Lana that since Michon had been giving directives to the therapists, circumventing Lana, Amber was beginning to wonder who she worked for, Michon on Lana.

Why was the Formal Grievance so delayed? Why was the Human Resources Department not responding? What was the EEO officer, Susan DeMasters, doing? Where was the Office of Special Counsel?

Lana was alone.

Azawi continued to circumvent Lana in an attempt to discredit her. Azawi had been communicating with therapists, mostly Gail Francis, Dennis and Amber, to generate reports which were a waste of time. At one point, Dennis began yelling at Lana about being "put in the middle". This behavior seemed a bit disingenuous to Lana because Dennis was "smiling" as he was yelling.

Later in midday, Azawi sent an email to Lana, telling Lana that she (Azawi) could not find Lana. Lana replied that she had left late for lunch, and that Azawi had seen Lana return. Lana wrote to Azawi that if she were to be late leaving for lunch, Lana would be glad to let Azawi know this. Azawi was reminded that Lana had a pager which Azawi could all at any time.

Lana then sent Azawi a long email concerning the fact that Azawi was giving directives to the therapists, by-passing Lana, requesting reports.

On the following day, Azawi started over again. Her email sent at 7:05am began with:

Wednesday, March 16, 2011 7:05am
I counseled you verbally regarding changing my clear instruction to the therapist for filling out the QA (Quality Assessment) forms. Michon had clearly given the details to execute the new therapist assignments in view of low work load. I do not expect changing or interfering with such clear instructions in the future. This is a reminder for both of us about this incident.

Azawi was running her game through Michon.

Azawi would not approach Lana for anything productive. She triangulated contact, always having a witness, and tried to make Lana appear to not be following orders by involving others to communicate to Lana, or bypassing Lana totally, going straight to the therapists. Lana knew what was happening, but was always nice and polite to Azawi.

There were 2 physicists for at least a month, and one dosimetrist in the department requiring 3 Eclipse treatment planning computers. The department had 2 computers. Dr. Azawi would not decide about getting the third computer. Having only two computers left a physicist unable to do treatment planning that she was hired to do since Dr. Azawi said they are "so busy." Hagan also stated the department needed 4 more radiation therapists as well. Dr. Azawi still would not make a decision.

What were the new employees, which Hagan said should be hired, supposed to do if they had no computer to use?

In an attempt to normalize the operation of the department, Lana emailed Azawi on March 28. Within the email was a copy of the table of contents of the Policy and Procedures from the VA Hospital in Tampa, FL. No response was received from Azawi; she was going to do everything her way.

Monday, April 4, 2011

On April 4, 2011, at 331pm, Lana emailed Michon Dean, asking her to explain why Lana's encounter report should not have been blocked.

Michon tried to block the Report of Contact because "any problem had to be fixed before the next day."

Lana replied that Michon violated the policy enabling reports of encounters to be entered within 7 days. Michon was left speechless.

Azawi sent an email asking Lana to enter leave time for all the doctor/psychiatrist appointments Lana attended since August.

Lana reminded Azawi that Lana was out on leave for PTSD for 3 months and that would not constitute leave time. Azawi was looking for anything she could find which would impeach Lana's credibility. It was constant but futile.

Dr. Azawi would find any way to impeach the credibility of anyone, just to make herself look good. On April 20, she sent out an email to Lana telling Lana to tell the therapists not to call Azawi and leave phone messages for Azawi to approve film. Well, after the patient had completed simulation, and film was taken at treatment, the doctor had to approve the film taken at treatment to insure the films (simulation and treatment films) matched.

That was the job of the doctor- approve the film. When the doctors left the department without making any announcement, and the therapists could not find the doctors, either the patient would not be treated, or treatment would be performed by the therapists without the doctor's approval. It happened.

On April 21 and 22 Gail Francis did not come to work. Lana asked everyone if they knew about Gail being out since they found notifications on 2 different calendars that she was out on leave.

With Lana as the supervisor, Gail was supposed to get the leave/absence approved by Lana before Gail entered any information into the computer program.

Gail had been sending emails requesting time off with the last one regarding an appointment for April 8, 2011. Lana requested Terry Girley, Timekeeper in Radiology, to report if Gail had requested the time off, and who and when it was approved.

Michon Dean replied, stating Gail had entered the request but did not say who or when it was approved. Michon wanted to know if the therapists had been given verbal or written instructions regarding a leave request and Lana replied that it was verbal, and the therapists were to follow instructions.

On April 25, Lana forwarded an email to Michon noting that Lana had given written instructions to Gail and Dennis regarding the request for leave and the procedures to follow.

This email was dated February 9, 2009, and the time of the email was 11:29a.m. Lana also emailed Terry Girley to notify Lana anytime Gail or Dennis requested leave time to make sure Lana had approved the leave. Michon did not reply.

Later in the day, Gail was at work and was on the workstation in the Trilogy control area. As Lana walked by the area and observed Gail, Lana reminded Gail to enter her sick day into Vista. (Lana had found out that Gail had planned a family gathering to attend, which was associated with her absence of April 22.) Gail did not respond to Lana.

As the morning progressed, there were certain tasks Lana needed Gail to complete and another which she needed to be reminded. At no time would Gail make any form of acknowledgement.

After over an hour of this behavior, Lana walked up beside Gail and asked Gail if she had heard the request and instructions given by Lana.

Gail answered "yes." Lana told Gail that Lana needed to know from Gail that she had heard and understood the instructions. She said, "I hear you." Gail became very defensive and insubordinate when she knew she was caught, but that still did not explain who authorized Gail to be absent. Veterans needing treatment suffered when this happened.

On the following day, April 26, Lana noticed Gail in the Simulator at the computer. Gail was a bit more talkative; Lana figured this would be a calm environment to discuss matters. Lana asked if Gail was feeling okay, and Lana decided to engage some coaching techniques. Lana closed the door.

Lana asked Gail, since Gail had been out sick, on leave, if Gail was feeling well. Gail replied that she was fine. Lana asked if things were okay at home with Gail and her son. Gail said she was fine, and that the only problem she had was work, and Gail became very angry.

Lana let Gail settle back and down and Lana talked about some changes in some policies and procedures, and if Gail would like to make some input with respect to making any changes.

Gail started yelling, saying she was tired of the disrespect and why didn't Lana treat her like everyone else. Gail was stomping her feet, screaming, waving her arms at Lana and said, "...[t]hat is why I do not like talking to you" and left the room. Gail yelled that she had warmed up the machines, but that was not true; not all of them were warmed up and that delayed patient simulation.

A few people heard Gail; one was Dr. Azawi and another was Donna Pikulsky. Lana told Dr. Azawi that a meeting to discuss this matter needed to be scheduled. Azawi's response was, "I don't want to speak to you. How could you get her into that state?"

Dr. Azawi and the others appeared to be in concert with respect to taking away authority from Lana, and making her look inconsequential as a supervisor.

There had been a problem with therapists leaving from time to time and not telling Lana when they were leaving. There was a computer program which the employees were to use when asking for leave, and another to use when they returned. It was not used as required. This caused major problem scheduling patients to receive treatment or simulation.

Patients did not deserve to be left in the waiting room for hours at the whim of therapists.

On April 29, Dr. Azawi sent an email to all the therapists, and sent a copy to Dr. Williams and Michon Dean. The email said the following:

Friday, April 29, 2011

Dear All:

This is a reminder that when calling in sick you need to talk to a live leave approving official. If you cannot get in touch with one of the approving officials [sic] you must leave a call back number where you can be reached.

Leave approving officials: Dr. Azawi

Dr. Williams Michon Dean

All these people worked for Lana. These people were supposed to be reporting to Lana. Azawi was driving the wedge between the therapists and Lana. It was gas-lighting again.

After this, on May 2, Azawi sent out another email to Lana, requesting that Lana enter all leave she had used for Lana's standing appointments with Dr. Schuder. Azawi stated she wanted the information by close of business on 4/5/11. The date had to be a typo, she had to have meant 5/5/11.

Azawi knew that for 3 months Lana had been out on leave, and those months did not need to be included when documenting "leave time". This was more harassment. This was the type of behavior which cause and contributed to PTSD being exhibited by Lana.

Azawi ran her department as she wished, and her behavior, yelling and screaming at Lana, was ignored by hospital officials. Azawi was doing her best to eliminate Lana from the loop of authority. Lana knew too much, and those outside the hospital knew that.

On May 3, Dr. Azawi asked Lana why a patient needed to be re-simulated. Lana researched the patient's simulation and discovered the patient had been simulated on February 17 and had already completed treatment. The patient was not Azawi's patient. Evidently, Lana's answers were not acceptable to Dr. Azawi, so after 5 emails, having extensive detail,

Azawi wanted to know who Lana asked and why the simulation had to be repeated. Azawi's motive for taking Lana's time to do this was consistent with the attitude of harassment.

Azawi was not the only person harassing Lana; Azawi was empowering others to do the same, even if the person was of the same level of authority or below Lana. Donna Pikulsky, the RN, had joined in.

Lana had begun training Ms. Gabbard in the CT simulator per orders from Dr. Azawi, explaining each step, documentation, and procedures. Lana needed to remain in the simulator during each procedure to guide Ms. Gabbard. When a patient with bone metastasis was scheduled, required documentation was checked but there was no imaging or pathology report to support treatment or simulation. Lana called Donna Pikulsky and asked Donna to print out the report for the chart.

Donna replied, "Dr. Azawi told me I only had to supply a pathology report. If you need it, print it yourself."

Documentation of this sort had always been required and provided by Ms. Pikulsky or the receptionist. This refusal to deliver all proper documentation which was in the patient's chart prior to simulation was inexcusable. This delayed patient care and added to the frustration of the patient, as well as Lana as she had to watch the patient wait for treatment.

Lana knew she had to cover herself at every move, so Lana sent a copy of an April 26, 2011 email she sent to Azawi, Williams, Michon Dean, Donna Pikulsky, and Mary Beth McCartan, to the EEO officer, Susan D. DeMasters. The incident occurred April 26, 2011 and was documented in the email that follows:

J.B. Simms

*From: Lana Miller
To: Susan D.
DeMasters Date:
May 9, 2011
This morning when I came in both treatment machines were not warmed up as required by the therapist assigned-again. In fact, this has been the issue when Gail Francis is assigned to the task. There is not problem being on time when others warm up the machines. Gail Francis stated she had the machines warmed up by 8am. This is not true. She began screaming at the top of her lungs, saying I treat her different and other things.
his is a complex issue. Do not take it on face value because things are not as they appear. Gail Francis does not like being correct in any fashion. She believes she is the only person that gets in touble [sic].I would hope we can discuss this to describe issues at hand. Please do not take what Gail Francis says as the only version because I assure you it is not.
Let's talk about this before you are convinced I am to blame... Lana Miller
Chief Therapist- Radiation
Therapy VA Long Beach
Healthcare System*

Lana knew that Gail would run to DeMasters and make some kind of complaint, just as she did when Gail's paperwork for her raise a year before seemed to be delayed. Azawi was the one demanding that Gail get the raise, Lana would not put her name on the document to approve it, and Gail became a puppet of Azawi.

On May 10, Azawi fired of another email to Lana asking for evidence of leave time having been entered for Lana's appointments with Dr. Schuder, her psychiatrist. Lana told Azawi that, subsequent to and pursuant to their conversation in Azawi's office, Lana entered leave requests for a month in advance, to leave at 3:45Pm each Monday.

Azawi resented Lana seeing Dr. Schuder because Azawi was the reason Lana was seeing Dr. Schuder.

Azawi had to be reminded that Lana did not leave early or have standing appointments with Dr. Schuder until after Lana returned from the 3-month leave, which began when Lana returned to work in December 2010.

Further, Lana stated:

"I will stop everything I am working on with critical deadlines and review the Leave Report that has been on my desk since April 18 and get back to you on any missed submissions. Please let me know if there is anything else you need me to do and I will be happy to do it."

The department was in utter chaos. Gail was insubordinate. Michon Dean and Donna Pikulsky became minions of Dr. Azawi, who both continued her harassment game. They wanted Lana out; gone. They knew that Lana was going to battle to keep the Veterans from being further harmed.

The next step for Azawi to "punish" Lana was to bring her out of her supervisory role and put her into a position as a therapist. Lana had many reports to do and had to supervise therapist who supposedly has been trained. Also, Dr. Hagan, the Chief Oncologist for the entire VA recommended at least 3 additional therapists be hired. Azawi was not going to do that. So, Lana had a meeting with Dr. Azawi on May 12 and was told that Lana would be treating all IMRT patients daily beginning Monday May 16. Lana was also to assist in creating a task list for the therapists.

Lana told Dr. Azawi that she did not need to work the IMRT machine to know what tasks each person would perform because Lana assisted Patti Hall in creating the procedure presentation in Washington, DC. for the entire VA system. Azawi resented the fact that Lana was so intelligent that nothing would get past her, and that Lana helped write the manual for the procedures. Azawi piled on the additional work. Lana was being set up to fall.

After Lana explained that putting her on the machine in order to know what the therapists were to do was ludicrous, and that Azawi had Lana working on other projects, a confrontation finally erupted.

Lana told Azawi that she was tired of her harassment, intimidation, and retaliation. Azawi's reply was for Lana to go file something against Azawi. Azawi asked Lana if Lana was raising her voice, and Lana said "yes."

Lana finally stood up against Azawi, but it took a toll. Lana sent an email to Dr. Schuder, her psychiatrist, and this became the subject of another Monday session with Dr. Schuder.

Dr. Williams was a passive person and allowed Dr. Azawi to run all over him. Occasionally Dr. Williams would show a glimmer of having a conscience, but never any backbone. If Dr. Williams needed to confer with Lana, he knew that his demeanor had to be different than it was during the time that Azawi had been demoted. Dr. Williams had become empowered when Azawi was suspended, but Dr. Williams had little or no initiative.

A glimmer of anxiety was exposed, along with another glaring example of patient neglect and harm, when Dr. Williams emailed Lana on May 18, 2011. Dr. Williams sent a copy to Dr. Azawi.

J.B. Simms

Dr. Williams to Lana:

Friday, May 18, 2011 1:59pm

An issue has surfaced that I think could have serious consequences. I recall a few weeks ago Dr. Azawi had a discussion with you about checking to see that daily images had been reviewed by the patient's physician. I believe that part of the discussion revolved around verification that the correct physician's name be assigned to the patient in ARIA (computer program).

So you can imagine my shock to discover an even more disastrous situation- a patient that had NO PHYSICIAN assigned. Why is this more disastrous? By having no physician assigned the images do not appear for daily "film check". Accordingly, this patient's images did not appear for physician review on 5/5/11, 5/6/11, 5/10/11, 5/11/11, 5/12/11, 5/13/11, 5/16/11, and 5/17/11. Today this patient's images appear on my list.

Apparently, a physician has finally been assigned-after the patient received 10 treatments! (I notice that the initial day's images on 5/4/11 were reviewed, which is likely because I retrieved them by name on the first day of ports.)

I have verified the above scenario by checking old "machine schedules" which confirm there was no physician assigned.

I have yet to approve the old images. Likely, they are all correctly aligned. However, the potential for a disaster is huge. If there had been a daily error, it would only result in only 200cGy of inaccurate dose. But in this patient it could have resulted in 2000 cGy inaccuracy, or worse if it had gone longer.

I think we need to discuss this.

A few moments later, Dr. Williams wrote again:

Also, with all this prompting me to look further, I see one of Dr. Azawi's patients is listed as mine and one of mine is listed as Dr. Azawi's. This is beyond a "random occurrence."

During this time, Dr. Azawi was reassigning Lana to different things, such as having Lana help, out front. Lana was the Chief Therapists, but Azawi was removing Lana's authority, and telling her she needed to go "out front" and help. This compromised patient care in a huge way.

After Dr. Williams sent out the email stating that a patient had been reviewed and obtained treatment before any doctor was assigned, Lana knew that a doctor was supposed to have been assigned where Michon Dean worked. Lana was up there from time to time but had been forbidden by Michon Dean to help train the personnel working up front on the patient program connected to schedules, treatment, films and treatment planning. After being forbidden to help or talk with the people up front, Lana was requested to provide written instructions on entering a new patient and scheduling patients.

The employees wanted Lana to create the program but did not want Lana to be privy to the workings of the input of the information. This was because Lana knew the appropriate manner to handle the patient, and it was not being done.

It was not a shock to Lana that the patient "fell through the cracks" because Azawi had taken away much of Lana's supervisory authority of the therapists, and Lana would be the person blamed for the lapse.

On May 19, Dr. Azawi sent out an email, claiming the situation was:

"...[v]ery disturbing and concerning and wanted to know how this situation could have happened."

On May 23, 2011, Lana sent a three-page letter to Dr. Azawi and Dr. Williams, detailing the incident of the "lost patient" and the patient care problem. It was determined that Dr. Azawi "had approved the films dated in red in Dr. Williams's absence." Also, if a physician had not been assigned to a patient, the provider (the doctor) should have been assigned or the front notified.

Later in the day, there was an incident in which Gail Francis was "driving" and Ray "charting" the new boost plan. The treatment plan was not checked against the computer and treatment record. The patient was treated with an incorrect field and the error was caught on the second field. The plan had not been pushed over to the treatment machine by "EF". Lana was supposed to be notified about any incident of the type but was not. Lana found out accidentally. No one wanted Lana to know that mistakes continued to be made.

From this time on, there existed a combination of understaffing and assigning therapists to areas which they were not trained. Gail was sent with Lana to do observation for CT in simulation, but Gail was only licensed to operate a CT in therapy, not simulation. Diagnostic CT was completely different than doing a simulation.

The lack of approved overtime left only one person to operate the therapy machine. Lana operated machine one day from 3:30 until the end of the day. This violated standards, but Azawi was not to be denied her power, regardless of the affect it had on the Veteran patients.

After Lana treated the patients, Lana emailed Dr. Williams, telling him that Gail Francis did not need to be observing in CT since it was of no benefit and a waste of VA funds. Lana further stated that there must have been a reason to have her there, but Lana did not know the reason.

During the time Lana was conducting the treatment, Gail was in an office with Dr. Williams and Michon Dean. When Lana found this out, she sent a message to Dr. Williams telling him that she (Lana) was the supervisor of Gail, and Lana should be privy to any meeting, especially since Lana was constantly told by Azawi that Lana should know what her subordinates were doing always. Azawi kept assigning different tasks to the therapists, putting a strain on the department and the treatment of the Veterans. The new therapists were not hired.

There were the constant emails from Azawi, referred to as the "where were you?" emails, sent out when Azawi did not see Lana directly in front of her. Azawi would send out these emails and not page Lana or make much of an attempt to find Lana. Azawi was simply looking for a way to document what she would deem to be uncooperative. It was absurd.

J.B. Simms

On May 26, Lana received an email from Dr. Williams, stating he went to deliver something and he could not find her. He did not call or page, just sent the email stating that none of the therapist had seen her that day. The time of the email was 8:51a.m. Williams simply sent out the "nasty-gram" implying Lana had done something wrong.

Lana replied at 10:18am, stating she had called Pat, and said she would be late. When Lana replied, she did not hit the key to "Reply to All" and simply replied to Williams although Williams had included Azawi on the email. Williams' reply at 10:22am was to chastise Lana for not including Azawi in the response to Lana's short tardiness and having called Pat to explain her short absence. Williams continued, saying that since Lana had not included Azawi in an email reply, she had "removed" Azawi's name.

Also, since Azawi's name was not included as a recipient of the email, Williams was going to have to verbally explain to Azawi the name of the person Lana called to confirm she was going to be late. What a reach in order to attempt to crucify a person.

After 2 weeks, on June 3, Lana and the therapists were called to the treatment machine, including Ms. Francis (Gail), coming from Radiology. All were handed assignments for the next two weeks signed by Dr. Williams and Dr. Azawi. Lana was assigned to work on the treatment machine 36 hours a week with 4 hours allowed for Quality Assessment tasks. Ms. Dean was standing there so Lana asked what was going on with this assignment. Ms. Dean clearly and flatly stated, "You were asked to cross-train the therapists in the simulator and you did not so this is the result." Lana wondered exactly what she had been doing the last month if not training Ms. Gabbard in the simulator. Lana was now going to be punished.

After Lana told of this interaction with Azawi and Williams, Dr. Schuder put Lana on leave again.

Dr. Schuder was saving Lana's life. Dr. Schuder, who trained in hospitals in New York City, could see the truth of the plan to psychologically attack Lana, and break her down. Others outside the hospital saw it (OIG, Dr. Hagan, Wendy Kemp, and other Chief Radiation Therapists) but no one was powerful enough to rid the hospital of the persons who were injuring the Veterans.

J.B. Simms

J.B. Simms

Chapter Fourteen:

Excuses by OIG; Schuder's Rescue

Doctor Suzie Schuder had seen enough of the abuse. of Lana.

Suzie Schuder, MD
Diplomate: Board of Psychiatry & Neurology

901 Dover Drive, Suite 204
Newport Beach, CA 92660
Tel: 949-722-9884
Fax: 949-722-9885

June 6, 2011

RE: LANA MILLER

To Whom It May Concern:

Lana Miller is a patient in my care. She has been suffering with a work-related acute stress syndrome that has continued and evolved into a Chronic Post Traumatic Stress Disorder. The work-related stress is due to the continued harassment she has suffered at the hands of Dr. Samar Azawi, the chief of the Department of Radiation Oncology who is also Ms. Miller's direct supervisor. In addition, Dr. Azawi has had a great deal of influence on some of the other people in the department who have followed Dr. Azawi's lead in harassing Ms. Miller.

Ms. Miller has been aware that there has been a rapid turnover of chief therapists in the department since Dr. Azawi has been chief for about five to six years. During this time span, there have been about five other people who have been in this position before Ms. Miller. Most left the job after a short while and one man died on the job of a heart attack. One woman in this position had repeatedly banged her head against a wall and had to be physically removed from the department. She did not return. Ms. Miller seems to have outlasted the prior chief therapists under Dr. Azawi's command.

Although Dr. Azawi has actually been physically violent with some of the contract therapists, she has not physically attacked Ms. Miller. Her tactics are more insidious. She undermines the authority conferred by Ms. Miller's job title in front of Ms. Miller's subordinates. She encourages Ms. Miller's therapists to join in demeaning and attacking Ms. Miller.

One of the many examples of Dr. Azawi's harassment tactics occurred in the summer of 2009. Ms. Miller had asked Dr. Azawi to meet with her to discuss how they might improve treatment accuracy with the treating therapists. Ms. Miller had expected that Dr. Azawi would follow the basic protocol of a military facility honoring a chain of command. Ms. Miller expected that after meeting with the department chief she would then present new treatment guidelines to the therapists for them to follow. Instead, what had occurred was entirely counter to basic protocol. Dr. Azawi had invited the three therapists in question to her meeting with Ms. Miller and told them to come prepared to point out Ms. Miller's role in poor treatment practices. Ms. Miller was informed of the new meeting parameters only about five minutes prior to the meeting time. The meeting then involved the therapist attacking Ms. Miller with comments saying that Ms. Miller lied about their inept and dangerous treatment protocols and that she did not know what she was talking about and was outdated. Their accusations were blatantly false as documented evidence showed. In spite of this, Dr. Azawi sat back and watched grinning from ear to ear encouraging the therapists in their attack of Ms. Miller. Ms. Miller sat in this meeting dumbfounded that her subordinates were not only allowed to debase her they were encouraged to do so. She mentioned to Dr. Azawi that this was inappropriate and to that Dr. Azawi said that she disagreed. Ms. Miller was appalled that Dr. Azawi did not believe she had to follow any departmental rules and felt she could get away with unprofessional management behavior because she was the doctor.

J.B. Simms

RE: LANA MILLER

This incident, one many to follow, had totally undermined Ms. Miller's authority and prevented her from doing the job she was hired to do. Whenever Ms. Miller tried to perform her duties and correct therapists' substandard patient treatments or point out inappropriate insubordinate behavior, the therapists in question would run and complain to Dr. Azawi who then told the therapists that it was no big deal and they should not worry about it.

Another particular instance was with a therapist, GF, who had mistakenly aligned the patient to a freckle rather than the treatment mark. This would have caused the treatment area to be missed by an area of 1.75 cm by 1.5cm. Ms. Miller instructed GF to line it up on the correct spot. Dr. Azawi was present and when all three left the treatment room, Ms. Miller said to Dr. Azawi that she was glad she had seen that. To which Dr. Azawi answered that GF "was not that far off". This concept is foreign to radiation oncology where precision and accuracy are crucial to patient treatment and is the standard of care.

She is also being harassed by other people in the department who are influenced by and would benefit from gaining Dr. Azawi's approval, by being the recipients of preferential treatment that includes salary increases. They took part in willful isolation of Ms. Miller especially during departmental events or meetings. One of many examples is the recent exclusion of Ms. Miller from a departmental holiday luncheon. In fact, her subordinates had avoided Ms. Miller so that they did not have to mention the holiday gathering because Ms. Miller had been purposefully excluded. She found out inadvertently by opening the door to the conference room to join her friends for lunch but was surprised to see the entire department, including the janitor, eating Pizza that was bought by Dr. Williams. She was actually even more disturbed by the stunned silence when she said, "Oh, no one told me we were having pizza." Her words were met by an awkward silence. Furthermore, when the holiday gathering ended, she overheard Dr. Williams say to the nurse that he could invite or not invite anyone as he pleased because he bought the pizza.

Ms. Miller has also been subjected to continued, unscheduled and unpredictable meetings with Dr. Azawi and Dr. Williams. This occurred and occurs almost on a daily basis without warning and without being given any idea about the topic that needed to be addressed so "urgently". It seems that the only purpose of these command meetings were in effect to intimidate, harass and demean Ms. Miller with false accusations and without allowing her to an opportunity to address any of the accusations.

One other example of how Ms. Miller has had to survive a hostile work environment is exemplified by being singled out as the only person in the department who is not permitted to exit the department through the back door. Dr. Azawi made this edict after Ms. Miller had notified Dr. Williams about a leather office chair and treatment device that had been removed from the department. Ms. Miller expected that something would be done to prevent further pilferage. She was dumbfounded at the response of barring only her from exiting through that door. This totally defied any logic and seemed to be another way to isolate and further harass Ms. Miller.

Although some types of PTSD are caused by a single trauma it can also be manifested by continued "prisoner of war" tactics. Examples of these tactics are described above and are insidious ways of harming another. Essentially Ms. Miller is being isolated and singled out as the only one to be harassed and "micromanaged" by Dr. Azawi who has bullied her and created an extremely hostile work environment as a way to exploit her power over anyone in the position of chief therapist.

J.B. Simms

RE: LANA MILLER

Ms. Miller has been thwarted from doing her job and has been given little control over her performance. She has been continually obstructed by being given useless reports to do along with the duty of endless documentation. When these reports are given to Dr. Azawi, she dismisses them with a wave of her hand, clearly without any intention of reading the report she requested. These pointless assignments take up much of Ms. Miller's work time. Furthermore Dr. Azawi assigns duties that are not within Ms. Miller's scope of her job description. This happens more frequently when Dr. Azawi is angry with her. She currently is being "punished" for some illogical infraction. Ms. Miller's response to all the inescapable bullying has created a sense of "learned helplessness" that has fueled her now severe, debilitating chronic PTSD.

Ms. Miller has lived under a tremendous amount of pressure at work to the point of having it affect her health necessitating her to take a three month FMLA. The persecution, lead by Dr. Azawi, has caused Ms. Miller to suffer from insomnia, nightmares, fatigue, back pain due to muscle spasms, nausea, headaches, high blood pressure and anxiety along with the inability to concentrate. She feels paralyzed, and has difficulty making decisions that had not been an issue for her in the past. Her health has been adversely affected by the hostile environment she faces on a daily basis. In that she has no more family leave time available and must be at work, I have advised her to take a few days off as sick leave because she will become ill to the point of being disabled.

As a psychiatrist working with people with PTSD, I am appalled that such an abusive of power is allowed to exist in the health care arena causing poor health in employees. Furthermore it is ironic that a military hospital specializing in treating soldiers with PTSD allows an employee to harass her subordinates to the point of causing severe PTSD symptoms even without the trauma of being on the battlefield.

Sincerely,

Suzie Schuder, MD

J.B. Simms

It had been 20 months since Lana filed the complaint with the Office of Special Counsel. She thought they had 240 days to respond, but she had received an e- mail asking for an extension about a year prior to this date. This was unfair, and cruel. Lana sent an email to the OSC telling them that Dr. Schuder had put her on leave again.

A copy of the email sent by Lana to the Office of Special Counsel is below:

June 3, 2011

Mr Bruce Fong By email

Office of Special Counsel Oakland, CA

OSC File No. MA-10-0159

Dear Mr Fong:

Thank you for the opportunity to respond to your letter.

Dr Azawi is abusive. When asked why she acts or does something way out of the norm, she has stated, "Because I can." That is her management philosophy and she is dedicated to it. Her unorthodox management style is the cause for her to run the Radiation Oncology department unlike any other similar departments within or outside of the VA system. Dr Azawi believes in intimidation, demeaning, lying, and berating as part of her management style. She threatens and intimidates the other radiation oncologist and is constantly accusing him of undermining her. There was a 5 month period when they would not speak with each other despite their offices being next to one another.

Dr Azawi deals with employees in a fashion that supports her agenda. If she wants you "gone" she will accuse you of acts that never occurred.

Likewise, if her agenda can be better met by using an employee to harass another one, Dr Azawi does not hesitate to use those tactics either.

Dr Azawi has accused many physicians of not caring about the patients as much as she does. She will also lie to physicians at conferences by denying certain symptoms could possibly be caused by radiation treatments.

Evidence proves otherwise. When asked about the side effects of radiation Dr Azawi and Dr Williams state the side effects (toxicities) (i.e. skin burns- erythema, burning on urination, constipation, diarrhea, dry mouth etc) are to be expected. This is true for 3-D conformal or standard radiation therapy treatments. However, with IMRT (intensity modulated radiation therapy) a higher dose can be delivered to the tumor without over radiating adjacent or normal tissue also referred to as organs at risk (OAR's).

This is possible because the extra area marked around the tumor is smaller therefore limiting the adjacent organ's radiation. This is one of the criteria of documenting the medical necessity for using IMRT. If a larger area is marked around the tumor for the "tumorcidal dose" or total dose prescribed, the adjacent structures for prostate treatment, bladder, bowel, rectum and penile bulb will received a higher dose as with 3-D treatments. So a total dose of almost 8,000 cGy is delivered in part to the bladder, bowel, rectum and penile bulb instead of the usual 6,600-6,800 cGy. So essentially IMRT which is supposed to be tissue sparing (protecting normal tissue, organs) ends up with the same side effects, (toxicities as mentioned above) as 3-D conformal treatments. IMRT will decrease side effects or their severity when the area around the tumor is properly outlined.

Therefore if some one inquires as to expected side effects, it can be said they are expected in IMRT but it must be clarified as to the severity and appearance at a dose level that must be detailed. That is the whole purpose of IMRT....to be able to deliver a very high dose to a tumor without unnecessary or very limited injury to the adjacent structures.

The patient chart is the history of a patient's care. If procedures and patient's condition are not recorded and not included in the patient's chart, it can affect a multitude of medical decisions and actions. There are also documentation requirements to support insurance and Medicare billing.

Additional documentation is necessitated by accreditation standards held by the hospital (Joint Commission) and specialty accreditations held by the department specialty of Radiation Oncology (ACR – American College of Radiology & ACRO – American College of Radiation Oncology).

ACR is the most demanding of the accreditations and was mandated through a Directive issued by the VA Central Office (VACO) due to bad publicity in a New York Times series of articles published in January 2009 which highlighted problems in the VA Radiation Oncology departments as well as other facilities.

Surrounding this time several VA Radiation Oncology departments were closed down completely or not allowed to treat any patients until the system was corrected. East Orange, NJ, Jackson, Ms and Philadelphia, PA were the ones immediately affected. Due to the awful details revealed and their negative impact on the VA, immediately following the Walter Reed Hospital debacle which was paraded in front of a congressional hearing, the VA was not too anxious to have any more negative publicity. However, instances of improperly cleaned scopes being used for colonoscopies and other improper procedures came to the forefront and the VA was ordered to contact patients involved with the scopes to inform them to be tested for HIV and Hepatitis due to the improper sterilization in between patient use. Since that time there have been other scenarios with the potential for bad outcomes for patients.

It was in this atmosphere at VA Healthcare Systems that more details of improper procedures should not come to light in order to save or protect the reputation of the VA. Congress mandated a review of all Radiation Oncology departments in the VA to have the OIG check each facility, physics QA documentation and radiation oncologist training credentials for delivering IMRT treatments to patients. Although neither of our radiation oncologists, Dr Azawi and Dr Williams, had been trained in IMRT, they had treated many patients with that method. Hence, unnecessary side effects and radiation injuries resulted. I will talk more about this later.

Radiation treatments for cancer must be accurate and reproducible every day. If the treatment is not delivered accurately but rather haphazardly due to the inattention of the staff delivering the treatment, the outcomes will not meet the standard of care. Similarly, if a patient undergoes a radical prostate removal for cancer and a small portion of the prostate is left behind, how comforting would that be?

But the physicians said they used the latest in technology, a new surgical robot, that can cut and rotate unlike the human wrist therefore allowing careful slices to enable nerve sparing, so that the patient will maintain the ability to have an erection. The only problem with that scenario is the surgeon is still controlling the robot, even though not truly trained but simply given an orientation to the procedure over a weekend. In one moment the quality of life, as the patient knew it, was gone. The nerve that controls erections was cut, although the surgeons used the latest technology. The doctors maintain that the latest surgical procedures and technology were used. A year later the patient's PSA has risen because of the small portion of the cancerous prostate left behind and now the patient has a recurrence of his cancer and must be treated with radiation and possibly hormones that will give him "hot flashes" just like women have.

Accuracy does matter. Training does matter. Willingness to do what is right matters. Technology does not replace training and skill. Ask the nurse in the operating room who knows what actually happened in the OR but also knows what the patient was actually told. Just ask the patient above how he now feels about his quality of life. No drug can help that patient because of the critical nerve that was severed. As long as there is no lawsuit then this incident is acceptable to hospital administration. Nothing is done about it. I ask you, what if you, a family member or even a friend had just been diagnosed with prostate cancer (or any cancer) at the hospital above? Would you want to accept treatment at that hospital or encourage your family member or your friend to be treated at a facility under those circumstances? I would not. Our department has some of the best treatment equipment. In fact many hospitals do not have the state-of-the-art equipment we have but our Radiation Oncologists are not trained in IMRT/IGRT yet patients are treated daily with this form of treatment.

This surgical example has been used for simplicity purposes. Radiation Oncology is complex yet basic. It is a specialty most people are not really familiar with including many hospital personnel. A common remark is, "I thought it was the same as x-ray." It is not.

The purpose of radiation is to deliver a high enough dose to kill particular types of cancer. Not all cancers respond to radiation.

Melanoma is resistant to radiation as well as nerve and muscle. Lymphomas, testicular and benign pituitary are treated to a lower dose since they are not resistant to radiation. Most other cancers fall somewhere in between. If a "tumorcidal" dose is delivered accurately on a daily basis, the tumor cannot keep multiplying and cells will die. This is good. However, if a high dose is delivered to the tumor with a larger than needed area around it, the healthy tissue will be unnecessarily injured. The Radiation Oncologist (physician) prescribes a dose and placement of the dose. Radiation Therapists (techs) deliver the radiation with a linear accelerator on a daily basis. If the patient were given the whole dose in one day, it would probably kill the patient depending on the treatment site. However, given a small amount each day the dose becomes therapeutic.

Radiation Oncologists are trained in the medical aspect of cancer treatment. Radiation Therapists are trained in the technical aspect of initial treatment position (simulation) and daily treatment delivery. Accuracy of replication of setup is paramount since measurements are in millimeters. Our specialty is based on accuracy, attention to detail, honesty, judgment and lots of double checking.

It also involves monitoring the treatment at the computer console when radiation is delivered as well as watching the patient on closed circuit TV while the patient is in the treatment room.

Any number of dangers can occur during this time. The IMRT movement of leaves can stick causing the dose to be delivered in one concentrated spot instead of spread across the organ being treated. The patient may become sick while the mask is secured and the patient's hands are pulled in a retractor. At any point, one of the radiation therapists may need to run into the treatment room to "free" the patient to prevent further harm or stop the beam if the IMRT malfunctions. Radiation Oncologists practice the art of medicine. Radiation Therapists deliver the accuracy of science and technology. Radiation Oncologists and Radiation Therapists do completely different jobs. They cannot be interchanged.

J.B. Simms

Honesty is mentioned because if an error has been committed by a therapist such as not including a treatment device or a field of treatment is not delivered, the therapist must notify the physicist and Radiation Oncologist.

Often an error in dose can be corrected if it is admitted by the therapist. It is the honor system. Honesty cannot be compromised.

When I was hired, I was told the Radiation Oncology department was real messed up and needed to be improved. There were 2 pages of technical policies and procedures consisting of a paragraph per policy or procedure. That is not acceptable even in a department that does not do IMRT. There was no system of checks and double checks. Nothing of substance, no accountability.

So begins the problems........

My job as Chief Therapist is to ensure accurate treatments are being delivered according to the physicians' orders. I developed a structure and system of guidelines, policies and procedures to ensure accurate treatment occurs. Of course the guideline, policies and procedures have to be in agreement with the Chief of the service, Dr Azawi and with staff physician, Dr Williams. I had requested weekly meetings for input, feedback to make sure we were all on the same page. There was resistance from both doctors, which I did not understand and had never run into in any other radiation department.

It became evident to me that there was a division between the front (Drs, nurse and receptionist) and the back (physicist, dosimetrist, and therapists). There was no communication between front and back. This lack of communication made proper patient care and setting up new treatments for patients very difficult. The back was never informed when a physician would not be in the office or if the physician would be in the office for a part of the day.

This created other problems in patient planning and treatments. As supervisor, I was never kept in the loop.

If Dr Azawi was not in and you asked the nurse if Dr Azawi was coming in, her reply would be "I don't think so." "Will she be in tomorrow?" "I don't know." Then somehow you find out that Dr Azawi will be gone for 3 days. One day I was in Dr Azawi's office as she was putting in a leave request. I asked if she would be in next week and her reply was "Yes." She was not there all week. Why the secrecy and lies? Departments cannot operate that way.

However, I was expected to ensure smooth operation under the circumstances.

Then the lying began. Dr Azawi accused me of refusing to do a simulation and sent an email to get me fired for it. Fortunately, a Radiation Oncology resident assigned to our department was with me when Dr Azawi gave us instructions regarding the patient. (see email dated 4-18-08)

Dr Azawi refused to insist on proper documentation or procedures because, "We were too small. We are not MD Anderson or Sloan Kettering." This phrase was repeated endlessly when attempting to discuss normal documentation requirements with her. All I could do was accept Dr.

Azawi's refusal to discuss the issue.

Her harassment escalated. She continued to accuse a contract therapist of not doing something right. The contract therapist apologized, but Dr Azawi kept yelling at her until she broke down in tears and repeating that she was sorry. This therapist was not the type to break down easily. Dr Azawi demeaned the contract physicist in front of others, but even then he did not react. At this point Dr. Azawi was attacking everyone in the back. Because of this incident I asked for a meeting to discuss problems (including supporting documentation) with Dr Szabo, who was Chief of our Medicine group DMM which included Pathology, Labs, Radiology, Nuclear Medicine and Radiation Oncology. He also was Chief of Staff of the hospital. Holding both positions was considered by many as a conflict of interest. Dr. Szabo was upset about what I told him and he promised to look at the documentation and talk with Dr Azawi. Nothing changed after my meeting with Dr. Szabo. Instead, more incidents occurred, and I asked for another meeting to update him. Once again Dr Szabo was disturbed about the facts I presented then he asked if others from the department would come see him.

J.B. Simms

Everyone was afraid to say anything because they know what Dr Azawi does to them if they do. After much conversation the dosimetrist, contract physicist, staff radiation therapist and the contract therapist agreed to go speak with Dr Szabo if he would protect them.

When they returned to the department, Dr Azawi asked the staff radiation therapist to come to her office and Dr. Azawi intimidated him. He came out of her office shaking and in tears.

Dr. Azawi had sent an email to the dosimetrist asking him where he was. Dr. Azawi said nothing to the others. However, the next day Dr Azawi had the contract physicist removed.

I notified Dr. Szabo and reminded him that he said he would not allow anything to happen to the people who spoke up. He did nothing about Dr. Azawi removing the contract physicist. The others were totally intimidated then and refused to say any more.

Temperamental physicians are not uncommon but Dr Azawi does not fall into that category. Her actions are purposeful and follow her "Because I can" philosophy. My employees cannot work in a stressful, hostile environment especially when we are treating cancer patients. After speaking to Dr Szabo a few more times and him saying it would take a while to get the situation corrected I contacted the Director's office to let her know I was thinking about contacting the OIG. Dr Azawi was removed as Chief of the Service pending an Administrative Investigation. As a result, Dr. Williams was made acting Chief of Radiation Oncology. It was during this time the Directive was issued by the VA for every Radiation Oncology department to go through the accreditation survey for the American College of Radiology (ACR). Dr Williams and I went through all of the standards to set up any policies, procedures, meetings and documentation required.

The department began operating as a normal radiation oncology department for the first time. Patient monitors were being tracked, more policies were written and procedures were put in place and followed. The site survey by the ACR was successful and when a few of the listed items were corrected, we were accredited. Being accredited meant everything had to be done correctly and in a collaborative manner.

Since we had the patient software one of the accreditation surveyors said we needed to go paperless. Dr Williams was going in that direction. However, Dr Williams was not sure if Dr Azawi would return as Chief after the investigation so he knew there would be hell to pay if he did something she would not like.

After 8 months of not being Chief, Human Resources had no choice but to reinstate Dr Azawi because Dr Szabo did not provide them with documentation concerning her "removal" as Chief of Radiation Oncology. He said he did not have any documentation.

What happened to the 2-3 inch tall stack of documents? What about his own documentation? Dr Szabo thought the problem would go away so he did nothing. This inaction is also common behavior for him.

So now Dr Azawi was back as Chief of Radiation Oncology and picked up where she left off. In the mean time she filed an EEO claim against Dr Szabo for discrimination based on country of origin. Dr Azawi is from Iraq. Because Dr Szabo did nothing to fight Dr Azawi's accusation and once again presented no documentation, Dr Azawi won the claim in court against Dr Szabo. Everyone concerned was furious and in disbelief especially since Dr Azawi perjured herself in court.

EEO wanted to appeal but the Director, Isabel Duff refused. Now things were truly in a mess. Dr Szabo could not say much to Dr Azawi or she would take him to court for retaliation or harassment. This presented a problem since Dr Szabo is her direct supervisor in the DMM medicine group previously described and the Chief of Staff of the hospital. Dr Azawi now had a free ticket to do whatever she wanted without consequence. All she had to do is yell "retaliation" or "harassment" and her improper incidents were and still not corrected - just ignored.

When Dr Azawi returned as Chief she began reversing everything required by the ACR accreditation. Required meetings were stopped, documentation was stopped, procedures were stopped. She was following her management philosophy "Because I can".

At that time the department had a new contract therapist and two staff radiation therapists. Morale was low because of Dr Azawi's return to power and the therapists are not paying attention to detail or accuracy.

I tried to reeducate the therapists. I worked one on one with the therapists in the simulator. A month was spent with each therapist, but to no avail.

There were so many problems with the treatment of patients because the new contract therapist was a "good time Charlie" who thought it was more important to have fun than pay attention to work. He kept the other therapists distracted from work.

At that point I went to Dr Azawi and explained the situation with the therapists, my reactions and attempts to reeducate them. I have worked with and ask for her input. Dr. Azawi asked if the therapists could review each other to try to improve themselves. I responded that the results of the review would be biased due to the therapists' lack of integrity. Dr Azawi then recommended re-education. I explained I had already worked with them one on one.

At that point I explained the team concept which was used at other VA radiation oncology departments.

In the team concept there are 2 radiation therapists in the treatment room setting up and aligning the patient for treatment. If one therapist forgets to check or move the patient correctly the other is the second set of eyes to ensure all parameters are correct prior to leaving the room to deliver the radiation treatment. If one therapist does something wrong or forgets a parameter the other therapist is there to correct it. Both are accountable for a mistake in treatment. In our department in the past, if 2 therapists were in the room setting up the patient, if one did not do something correctly the other would just watch and do nothing. When I would say something about the error they would blame each other or refuse to admit to the error. This behavior had to stop so Dr Azawi agreed to the Team Agreement.

After receiving her consent I met with the therapists to introduce the Team Agreement and have them sign it. Then I showed the therapists the Variance Report that would be signed.

The entire procedure was discussed and cleared by Human Resources prior to my discussion with Dr Azawi and later with the therapists.

With the agreement of the therapists and initiation from DMM, the yearly evaluations would be objectively scored in relation to the number of mistakes made as recorded and signed by each therapist. Each staff therapist understood the scoring on the evaluation and participated in the creation of it. As long as the Variance Reports were not punitive or considered a written counseling of any type this scoring was acceptable.

During June and July two of the staff therapists would be gone at different times for vacation.

The day after the agreement was signed by all, each staff therapist came to me separately and said they did not want to work with the other because they did not want to be held accountable for mistakes made by the other therapist. I explained the Team Agreement to each of them again restating the necessity for the therapists to speak up during treatment to correct any problems. Not doing so would make them accountable. Within 2 weeks the first problem occurred. Then the Varian Incident happened. (see emails and Report of Contact)

Remember the part about honesty and the importance of it? Honesty is required to report an FDA alert not only for injury to a patient but when a medical device (especially one that emits radiation) malfunctions.

According to the therapists, the treatment table moved on its own causing treatment to be delivered to the wrong spot. If that was true it would be an FDA alert dealing with a malfunction of equipment. This would be determined by the vendor after extensive investigation. If you go to the website on FDA alerts dealing with medical equipment you will find reports of malfunctioning devices including treatment planning computers and linear accelerators. It was never about injury to a patient. When I told Dr Azawi it was determined the therapists had lied we were both disappointed. Since there were serious problems with sloppy patient setups by the therapists and inaccuracy on their parts, I recommended removal of the 2 therapists. One was a contract therapist and the other was still in the one year probation time frame. I told Dr. Azawi I would also get a recommendation from another Chief Therapist at another VA about how they might handle this situation. Dr. Azawi agreed.

When I gave Dr. Azawi the other Chief Therapist's recommendation, she told me to proceed in finding replacements and let her know how long it would take. Azawi asked me to have the Business Manager contact the Agency who supplied the contract therapist to ask about the time it would take to send another therapist. I was told by Dr Azawi to contact Human Resources to get paperwork for removal of the staff therapist on probation, which I did. But then things took a bad turn when the nurse involved herself in the situation by discussing it with Dr Azawi.

Later that day Dr Azawi had the receptionist and the nurse in her office and told them I recommended the therapists be removed but failed to mention she had instructed me to move forward with the decision.

Apparently Dr Azawi changed her mind but did not inform me. The nurse and receptionist immediately went and told the therapists what Dr Azawi had told them. You can imagine what happened then. There was a mutiny instigated by the nurse and encouragement from the receptionist. It did not matter if the nurse and receptionist did not know all the facts.

That is how Dr Azawi runs the department. It was hostile before this situation, but even more so after this.

During this time I was given my mid-year evaluation by Dr Azawi.

During my evaluation nothing was written or said about the serious items that supposedly happened prior to the date of the evaluation and only later appeared as the basis for my reprimand at the hand of Dr Azawi. At no time was I ever asked anything about the supposed incidents or was anything ever said to me about the accusations. The two therapists in question were now doing whatever they wanted and if I said anything to them they would complain to the doctors. The doctors would then tell me basically stop working with the therapists.

Then Dr Azawi told me to be with the therapists at all times. I followed Azawi's orders and then the therapists would complain so Dr Azawi would reverse herself and tell me to again stop contact with the therapists.

J.B. Simms

This behavior of reversing herself was constantly happening. The atmosphere was more bizarre and hostile than ever

I showed Drs Azawi and Williams on the images the inaccurate treatment being delivered by the therapists but the doctors did not react. The only thing said was if the therapists were supposed to treat a lung and treated a leg instead THAT would be a problem. Unbelievably, to this day, the doctors still do not understand what the problem was and is according to the images. In any other facility, with any other radiation oncologists, the problem with the quality of work and the inaccuracy of treatment by the therapists would not have been allowed to continue.

And I would not have been harassed and retaliated against for bringing the problems to the attention of the doctors. Drs Azawi and Williams say I do not understand IMRT. However, they are the ones that do not understand how radiation injuries can occur to healthy tissue if the patient is moved (shifted) too much in one direction. I have given them multiple papers on the subject but they refuse to read them.

Your letter to me states "in the absence of your disclosures, management would have taken the same action to reprimand you, lower your performance appraisal and more closely monitor your supervision." I most strongly disagree.

The only way I can understand the statement is to assume I did not make myself clear in presenting the facts. How can I protect myself against false accusations?

Because of all the lies made by others I contacted a polygrapher to see about taking a polygraph test because I knew it would come down to "he said-she said." I was told by Human Resources that I could not present that evidence, so how do I prove or disprove any of this?

To insure proper treatment of our patients my job is to ensure accreditation standards are followed, that all documentation required is present and to insure the therapists deliver accurate treatment according to the standard of care. Trying to fulfill the requirements of my job description is where the problem occurs.

J.B. Simms

Not knowing who else to ask I will ask you this: If I know something is not correct and it is my responsibility to correct according to my job description, do I correct it? Do I continue to attempt to discuss it with Dr Azawi? What are my obligations to report serious matters when Dr Azawi refuses to discuss matters with me? Am I protected if I do nothing as long as I have reported the matter to my superior? What about the patient? Do treatments continue as prescribed by the Drs although it is obvious what will happen to the patient? What if it were you or a family member? What would you say then?

Let me give you an example: It is required chart documentation to have a tissue pathology report for a primary cancer before a patient can be treated. Departments require that this documentation is in the chart prior to simulation (setting up the patient for CT and treatment planning prior to treatment.

If the patient is diagnosed with metastatic disease (cancer which has spread from the primary cancer to the bones or brain) then a radiology report must be placed in the chart to show there are tumors in the brain or bone. A brain biopsy is usually not done for metastatic disease. On occasion there might be a bone biopsy, but that would just be for special cases. This tissue pathology report is a record to show the patient actually has the primary disease that is being treated. A couple of months ago I was checking chart documentation before performing a simulation on a patient who had metastatic disease to the spine. There was no supporting documentation for treatment in the chart. I called the nurse as I have done on other occasions to get a radiology report.

She said I did not need one. I reminded her that we always need the report. She sent the resident physician down to the CT to tell me the primary pathology was in the chart so why did I need the radiology report.

The nurse then told Dr Azawi I was requesting the radiology report for the metastatic spine. Dr Azawi called me and told me I do not need it. That is not true. I was told that if I needed the report to get it myself.

Recently I was going to simulate a patient with metastatic brain tumors. I called the nurse again to request a copy of the imaging report. The nurse told me that Dr Azawi told her to just give me the pathology report.

This is not correct chart documentation. This has not been an issue of obstruction until the last few months.

Although the 2 current contract therapists were not hired to simulate patients (which is a specialty in itself) Dr Azawi decided they must do simulations. I told her they were not hired to simulate patients. Dr. Azawi and Dr Williams were both at the contract discussions before hiring the two therapists and no one brought up the need to have the contract therapists simulate patients. It never has been an issue. Contract therapists are hired to fill in on the treatment machines. Very seldom are they even asked to simulate on a contract position. If necessary a staff therapist will go to the simulator and the contract therapist on the treatment machine because of the important and tricky nature of simulation. The most a contract therapist would be asked to do would be to assist in a simulation. I explained all of that to Dr Azawi and Dr Williams. Dr Azawi decided there should be a skills list for the contract therapists.

I told her there was, but it consisted of the type of equipment they were able to use. Nothing is stated about procedures the therapists are able to perform. Dr Azawi told me to create a skills list for procedures on the contract therapists including simulation.

The contract therapists completed the skills list for simulation. Neither of them had performed a simulation in over 9 years alone and very seldom assisted with one. Contract therapists do not perform simulations.

Unfortunately, the contract states they are contracted to do any number of tasks that do not even pertain to their specialty. So Dr Azawi is using that contract statement to force the therapists to perform simulations.

One of our therapists is off for 2 months with shoulder surgery so we are short handed now. I informed the contract therapists about rotating through the simulator as was now required by Dr. Azawi.

Since neither therapist had operated the CT simulator before, it was necessary to show them the procedure. I proceeded to show the therapists how to set up treatment parameters for different simulations we performed, the use of immobilization devices, how to set isocenter, etc.

That task is very time consuming since it is totally different than treating patients.

Documentation is different as well. One of the contract therapists had a few days off to go home so I was going to fill in doing simulations until the following week when I would train the other contract therapist. In the mean time the staff therapist who constantly complains to Dr Azawi about me was working with one of the contract therapists. Without prior notice or discussion with me, Dr Azawi decided to send the staff therapist to Radiology to observe in CT. When I asked Dr. Azawi why she was doing that, she told me it was to help her with CT and simulations.

That is absurd. First of all, this particular therapist is not even credentialed in x-ray. The only reason she can do CT's in our department is because it is a simulation – not a diagnostic CT that operates differently and whose procedures are not comparative. Dr. Azawi's decision left my department shorthanded with only me and a contract therapist for 2 days.

During those two days we sometimes would be treating on 2 different machines at the same time. This is unsafe for the patient and not normal procedure.

Other times I would have to go treat on a completely different machine for skin cancer in another area. I asked to have the therapist return to the department at 3:30 since the contract therapist was leaving at that time. There were still patients to treat. Dr Williams had strict instructions not to let her return that day. That therapist stayed in Radiology "observing" CT for 2 weeks. Friday we were given instructions that one of the contract therapists would go to CT to "observe" for 2 weeks. The staff therapist would be in the CT simulator whether she was needed on the treatment machine or not. Two weeks after that the other contract therapist is supposed to go to CT to "observe".

Since Dr Azawi has not been in the department since she ordered the therapist to observe in the CT, I asked the acting Administrative Officer why my therapists were wasting their time observing in CT. Her response was that Dr .Azawi had asked me to train the contract therapists in the simulation and I didn't do it so this was the result.

I wonder who I was training in the simulator the last 3 weeks prior to this? It was a contract therapist.

So now I get punished like a child? And based on an outright lie? These bizarre decisions by Dr. Azawi are not in the best interest of the safety of our patients. In addition, this is harassment, unsafe patient care and increasing the hostile environment. But it does not matter "Because I Can."

The department just got in trouble by the head of the VHA Department of Radiation Oncology for not having enough therapists in the department. According to ACR there should be a minimum of 3 therapists per linear accelerator. We have 2 linear accelerators. The hospital was instructed to hire 4 more therapists. They have not and are making no attempt to do so. Dr Azawi said the only people that were getting hired was a physician to help the doctors with their case loads. According to the same ACR guidelines there are already too many radiation oncologists.

Recommendations to hire more therapists are not being followed and yet Dr Azawi wants to hire another physician when there is no data to support such a decision.

Dr Azawi and Dr Williams block everything I mention that is required by accreditation and hospital standards then harass and intimidate me for bringing it up to them. Then I am asked by the doctors why I did not do the thing I asked and was refused. I constantly get accused of things I never said because Dr. Azawi twists my comments into something else. One minute I am responsible the next minute

I'm not but responsible for something else. Sometimes it feels like the game "Wack a Mole". Go do this. Why are you doing that? Do this? Why are you doing that? Don't contradict a Dr's order. Why didn't you override what Dr Williams approved? Not my authority. Why didn't you override what I approved? Not my responsibility.

Why did you make that patient come back so many times for the same procedure? I cannot override your decision. It was a research patient...Dr's decision. Why did you say.......? I never said that. Why didn't you do ……? You said not to. What was a certain staff therapist doing a month ago? Why wasn't he helping the other therapist? I don't remember. I would have to look at my calendar of which you have access to. But that is not enough.

Dr Azawi calls me into the conference room or emails the same question 4 times and I respond 4times. She tells me to keep up with the reason so many patients are needing a 2nd simulation. I asked her one day why a patient was being resimulated and she screamed at the top of her voice "I don't have to tell you anything." Weeks later she asked why a patient was simulated the 2nd time. I respond by email but that response was apparently not good enough. She asks again. And again. I respond again. And again. I send her emails and she complains that I send too many. She tells me to email her something. I do but she doesn't read it. Instead I get called into the conference room to ask why I did not respond to her email. This goes on constantly. She calls me in on short notice. Drs Azawi and Williams are on one side. I am on the other. He is taking notes while she yells at me. I have no chance to write notes.

Dr Azawi yells at me and tells me I am supposed to know everything my therapists are doing. I see them working on something not assigned by me so I ask them. It is something that Dr Azawi gave them to do but of course she did not tell me. They are working on the same thing independently. They got upset because I asked them and they feel put in the middle. She will also ask 3 different people to write up the same policy. We find out about it later in the day that our time is wasted. Once again - "Because I can."

This is how she has run off past Chief Therapists who normally last only about 2 years. There have been several. Dr Azawi does not want anyone to have any authority but her. She does not understand the chain of command. She does not understand how a Chief Therapist helps the department run smoothly. Why does she want to lower herself from Department Chief to do my job? She is not trained in my job.

If I am just a treating therapist, I am no different than my subordinates unless she chooses to use something against me.

At that point she will say that I am their supervisor, I should take care of it.

The continual accusations are difficult to deal with.

For example: I sent an email to the nurse to "try not to schedule any simulations on Friday morning" since I have a weekly supervisor meeting with Dr Szabo (including the Chief Tech from Radiology, Manager of the Lab, Business Manager of DMM and the Administrative Officer of Radiology.)

What happened next? Dr Azawi and the nurse come to the control area and Dr Azawi accused me of telling the nurse not to schedule simulations on Friday morning. Those are completely different statements but this is typical of Dr Azawi's accusations. They are twisted from what is said. She continued to yell at me and demean and berate me in front of my employees while the nurse stood by her side smiling. Of course Dr Azawi's actions send multiple messages to those in the immediate area. She has no respect for me and will not hesitate to harass me in front of others.

Everyone in the "back" knows they had better not say anything to anyone or they will be treated like me. Very seldom is anyone given an opportunity to speak in response to Dr Azawi's accusations.

She is not willing to listen because that would diminish the affect of her intimidation and harassment. When she is accusing me of ridiculous or twisted statements I have to ask for permission to respond. When I ask if I may respond, her answers range from "NO" to "Briefly" or simply a head nod. I don't know why I even bother to respond because she does not care about the truth of a situation. These tactics are meant solely to harass and berate me, many times occurring in the presence of my subordinates which serves only to further erode and diminish my authority. I am often humiliated and demeaned in the presence of others.

Another example is the time I got called in again to the conference room and asked why I had harassed a therapist for filing an EEO complaint. That accusation was way out in left field. I tried to explain to the doctors about the conversation they referred to which was between the therapist and myself.

The therapist had asked during her yearly evaluation how we could work together better. This is the same therapist who complains to Drs Azawi and Williams any time I say anything to her regarding any aspect of her work performance. She is also the one that moved the table, lied about it and caused the Varian Incident. When the therapist asked how we could work together, I told her open communication would help along with several other possibilities like coaching/mentoring her. I then asked her why she did not come to me about her complaints, which included a complaint she had about her grade increase being held up. That was news to me since I had given the paperwork for the increase to Dr Azawi for her to sign weeks before the evaluation. I was not the one holding up the paperwork.

(I was not in agreement with the proposed grade increase, but Dr Azawi had ordered me to fill out the SF-52 and told me what to write about how wonderful the therapist was.

I removed my name from the form and replaced it with Dr Azawi's name in the place for signature since I was not recommending the increase. The form was sent to Dr Azawi for her to sign and submit which she did not do until the therapist filed the EEO.) See emails.

Yet another example: Last summer a staff therapist who had injured his left shoulder at work had surgery and was on light duty.

Shortly after returning on light duty the therapist said he had re-injured his right shoulder from an injury in 2006.

He was taking too many pain pills and was not in good shape. I spoke with the Drs concerning the matter. They were not anxious to do anything about it. If I take an action they are not in support of, I get in serious trouble with them and end up harassed, berated etc. At this point the therapist decided he could not even operate a mouse because of the pressure he would have to exert to press the button. It was an outrageous situation so I contacted the Employee Relations rep as well as the Worker's Comp person to get guidance. Because the therapist was suddenly refusing to do tasks not included in the limitations issued by his physician it became a conduct issue. Furthermore, if the condition of his right shoulder was that bad he had options. I discussed with the therapist these options given to me by Human Resources: Look in to medical retirement,

Fitness for Duty, face insubordination for refusing to perform within his physician's documented limitations or perform his job as agreed. It was his choice to make. I then called him in to my office to tell me exactly what he felt he could do in the department considering the different limitations for each of his shoulders. An extensive list was recorded as stated by the therapist. It was truly amazing. He even stated he felt unsafe to do his job at times because he had to take so many pain killers, but he was trying to wean himself from them. At that point I offered him help through the Employee Assistance Program (EAP) or more extensive help in rehab. He refused saying he would do it himself. I retyped his statements, emailed the document to Drs Azawi and Williams then discussed it with them. A few days later I was called in to the conference room again and accused of telling the therapist to retire.

Then the therapist decided to request accommodation for ADHD. I contacted EEO and documents were sent to me for him to fill out, sign and submit which he never did. How can multiple emails to the Radiation Oncologists, meetings with the Employee Rep and the Worker's Comp person get twisted into me telling the therapist to retire? I'll answer that for you. Because of Dr Azawi and her "Because I Can" attitude. Since Drs Azawi and Williams kept the therapist upset by saying I told him to medically retire.

I went back to the Employee Rep who recommended sending a Fitness for Duty letter (339 letter) to the therapist's physician regarding the actual condition of the therapist's shoulders and ability to work. This was discussed with Drs Azawi and Williams. Dr Azawi agreed to this, but would not put her name on the letter. I had to sign it. That was no problem since I was his supervisor.

Dr Azawi did not want her name associated with any of it so she could use that against me as well.

Mr Fong, I could write endless examples of the problems in the department but what I would request of you is to talk to a few people that are willing to speak up but only if they are contacted. If you do not contact them, the investigation is incomplete. The entire story needs to be told. There is a serious problem and you are the last hope in the system.

J.B. Simms

I would be more than happy to point out key people that deal with Drs Azawi and Williams on a regular basis and on many different levels. Please allow these people a chance to speak.

In case you did not know, when the OIG came for the Congressional Mandated Review of Radiation Oncology departments of the VA regarding physics, IMRT training and treatment, one of the investigators asked me a question after Drs Azawi and Williams tried to blame a documentation problem on me. Another issue came up where I was blamed again.

Fortunately I could show them documentation supporting my statements. The subject came to patient care and after much cajoling, I gave them names of patients that had problems from the radiation. They assured me it would be kept confidential.

My identity would not be revealed. A few weeks after the OIG visit I was put on FMLA for a total of 3 months by my Dr. for work related PTSD. While I was off work the OIG returned to the department to investigate the patients I mentioned.

I was told everyone was questioned and of course evade answering truthfully out of fear. Drs Azawi and Williams were told that someone scheduled in the afternoon was the one that reported the problems to the OIG. That would have been me or a contract therapist.

They told me I would be put on the list as a decoy listed as a phone call instead of in person. They had already spoken to me prior to their arrival so they had no intention of calling me that day anyway. The physician that reviewed the charts was not a Radiation Oncologist. I knew that would be a problem. As they say, it takes one to know one. The physician did not obviously understand radiation oncology – just the management of patient side effects. However, he did get them in trouble for not having lots of required documentation in the chart such as end of treatment summaries. I would imagine that very few of the charts have a summary among other things.

Because of what the OIG found, the head of the VHA Radiation Oncology Program came for a visit. I was dumbfounded by the letter he wrote until I personally spoke with him the day after it arrived and was presented at the Quality Management meeting my first day back after 3 months.

He said he wrote what the Drs had told him but he also insisted the Drs receive training in IMRT and other things involving treatment.

He then told me after his visit he met with the hospital Director, Isabel Duff, privately for 45 minutes and suggested the radiation oncology department be closed down. He did not have the direct authority to do that but that was his conclusion after all he had seen and heard. After that he did have an exit meeting with the rest of the people on the QM Committee to let them know many changes had to be made.

He did not, however, tell them he recommended closure of the department as he did privately with Ms Duff. After he left, Ms Duff had a meeting with Dr Szabo and Dr Moran who is the head of the American College of Surgeons accreditation program. If the department was closed, that would be the end of the American College of Surgeons program so Dr Moran was definitely against it. I'm not sure of the details of the other two.

A few days after I returned to work after 3 months on FMLA, Dr Williams made a rude remark to me in the hallway about me being the one that called the OIG on them. I tried not to get involved in the conversation but he was very adamant saying it was someone in the afternoon that turned them in. I told him I did not speak to anyone from the OIG in the afternoon. He said they knew who called. I finished the conversation and returned to what I was doing.

At the next QM meeting, of which Dr Azawi never wanted me to be on since I was the evil tattle tale in her estimation as well, Dr Williams was sitting next to me and said that I was the reason they had to do all of the things required by the OIG. I was the one that had caused the trouble. He said this loud enough for the Lab Manager sitting on the other side of me could hear.

They have made it quite clear I should have kept my mouth shut from the beginning starting with the initial report to them regarding the sloppy and dangerous ways of the therapists. They make me pay regularly and harass me. I do work in a hostile work environment but I am pretty sure that you did not receive any of that information during the investigation.

J.B. Simms

The OIG report also states that the hospital administration had no idea there were problems in the radiation oncology department. That is a blatant lie and I have documentation to prove it.

I spoke with Dr Szabo at our weekly meetings and the problems with patient care and harassment, hostility etc were always discussed. He wrote notes about it.... supposedly. He would write something down in a bound book or on an Outlook calendar page. This can also be confirmed by people if you would contact them. Ms Duff knew as well because Human Resources notified her I would be telling her about the treatment issues etc during my Formal Grievance Hearing. Although she was not the hearing officer many documents were presented she had to have seen since she was the deciding official and signed the Formal Grievance response.

This is the first time I have ever worked for any government agency. My work experience is in the "outside world". I have been employed at the Long Beach VA for 3 ½ years and have been told by others at other VA Radiation Oncology departments their hospital is not like mine. I hear this from others that have transferred to the Long Beach VA as well. There is a system wide problem here. Not a VISN problem but a specific facility problem.

I do wish they would close down the department if administration will not tell Drs Azawi and Williams to straighten up and act like professionals, treat the patients with care and stop the nonsense.

I know that would mean I would not have a job but you cannot imagine how horrible it is to work there and see the lack of caring that goes on.

It's just a game to the "Front". It would be wonderful if Drs Azawi and Williams would follow the standard of care and operation then say "Because I can" do what is right.

I will be sending you some copies of emails but since I was not feeling well for the last several days and the Dr has put me off work until Thursday I will have to go to the department after hours to print some emails I do not have available at home. I will get some to you tomorrow but I will have to scan one page at a time so I doubt if it will be many of them.

J.B. Simms

Hopefully tomorrow evening I will be able to get all of them to you.

Thank you for your time and patience. This is a very frustrating and sad situation that needs to be fixed for the patients' sake.

Respectfully

Signed electronically Lana Miller

I will also be enclosing some graphics for you to see what is being discussed.

Bruce Fong, a worker at the Office of Special Counsel, replied:

From: Fong, Bruce
Sent: Wednesday, June 08, 2011
4:46 PM To: 'Lana Miller Boyer'
Cc: Wells, Vivian
Subject: RE: OSC File No. MA-

10-0159 Dear Ms. Miller

Boyer,

"I have read both your letter and your doctor's letter. I am appalled by the behavior of Dr. Azawi that you have described. I think, based upon your vivid accounts, that your description of her as "abusive" understates the matter. Nothwithstanding that, there is little that my field office can do for you.

We were tasked to look into your reprimand, evaluation, and interference with your duties. I do see that very recently you have had contact with the OIG and as a result, you have received hostile remarks concerning whether or not you are the suspected whistleblower.

But all of that does not help us in the 2009 timeframe that your OSC complaint concerned.

When I wrote in my letter of May 4 that actions in your complaint would have occurred in the absence of your disclosures about your subordinates' dangerous practices to your superiors, I did not mean to imply that Dr.

J.B. Simms

Azawi's mistreatment of you was excusable. I'm sorry to have given you that false impression. Rather, I meant to say that in the absence of your complaining about your employees, Dr. Azawi likely would be the same abusive manager that she apparently is based on your detailed descriptions of her behaviour. I understand that you are in a classic hostile environment. Without doubt, your grievances deserve an adequate investigation. I don't think, however, that OSC is the proper entity to do it. We have limited jurisdiction in your complaint. We must prove that regardless of the elements of hostile work environment, that you and others have experienced, the challenged personnel actions were taken because of a protected whistleblowing disclosure.

But, as my letter states, we've concluded aas [sic] a amatter [sic] of law that your discussions with your supervisors about your subordiantes' practices, which they clearly concern patint [sic] health and safety, are not protected by our statute because of a line of court decisions that have excluded from protection disclosures made in the regular course of one's duties. As a supervisor, your discussions about your staff's practices did occur in the normal course of your duties. Now I don't personally agree with the logic of those cases, but that is the current state of the law ansd [sic] we have to obey legal precedent.

I, however, do see clearly the hostile environment and the employee abuse and general danger to patient health and safety that you have described. I don't want to close your file and just leave you hanging.

So, today, O written to inquire of my colleague in our Washington, DC office if trhe [sic] is a way OSC could get the DVA's attention at a high level and try to spur either the current OIG investigation or another investigation and fix the working conditions you face in the radiation oncology department. I know that the OIG is currently looing [sic at the matter and maybe that office is ultimately the proper entity to look at your situation.

OSC does not have the authority or the expertise to investigate the massive disfunction [sic in your division.

I know this email is not the response you were hoping for, but unfortunately it is the only one I can give you.
With warm regards, Bruce Fong
Field Office Chief

J.B. Simms

This letter from Mr. Fong was sent to Lana 20 months after Lana filed her Whistleblower complaint in October 2009. Twenty months? Lana had to experience the abuse of Azawi and others for twenty months while the OSC, in their wisdom, "investigated" Lana's complaint.

In the second sentence, Fong said he was "appalled by the behavior" of Azawi, and that Lana's account "understates the matter." In his next sentence, Fong stated there was "little" he could do. Well, what was the definition of the "little" he could do? Was Fong willing to tell Lana the best way to stop the abuse and save "patient care?"

Fong went on to state that even if Lana had not made the complaint, Azawi would still be the abusive manager described in Lana's report, and that "you are in a classic hostile environment" and your "grievances deserve an adequate investigation." Fong is confirming Lana's complaint, but where is the "investigation" which the OSC was supposed to perform?

What was Fong saying? was he saying the OSC could do something but won't, and that the OSC is not the proper entity?

Lana had filed more than just a Whistleblower Complaint. She also filed a Prohibited Personnel Practices complaint (PPP) in which all the understated abusive behavior of Azawi would be addressed. Fong is in the Whistleblower section. Vivian Wells, was supposed to be handling the PPP claim.

Fong dismissed the Whistleblower claim because, "in the course of" her employment, Lana gave the information about the therapist conduct to her supervisors. There was more than just the behavior of the therapist; there was the cover up.

Fong later admitted that he clearly saw the hostile environment and the subsequent danger to patient health and safety.

He was going make an inquiry to an associate in Washington to see if there was a way to get the attention of the high- level persons at the DVA.

Fong also stated, *"I know the OIG is currently looking into the matter..."* and since this email was dated June 8, 2011, Fong must have had been in touch with someone at the OIG, but who?

Lana had no idea that the disclosure of the errors made by the therapists was part of her duties as their supervisor. That was the reason Fong turned down the Whistleblower complaint. The same question came up on Page 6 of the 11- page form filed by Lana.

On the last page of the Whistleblower complaint, Lana dispelled the theory that Fong used to reject the Whistleblower complaint; she alleged that Azawi and Williams "protected the radiation therapists in question regarding my statement about the therapists being dangerous."

Fong dismissed the complaint and ignored the fact that the therapists were being protected. This was also ignored by the OIG.

J.B. Simms

Chapter Fifteen:

HR Bill 2104 June 11, 2011

Lana had been through hell. After the Varian incident in 2009, and Lana's abuse at the hands of the doctors and administrators in the Long Beach VA Hospital, Lana thought no one was listening. Lana had gotten someone's attention, but she was never to get the credit for being the person who exposed the inadequate treatment at the Long Beach VA Hospital. The Office of Inspector General dropped the ball and covered up the culpability of the doctors and administrators at the Long Beach VA Hospital, noting inadequate care in nine of ten test patients. Evidently there was some quiet maneuvering in Congress, behind the scenes, to make doctors and administrators accountable, but the matter of inadequate care and abuse of patients at the Long Beach VA Hospital was never directly mentioned.

After Azawi was demoted, used personal leverage to regain her position, then covered for the immoral therapists during and after the Varian Incident, someone in Washington, DC must have been watching.

Below is an abbreviated version of H.R. Bill 2104, which was "...to make the provision of technical services for medical imaging examinations and radiation therapy treatments safer, more accurate, and less costly."

The entire Bill can be found in the Index.

To amend the Public Health Service Act and title XVIII of the Social Security Act to make the provision of technical services for medical imaging examinations and radiation therapy treatments safer, more accurate, and less costly. Be it enacted by the Senate and House of Representatives of the United States of America in Congress assembled,

1 SECTION 1. SHORT TITLE.

This Act may be cited as the "Consistency, Accuracy, Responsibility, and Excellence in Medical Imaging and Radiation Therapy Act of 2011".

SEC. 2. PURPOSE.

The purpose of this Act is to improve the quality and value of health care by increasing the safety and accuracy of medical imaging examinations and radiation therapy procedures, thereby reducing duplication of services and decreasing costs.

"SEC. 355. QUALITY OF MEDICAL IMAGING AND RADIATION

THERAPY.

"(a) QUALIFIED PERSONNEL.—

"(1) IN GENERAL.—Effective January 1, 2014, personnel who perform or plan the technical component of either medical imaging examinations or radiation therapy procedures for medical purposes shall be qualified under this section to perform or plan such services.

"(2) QUALIFICATIONS.—Individuals qualified to perform or plan the technical component of medical imaging examinations or radiation therapy procedures shall

"(A) possess current certification in the medical imaging or radiation therapy modality or service they plan or perform from a certification organization designated by the Secretary

pursuant to subsection (c); or "(B) possess current State licensure or certification, where—

"(i) such services and modalities are within the scope of practice as defined by the State for such profession; and "(ii) the requirements for licensure, certification, or registration meet or exceed the standards established by the Secretary pursuant to this section.

Lana had been through hell trying to get the attention of the OIG, OSC, EEO, and her VA Hospital. No one would validate her claims. Does it not seem odd that the HR Bill copied above was enacted? What prompted this?

Someone was listening, but no one was brave enough to become an ally of Lana's and fight the good fight. Someone would take the credit, but we knew the identity of the real hero.

J.B. Simms

J.B. Simms

Chapter Sixteen:

Statement of Lynne Roy

Statement of Lynne Roy
Director of Medical Imaging, Cedars Sinai Hospital, Los Angeles, California
Chair, Scope of Practice Task Force for the Society of Nuclear Medicine Technologist Section
House Committee on Energy and Commerce
Subcommittee on Health
Hearing on "Examining the Appropriateness of Standards for Medical Imaging Technologists"
Friday, June 8, 2012 at 10:00 a.m.
2322 Rayburn House Office Building

Chairman Pitts, Ranking Member Pallone, my name is Lynne Roy, and I serve as the Director of Medical Imaging at Cedars Sinai Hospital in Los Angeles, California. I am submitting this testimony in my capacity as the Chair of the Scope of Practice Task Force for the Society of Nuclear Medicine Technologist Section, and I am a certified Nuclear Medicine technologist. Thank you for allowing me the opportunity to submit comments for the record regarding "the Appropriateness of Standards for Medical Imaging Technologists, " and to give my enthusiastic support for H.R.2104, the "Consistency, Accuracy, Responsibility, and Excellence in Medical Imaging and Radiation Therapy Act of 2011," known simply as the "CARE Act."

The Medical Imaging Department at Cedars Sinai where I work treats and diagnoses over 330,000 patients per year. Physicians refer their patients to our department to determine a myriad of diagnoses, from what is causing a persistent cough to identifying heart disease and cancer. Advances in imaging have been very exciting in recent years, including the enhanced ability to determine if a particular chemotherapy agent is working after just one day. This can save a patient months of needless suffering, not to mention savings to the healthcare system.

The patients who come to our department rely on our 180 imaging technologists to take the right picture at the right time so our imaging physicians can deliver vital diagnostic information or treatment. All of our X-Ray and Nuclear Medicine technologists are licensed by the state. All ultrasound and MRI technologists, unless in training, are certified by the American Registry of Radiologic Technologists (ARRT) or the American Registry of Diagnostic Medical Sonographers (ARDMS). Therefore, patients who come to Cedars Sinai Medical Center for their imaging procedures will be treated by technologists that have met the minimal educational and credentialing requirements for medical imaging set by the state of California.

However, that is not the case in all areas of the country. For the past decade, the Society of Nuclear Medicine Technologist Section (SNMTS) and the Alliance for Quality Care and Radiation Safety have worked hard to raise awareness of the need for quality education and standards for the technologists performing diagnostic imaging tests.

In the case of nuclear medicine, 20 states do not regulate the nuclear medicine technologists that are delivering radiation to patients. Additionally, there are 11 states that do not regulate X-Ray technologists and no state regulates MRI or ultrasound technologists. That means imaging providers in hospitals and freestanding centers are able to hire someone off the street to deliver radiation to patients. The CARE Act, which currently has 122 cosponsors in the House, would require all those who perform medical imaging and radiation therapy procedures to meet minimum education and credentialing standards in order to receive Medicare reimbursement.

We believe that the CARE Act is vital to ensure the best treatment possible. Most Americans know very little about the technical aspects of medical imaging and radiation therapy treatment and assume the individuals performing these tests are qualified and competent. However, this is not always the case as inadequately trained personnel perform medical imaging and therapeutic procedures in many areas of the United States every day.

Under current law, minimum education and credentialing standards are voluntary in some states, allowing individuals to perform imaging procedures without any formal education. Poor quality images can lead to misdiagnosis and/or additional testing often times with additional radiation, delays in treatment, and increased cost.

The CARE bill will regulate all imaging technologists and radiation therapists. Since I began my career in nuclear medicine, and have spent the last 20 years directing the imaging department of a very large medical center, I would like to explain the responsibilities of imaging technologists and why it is so important that individuals performing these tests have received the education that is needed to be competent and to provide the patient a safe environment.

X-Ray and CT use X-Rays to produce anatomical pictures. This records a snap shot in time of what the body part looked like. However, just as in photography, if the settings, in this case dose, are not correct, any abnormalities in the organ may be hidden because it is too bright or too light. If the technologist does not interview the patient, or review the history, the incorrect angle or "pose" may be chosen, which could also obscure an abnormality. The resulting image could be non-diagnostic, a false negative, or a false positive. The patient may have to return for additional imaging which is costly, delays treatment and delivers the patient an additional radiation dose.

Nuclear medicine uses radioactive materials, known as "radiopharmaceuticals" that can image how an organ works. Rather than a snap shot in time, nuclear medicine uses "time lapsed photography" to trace what happens to an organ over time, or to see how it responds to a certain stimulus. Nuclear Medicine studies provide physicians with molecular level—not only anatomical or structural level—data that can help personalize treatment.

Nuclear medicine and molecular imaging technologists are responsible for performing a wide variety of highly specialized procedures. Because nuclear medicine looks at bodily functions, it is critically important for the technologist to understand how the radioactive medicine works and how a patient's own medications or diet could interfere with the study. For example, many medications and food contain caffeine. Caffeine interferes with the way heart vessels expand and contract. If some nuclear heart scans were to be performed on a patient who unknowingly did not discontinue caffeine, the picture could appear normal, even though the patient has coronary artery disease.

Like CT and X-Ray, MRI records a snap shot in time. Rather than using X-Rays to produce the image, magnetic radiation, combined with radiofrequency, can create a very detailed display of what an organ looks like. Based on the history of the patient, the technologist must select the correct settings, called sequences, to image. If the technologist does not fully understand anatomy, they can fail to capture the correct area or cut off part of the organ, making an accurate diagnosis impossible. In addition, if the technologist fails to conduct a thorough safety interview with the patient or does not provide adequate security against metal objects entering the magnet, the patient can be seriously harmed.

Ultrasound technologists use ultrasound waves to create images. Some of these images can be like a video that records the movement of blood through the veins and arteries. Other images record pictures of abnormalities in an organ. Unlike X-Ray that captures the entire organ in one picture, the ultrasound technologist scans the entire organ until an abnormality (or not) is found. The technologist selects the images to be recorded. If they did not program the scanner correctly, they won't see the differences between normal and abnormal tissue. If they do not have an excellent understanding of anatomy and pathology they will not be able to identify abnormalities and record them for the imaging physician to interpret.

As you can see, these are not simple tasks that can be performed by unqualified individuals. When performed properly, an imaging study can provide unique information that allows doctors to better diagnose, guide management of, and treat diseases. If a scan is performed incorrectly, a poor-quality image may be produced. This can result in the misdiagnosis of disease, delays in treatment, and needless anxiety for the patient. If additional testing is required, patients are exposed to an increased amount of radiation. While imaging can be an invaluable tool, the procedures do carry a potential health risk, and radiation can be harmful if administered improperly. Without proper safety precautions and careful patient screening a patient can be harmed in a MRI scanner.

It is clear that mandatory, stringent education and certification standards must be enacted for technologists performing imaging scans to ensure excellent patient care, safety, and effectiveness.

In 2006, there were roughly 395 million imaging procedures performed in hospitals and medical settings across the United States [1]. This is because imaging is a valuable tool that allows physicians to obtain unique insights into a patient's body that allow for a more personalized approach to the evaluation and management of all diseases. With early detection, heart disease, cancer, and other diseases can be successfully diagnosed, treated, and even cured. Yet despite the important implications these procedures can have for patients' health, in many states technologists are not required to have certification or a license to perform these tests.

Certification and ongoing registration in radiation imaging is managed by the American Registry of Radiologic Technologists (ARRT). In addition to the ARRT, Nuclear Medicine Technologists can also be certified by the Nuclear Medicine Technology Certification Board (NMTCB). MRI Technologist certification is through the ARRT. Ultrasound certification is managed by the American Registry of Diagnostic Medical Sonography (ARDMS) or the ARRT.
All of these certifying agencies require technologists to have successfully completed an educational program that is accredited by an acceptable mechanism.

Beauticians, cosmetologists, and insurance agents are a few examples of professions that are regulated in every state. However, medical imaging technologists and radiation therapists are not. To improve the quality of medical imaging, the CARE Act must be passed. If enacted, this bill would require those who perform medical imaging and radiation therapy procedures to meet minimum education and credentialing standards in order to receive Medicare reimbursement. As a result, institutions that provide medical imaging or radiation therapy to Medicare patients would need to employ personnel who meet or exceed these standards. Currently across the country, individuals with possibly little or no training are performing sophisticated medical imaging procedures that, if performed improperly, could harm patients and cost the health care system millions of dollars. It is time to take a stand and fight for the safety of these patients. It is time for Congress finally to pass the CARE Act.

J.B. Simms

Chapter Seventeen:

Lana's Parting "Dear All" Shot

Lana was still hurt and angry that Dr. Hagan all but named her in his report of the VA Hospital in December 2010. Lana emailed Wendy Kemp to find out why Dr. Hagan had written those things about Lana "not knowing IMRT" (we need to find the specific language) in his letter that was distributed at QA.

Later in the evening of June 8, Lana sent a long email to Szabo, Duff, and McCartan. The email began, "Dear All".

From: Lana Miller Boyer

Sent: Wednesday, June 08, 2011
7:53 PM
To: Duff, Isabel M (SES); Szabo, Sandor Cc:McCartan, Mary Beth; susan.demasters@va.gov Subject: Important

Importance: High

Dear All –

By now you have received and hopefully read the letter from my Dr.; however, I believe it is important for you to receive additional information. If I sound angry at times, well, I am. I hope none of you ever have to experience what I do each and every day with the resulting PTSD due to some of the below. This is really a tiny glimpse. It goes on and on.

After all my meetings with you in which I brought to your attention the many problems involving the quality of patient care being delivered to our patients and her unorthodox management methods, I do not know or understand why basically nothing has been done to stop the vile actions of Dr Azawi and others she encourages to follow her example. I have to believe that a simple directive such as, "You will not do that again", or,

"You will operate this department professionally using other VA's as an example" would have been reasonable Instead, apparently as a result of my efforts to bring such matters to your attention, as I believe my job

description requires, I have been subjected to harassment and having to work in a hostile work place.

J.B. Simms

Even, after many attempts to get you to halt her harassment of me and the hostilities directed at me etc have been ineffective which is sad. We all know you do not want Dr Azawi to remain as Chief or would like to get rid of her. Since the EEO case was lost, perhaps, are you afraid of her lawyer and a retaliation case. I believe you must be, otherwise how else am I able to understand the lack of an effective response to the problems I brought to your attention.

I believe Dr. Azawi feels emboldened by her EEO case and is counting on your concern as to her possible legal actions in the future. You can get rid of me but that will not stop her erratic behavior and actions and you are aware of this as well. That will empower her more and you will have your hands even more full. Furthermore, what is going on in the department currently goes against all norms in Radiation Oncology. We were supposed to obtain adequate therapists to cover both machines.

Instead Dr Azawi says the only people that will be hired is a physician (I also heard Nurse Practitioner) to help them because she believes that her case load is too high. The data indicates that is not so. (see attached ACR staffing recommendations). Surely you are aware that another physician would over staff the department even more with radiation oncologists and the radiation therapy department would still be short of the number of therapists the ACR recommendations state and Dr Hagan said we should have.

Dr Azawi is being encouraged (or not discouraged) to continue in her ways just as she did before we had any outside visits. This is just wrong. In an attempt to help and follow what Dr Hagan recommended, you have created and added to the difficulty of the departments by putting a person in a temporary position who is issuing edicts without any rudimentary understanding of how anything works in a therapy department. She is making technical staffing decisions, and playing out her personal agenda to gain favor and exhibit power that I believe goes beyond her authorization, understanding and knowledge. As a result, the department is more disorganized than ever and continues to deteriorate because of decisions made.

What about the team building that was supposed to take place? I know Mary Beth has sent emails to me and Dr Azawi, but it goes no farther. There has been increased division between the front and back, making it nearly impossible to improve the way the department operates. Irrational decision making appears to be encouraged. Why would you place someone in the department who knows nothing about radiation oncology and have her attempt to "restructure" it?

J.B. Simms

She has only added to the problems because of her ignorance of a radiation oncology operation. Sending her to Washington D.C. did not give her any understanding.

One day she decided she would shadow me to see what I did all day. We were in my office while I did some QA, checked on a sick patient that was supposed to come for treatment and followed up on images taken. After less than 2 hours she determined that all I did was check on what others did and left. Yes, that is part of my job. She thought it was a waste of time. After the time she spent she determined she knew exactly what my job was. Right. If procedures are not monitored, actions can get out of control but that did not enter her mind.

Because she does not know what the requirements are for radiation oncology, she ends up encouraging improper procedures just because they are different. We have enough bad in the department now.

Dr Azawi absolutely does not even know how a radiation department is supposed to run. Sounds astonishing but it is true. She does not even understand how the work flows. This is mind boggling to me. Maybe it is her management philosophy of "Because I Can" that she so firmly practices. With that philosophy nothing has to make sense. Dr Williams is too afraid of Dr Azawi to do what is right.

Donna's contribution is to stir up problems constantly by running to the Drs to report on matters she does not understand. Donna's goal is to put off her work on everyone else. Donna wants to do the minimum even when she is supposed to be working with patients. Donna is not a professional, has no bedside manner and is very rude to patients. She does not follow HIPAA laws and talks about patients in front of other patients.

Donna does not keep patient charts confidential, especially on weekly Dr visit days, but leaves them scattered around her office with patient names showing. Paper schedule books for simulations are lying open on the table as well as the charts where patients often sit.

But as long as the charts are locked up at night there is not a problem. Right?

She obstructs patient procedures either because of ignorance or perhaps because she would rather play one of her silly games. You should see her try to give an injection. I observed the time she kept telling the patient not to be nervous so many times as she prepared to stick him that he turned to her in frustration and said he thought she was the one that was nervous. And she is a Nurse III? How did that happen? Mima, when she was here, was more than happy to join in the immature behavior. Where was their professionalism?

J.B. Simms

Only Drs Azawi and Williams and Donna are informed as to when Dr Azawi will not be in. Neither I nor my therapists are aware. Even when we ask we are never told truthfully when she will return to work. This is unprofessional and delays patient care.

The Drs say they are interchangeable. Then, if this is true, why are the treatment plans not contoured and treatment plans completed so the patient can be treated?

Perhaps they are not as interchangeable as they like to say. The physicist and dosimetrist seldom know either when one of the Drs will be out. They are the ones working with the Drs on the treatment plans. The physicist and dosimetrist are constantly waiting on the Drs to do their jobs of contouring so plans can be presented for approval. But the Dr is frequently not in and we are not informed when the doctor will return.

What if you were the one with cancer waiting to be treated? Why do you think patients are always calling their Congressman to ask for their help in getting treated. You know this is just the tip of the iceberg.

Many times I have provided information to you regarding the multitude of problems in radiation oncology and still I do not see any change which leads me to believe that nothing, other than superficial attempts, have been done to address the problems much less than solve the problems. Dr Azawi and company are apparently free to operate in any manner and apparently without being accountable to anyone. Am I to assume that expecting anyone to be interested in addressing my concerns about problems in the department are merely an irritation? Because of the inattention to matters I bring to your attention I am led to presume that you prefer not to have to be concerned about whether or not the

department has professional oversight and run properly. The attitude in the department defies explanation and the atmosphere is more like you would expect in a Jr. High or a social club. No one is accountable or responsible for any task. The lack of professionalism and desire to do the best job possible is palpable. Or how about just doing their job. What a novel idea!

So you say I am not a "team player". I am not cooperative. Let's examine that. I am expected to keep my mouth shut when ordered not to follow documentation procedures. I am ordered to allow therapists to be sloppy in their work. If I believe the data supports that the Drs are causing harm to patients and report my findings to you or Drs Azawi and Williams, I am ridiculed, demeaned, berated, harassed for bringing the information to you.

J.B. Simms

You may be correct to say I am not a team player under those conditions. Who can blame me if I have not been a team player or cooperative under those circumstances? I should just turn a blind eye, pretend nothing is wrong and agree with the radiation oncologists. They are doctors.

How can a doctor not know what they are doing? Right? It does not matter what goes on in the department. Even if it involves patients. I can say I was "just following orders." Does that sound familiar? Perhaps from the 1940's? No responsibility. No accountability.

Why are Drs Azawi and Williams allowed to continue to treat Head and Neck patients with IMRT? Dr Azawi herself said in a QM meeting that she was not supposed to be treating them. If the doctors are so competent, why are they having to receive training in IMRT? Shouldn't they have already been trained in IMRT dose distribution and prescribing IMRT treatment? We are still having patients with unnecessary skin reactions due to improper dose using a bolus. This is impossible for anyone to deny when the burn is in the shape of the bolus. Yes, there will be skin reactions, but not to this extent especially when it is so obvious.

Even if the dose prescribed is correct, it is the way the Drs want the dose distribution that is causing the harm for one thing. Knowing what I know to be true I would not allow myself, a family member, or a friend to be treated under these circumstances.

I have tried to work within the system. I have discussed these issues ad nauseam with Dr Szabo, regularly if not weekly, both in person and email. He should have copious notes from those supervisor meetings. I have done the same with HR and they have discussed these issues with Ms Duff.

Furthermore, Ms Duff knew of the treatment and patient care issues along with the environment in the department since she had to read some of the documentation from the Formal Grievance and come to a decision be it a year late. EEO can only do things to a certain extent if administration does not encourage a responsible and accountable workforce. Out of frustration and continuous inaction on the administration's part and because I had continuing concerns about patient care and all involved issues, I contacted Dr Hagan's office, since he is also a form of supervisor to Dr Azawi as head of the VHA Radiation Oncology Program. At the DMM supervisor's meeting I endlessly discussed a multitude of issues including patient care, Drs Azawi's and Williams' unorthodox management styles, deficiencies in documentation and required ACR meetings in the department. Evidently accreditation standards seem to mean nothing to the facility when it involves radiation oncology and the ACR.

J.B. Simms

I know that when there is going to be a CAP survey in the lab everything comes to a halt to ensure everything is done properly and all documentation is complete. Why isn't the same level of concern extended to radiation oncology? I tried discussing issues with Quality Management and Patient Safety. To my knowledge none of my concerns were addressed for one reason or another.

In fact I was retaliated against by Dr Azawi because Donna informed Dr. Azawi that she had observed Lynette Fox and I talking outside.

We were discussing the problems in relation to the Varian Incident. That is why I had to contact Dr Hagan's office.

I wanted ACR to come do a surprise inspection in the hopes that if nobody wanted to listen to my concerns that they might be willing to address the same concerns if the concerns were brought to your attention by someone other than me That was what I was referring to when I sent an email to Susan D last summer asking for a meeting with her, Ms Duff and Dr Szabo. There appeared to be no evidence of any concern on your part or even a reply.

Remember the Varian Incident? The possible FDA alert? I was accused of going "outside". I stayed in the system. During the Varian Incident I asked for a recommendation (with Dr Azawi's permission and instruction) from another Chief Therapist about how they would handle a situation where therapists lie about their actions and end up losing patient treatment days.

The lie of one therapist and the cover up by the other caused Varian to send a national team to examine computer logs and involved their main programmers and software experts in California as well as Baden, Switzerland. These are the same therapists that refused to align patients properly. These are the same therapists that Dr Azawi told Mima and Donna I wanted removed (which the other VA Chief Therapist agreed was the proper response) Donna and Mima proceeded to tell the therapists they had been told by Dr. Azawi that I wanted them removed. This was a personnel matter that should have been held in strictest confidence between me, the supervisor, and my boss, Dr. Azawi. How well do you think that went over with those therapists? Dr Azawi neglected to tell Mima and Donna that she had instructed me to have Cindy contact the agency to find out how long it would take to replace the contract therapist and that I was to contact HR to find out procedures for removing the staff radiation therapist on probation. Dr Azawi also did not tell me that she had changed her mind about removing the therapists. Instead of continuing on with our mutual decision regarding removing the therapists, the result was that Dr Azawi then became their protector and I was the "evil" one.

J.B. Simms

Good Cop – Bad Cop. Playing Mom against Dad. However, you would like to put it and they took full advantage of it.

You will recall that the focus of the problem was redirected and everyone began concentrating on the dose received by the patient and the explanation was that the dose received by the patient was not critical? It was NEVER about the dose to the patient when the table moved.

The entire possible FDA alert was based on equipment malfunction – a treatment table moving on its own while radiation is being delivered. If anyone had checked (because I did state it), any time a medical device, especially one involving radiation, malfunctions, it is serious. An investigation must be done by the vendor to see if an FDA alert needs to be issued. That is why Varian had all the stops pulled for a complete and thorough investigation. All because a therapist lied and the other covered up the lie.

Before contacting Varian I asked both therapists several times to explain what happened. I even told them that if they did not remember to say they did not remember. Anything involving radiation treatment to a patient MUST be reported (confessed) to the Chief Therapist, Physicist and treating physician so a dose correction can be made. It can be corrected for the patient. It was never the dose. It was equipment malfunction. And yet I was accused of going "outside" on this issue. In spite of the lying and addressing the incident, the therapists were unbelievably exonerated and I, the messenger, was criticized.

The thing that most saddens me is the OIG report: Issue 2: Communication with Facility Leadership

We substantiated the allegation that senior leaders were not aware of RT patient outcomes. VHA expects that "peer review done for quality management fosters a responsive environment where issues are identified, acted upon proactively, and in ways that continually contribute to the best possible outcomes and strong organizational performance".14Facility staff confirmed that RT peer reviews had been performed. However, results had not been communicated to facility leadership nor was action taken to correct deficiencies identified in peer review. How could it be said Administration did not know what was going on in the department regarding patient care after the multitude of documentation, emails, Formal Grievance documents and meetings that were in your possession and was recorded in notes?

..."Radiation Therapy and Oncology Quality Management Committee" which would focus on clinical care monitors such as unplanned interruptions during treatment, unusual, severe, early, or late complications of treatment, and unexpected deaths during RT care.

Donna protects the Drs. Current items are not tracked correctly now in the charts and they are not as important as clinical monitors. There is no integrity in the process due to this issue.

Conclusions

...We also substantiated that facility leaders were not aware of patient outcomes in RT nor was action taken to correct deficiencies identified in peer reviews. This is very sad....

We did not substantiate the allegation that radiation oncologists lacked competence. The C&P folders and profiles of the radiation oncologists complied with VHA policy.

Is a nurse competent just because he/she holds a license/credentials. Is licensing/credentialing a basis for declaring competency. Can doctors who are not trained for IMRT truly be declared competent based on their licensing/credentialing alone? We all know if we need to see a physician we ask the people that work in that specialty because we KNOW just because a physician is licensed does not mean we want them to treat us. Our Drs are deemed competent because of C&P folders and VHA policy? They are not trained for IMRT yet they do it. How many physicians are allowed to perform surgeries/procedures they are not trained in? Do they have privileges to do them? Would you allow a general surgeon to do a heart bypass procedure? What if he went to a weekend training seminar to learn? I am sure that Dr would be the first one you would call to operate on your family member. Competent?

Director's Comments to Office of Inspector General's Report

Recommendation 3. We recommend that the VISN Director require that the Facility Director ensures that RT medical record documentation complies with VHA policy and ACR guidelines.

Concur Target Completion Date: August 18, 2011 Facility's Response:

The Radiation Therapy Quality Management Committee developed and implemented a Clinical Quality Plan detailing quality assurance and oversight activities for the Radiation Therapy Service. The action plan includes documentation improvement and monitoring. Specifically, it addresses the ongoing review of medical record documentation to ensure compliance with the VHA and ACR guidelines.

The Radiation Therapy Nurse audits the medical records daily to ensure progress notes, treatment summaries, radiation doses, and treatment modifications are completed within 7 days after the last radiation therapy treatment. Documentation discrepancies are addressed in the weekly chart round meetings.

J.B. Simms

The Radiation Therapy Chief reports medical record quality assurance aggregate data to the Radiation Therapy Quality Management Committee on a monthly basis and will continue to do so until 95% documentation compliance is sustained for a period of 6 months. Given the radiation therapy nurse's close ties and alliance with the doctors, this is not possible since she will protect Drs Azawi and Williams. Also she does not know what is required documentation for technical and obviously does little about the standard documentation like summaries, consents, consults. Otherwise, why are so many documents not in charts – over years. She blocks me and runs to Dr Azawi to cause trouble when I need appropriate documentation for the chart for what I do.

They do not want me near charts or documentation because I will request the missing items. They do not like that. So why allow the fox to guard the henhouse? She does not audit the charts daily. She does not know what a treatment modification even is. How can it be audited?

Status: Open

Recommendation 4. We recommend that the VISN Director require that the Facility Director ensures that Radiation Therapy (RT) patient outcomes are monitored by the Quality Management program and others external to the RT department to oversee the implementation of corrective actions for all adverse patient outcomes.

Concur Target Completion Date: August 18, 2011 Facility's Response:

Patient outcomes related to the delivery of radiation therapy are collected using clinical monitors. The Radiation Therapy Quality Management

Committee provides a summary of all adverse clinical outcomes, which

include, but are not limited to, skin breakdown, hematuria/radiation cystitis, and unexpected treatment interruptions, to the Medical Executive Committee quarterly. The report includes an analysis and summary of clinical monitors, unexpected complications, and adverse outcome

This report, further assessment and recommendations are also reported to Executive Leadership & Quality Board (chaired by the Medical Center Director), where this information is further reviewed, and analyzed quarterly. To further ensure patient safety and quality of care, a corrective action plan is required within 10 days for all deficiencies identified.

The Radiation Therapy Administrative Officer (currently an Acting is in place) ensures timely completion of the corrective actions.

J.B. Simms

The Chief of Diagnostic & Molecular Medicine Healthcare Group reviews outcome data quarterly, and will implement Focused Professional Practice Evaluation when there is a concern regarding a practitioner's ability to provide safe, high quality patient care. Fox guarding the hen house. The nurse is not tracking items correctly in the charts and they are not as important as clinical monitors. There is no integrity in the process due to this issue. Donna protects the Drs. There is no integrity in the process due to this issue. Are they assigning toxicity grades or side effect scores? It cannot be properly tracked without a system for comparison. How do you compare erythema with moist desquamation then say there is an improvement? Not very scientific. Not trackable since there are no descriptions assigned to grades.

This is standard procedure in Radiation Oncology departments where Drs are not afraid of data. They look at it as an opportunity to improve processes. Drs Azawi and Williams take it as a personal attack.

I make the mistake of thinking that eventually administration will do what is right and fix the department. Not half-heartedly like is happening now. (I believe the term for that is Pathological Hope) That will not fix anything and has caused a multitude of additional problems because a few people have visions of personal aggrandizement without thought of the patient. I thought that was why we worked at the VA. What about our mission? Does the phrase "close enough for government work" truly apply at Long Beach VA? We are better than that – aren't we? A familiar statement often heard is "It's not the problem that will take you down – it's the cover up." You know the problems in the department.

Like I said above – you can get rid of me if you want but that will give you a problem you cannot or will not be able to handle in radiation oncology. Then the problem will become impossible to correct later as it continues to feed on itself for strength.

The P.O. for the new linear accelerator (Trilogy) and associated software we still do not use much was $3.2 million. Guess how many patients have been scheduled for treatments on that machine? If I remember correctly, a year ago there were approximately 8 patients over a period of 4-5 weeks. Now it is used if the schedule gets behind. Usually there is only one therapist available to treat on the machine. Sometimes there is one therapist on one linear accelerator and one on the Trilogy. We have to have a therapist to do simulations as well. Oh, I forgot...if the 2100iX is down the Trilogy is used. That is a very expensive purchase for the number of patients that have been treated on it. I believe physics has spent more time on it doing the monthly QA than we have using it for patient treatments.

Besides we do not have enough therapists as Dr Hagan said.

J.B. Simms

I guess that I made the mistake of thinking that eventually the administration would fully address the concerns had for the department(I believe the term for that is Pathological Hope) and not just half-heartedly as is happening now. This half-hearted approach will not fix anything. In fact, it has actually caused a multitude of additional problems because a few people have visions of personal aggrandizement without thought of the patient. I thought we worked at the VA to serve the patients with the best care we are able to provide and which the patients have a right to expect from us. What about our mission? Even though I detest this phrase, does the phrase "close enough for government work" truly apply at Long Beach VA? We are supposed to be better than that. A familiar statement often heard is

"It's not the problem that will take you down – it's the cover up." You know the problems in the department. They continue to go unaddressed and the status quo remains. I get the feeling that you would prefer to get rid of me than to redress the concerns I have for our department and our patients. Getting a new Chief of Radiation Therapy will not make the problems go away and could even prove to be even more of a problem down the road.

Problems that are not dealt with now could become impossible to correct later as the problems continue to feed on themselves and gain strength.

At this point my opinion is that, for the sake of the patients, if the problems are not going to be solved, the department should be closed down. I believe the public, VA, Congress, patients and employees would applaud you for doing the right thing. To be clear, the problem is not me – I am just a messenger. Killing one messenger does not stop the message from going out. Correcting the problems would be seen by the good professionals in our hospital, and other people, as something to respect and admire. Please do what is right. These patients may not be your relatives but they are someone's father, husband, brother, son, daughter, sister, mother, wife, loved one or friend.

Just because these problems do not touches[sic] personally should not matter.

Administrators are responsible for every treatment given, every patient seen, every incompetent action taken by doctors, nurses, kitchen workers, etc. It is too easy to get caught up in paperwork, numbers, meetings and general bureaucracy to the point that it is easy to forget about the most important asset we have: soldiers coming to be cared for after they have sacrificed for us. Without veterans there would be no need for any of us.

J.B. Simms

Let's treat our ASSETS (Veterans)with all the respect they deserve, like we value them. Let's not just deliver VA-good-enough care. Let's not walk the line of average in order to protect ourselves and feather our own nests at their expense

Shame on everyone! Lana Miller

Chapter Eighteen:

Lana Transferred, OSC in Denial

In a spiritual sense, this was no coincidence, and the powers-that-be knew Lana had a hand in this.

It was time for Szabo to cover himself.

From:Szabo, Sandor
Sent: Thursday, June 09, 2011 5:04 PM
To: 'Lana Miller Boyer'; Miller, Lana (Long Beach)
Cc:McCartan, Mary Beth; 'susan.demasters@va.gov'; Moisa, Herbert Subject: RE: Important

Ms. Miller,

This is to acknowledge receipt of your email dated June 8, 2011, sent at 7:53 p.m.
In your message, you raise numerous claims and appear to reach several conclusions, all of which constitute serious allegations. As I previously advised you, all of these claims and allegations will be investigated thoroughly. Many of these allegations were investigated by the Office of the Inspector General (OIG) in November 2010 and by Dr. Hagen, Office of Radiation Oncology, and VACO. Each allegation will be investigated in connection to your comments in the email of June 8, 2011.
As I indicated in my reply sent June 8, 2011, you are temporarily reassigned until further notice to the Office of Quality Management, supervised by Nancy Downey, NP. Should you have any questions regarding this temporary reassignment, you may contact Denise Sodaro, RN at extension 3193 who is Acting Chief, Quality Management through June 16, 2011.
Sandor Szabo, MD,
PhD, MPH Chief of taff
VA Long Beach Healthcare System

Great. Szabo was going to investigate; investigate who? Was Szabo going to investigate Azawi, the person he fears, and who named Szabo in a lawsuit?

What a joke, and what a bunch of cowards. These people should be ashamed of how they ignore the Veterans. All they were doing is covering themselves.

Lana replied to Szabo, stating that Dr. Schuder was not allowing Lana to work, and supplied documentation.

Szabo then changed Lana's assignment from Quality Assessment to Mental Health. Lana would be leaving the job and position which she had trained

Dr. Szabo, the Chief of Staff, assigned Lana to Quality Management, then 2 days later to Mental Health to work due to an impending AIB investigation to be held regarding the hostile work environment.

Lana had lost her job because Azawi and Szabo did not want the truth to come out, and neither did Duff or Mary Beth McCartan.

A bit of vindication was received, but it was short lived.

On June 10, Bruce Fong of the OSC sent Lana an email stating that he agreed that the behavior of the administration against Lana was bad, and that it was a hostile work environment. The email from Fong revealed that Fong's impression of the Whistleblower claim was without merit because "reporting of the actions of the therapists fell under Lana's job description." Lana reported the bad behavior, to her superiors, which she was supposed to do. Lana did not include the fact that her superiors, Szabo, Azawi, McCartan, and others, failed to pass the reports to the next level, thus making the issue a cover up.

Also, Fong knew nothing about the PPP (Prohibited Personnel Practices) claim, which was the claim of hostile work environment. Fong went looking for the file since a different person was (Virginia Wells) the person who was supposed to be working on this matter.

Following are the emails received by Lana from Fong:

J.B. Simms

From: Fong, Bruce
[mailto:BFong@osc.gov] Sent:
Friday, June 10, 2011 12:01 PM
To: Lana
Miller Boyer
Cc: Wells,
Vivian

Subject: RE: OSC File No. MA-10-0159

Dear. Ms. Miller Boyer,

This follows up on my email below. I have heard back from the Chief of our Disclosure Unit at OSC Headquarters regarding my inquiry.

Unfortunately, OSC does not have authority to request a separate investigation by DVA of abusive management practices at your hospital. Apparently, abuse of authority is not sufficient for us to refer your situation to Secretary Shinseki for an investigation. However, I did learn that you could fashion your allegations strictly as patient care issues, and in particular issues concerning danger to patient health and safety -- not as an employee abuse or hostile environment matter – and our Disclosure Unit might request an independent investigation on that basis.

To do this, you would need to go here: http://www.osc.gov/ and click on "Whistleblower Disclosures" and this will take you to a new web page.

Review the information on that page, but fill out the "Disclosure Form."

You can file it on line and you can reference your OSC complaint file No. MA-10-0159. We could then share our file with our Disclosure Unit.

Today, however, we are closing your investigative file. I am sorry that we were unable to address the serious hostile environment at your hospital.

With regards, Bruce Fong

Field Office Chief

Fong stated Lana could "fashion your allegations strictly as a patient care issue and not as an employee abuse of hostile work environment."

Employee abuse is a prohibited personnel practice, and the patient care matter seems to be a Whistleblower matter, along with the subsequent cover-up.

The letter then directed Lana go to the OSC website, and click on "Whistleblower Disclosure" and follow the directions.

> "Today, however, we are closing your investigative file. I am sorry that we were unable to address the serious hostile environment at your hospital."

Fong just admitted that a "serious hostile environment" existed at the hospital. Who was supposed to address the problem? If the OSC was not going to address the admitted "serious" hostile environment, precipitated by "prohibited personnel practices", then who was going to take command of the matter? Who cared that the Veterans were being abused on a daily basis?

From: Lana Miller Boyer
Sent: Friday, June 10, 2011
12:09 PM To: Fong, Bruce
Cc: Wells, Vivian
Subject: RE: OSC File No. MA-10-0159

I will wait for you to read what I just sent. Please do not close until you finish the documentation I just sent.

Much Thanks Lana Miller

J.B. Simms

Following is another email from Bruce Fong

From: Fong, Bruce [mailto:BFong@osc.gov] Sent: Friday, June 10, 2011 3:50 PM

To: Lana Miller Boyer

Subject: RE: OSC File No. MA-10-0159 Dear Ms. Miller Boyer,

I have digested reasonably your emails from today. Let me try to address them quickly.

I see that you raised your allegations of substantial and specific danger to public safety in your original OSC complaint. I don't think we missed it when it came in, but we might have. It's right there in the last paragraph of your narrative and reference appear prominently in the accompanying chronology. I think the problem is bureaucratic and is on our end. We don't have a smooth mechanism for one side of our agency to talk to the other. It can happen, but not always. We receive over 3000 invidual [sic] complaints in a fiscal year and each one has to be looked at an accessed. Our complaints examiners are always working from behind.

If you visit our web site, you'll notice that there is a menu of possible complaint avenues. You chose to file a prohibited personnel practice complaint. That was correct and anyone in our office who read your materials would have understood that you meant to file a PPP complaint. Your complaint in simple terms challenged the way DVA officials had treated you as an employee (hostile work environment, abuse of authority, etc...). As I pointed out in my earlier email today, OSC has another complaint avenue: Whistleblower Disclosures. That is where your allegations of danger to the patients belong. But because those allegations were contained in your PPP complaint, they never made it to the other side of our house. When I called my counterpart about your situation that probably was the first time anyone in our Disclosure Unit might have been contacted about potential patient issues at your hospital.

Having said that, I can see by your other emails today that both the OIG and Dr. Hagen from VA HQ have been to your facility to investigate your division. OIG is normally the investigative entity that will investigate whistleblower disclosures that we refer to the Secretary. So it could very well be that had we referred your initial complaint to the Secretary, the results would not have changed. I don't know this for a fact. And based on your responses to management in the emails, it is apparent that you have issues with the adequacy of OIG's work. (I inferred that you were not satisfied that the audit accomplished what you had hoped for.)

I sincerely hope that your personal situation improves for your own health and that the situation for all VA patients at your hospital improve. I doubt that anything I have said will be of any consolation.

With regards, Bruce Fong

Regarding the above email, parts of the email deserve a few comments.

"I see that you raised your allegation of substantial and specific danger to public safety in your original OSC complaint. I don't think we missed it when it came in, but we might have."

What did that mean? Did they misread or ignore something? Fong continued:

> *"I think the problem is bureaucratic and is on our end. We don't have a smooth mechanism for one side of our agency to talk to the other."*

What type of inadequacy if Fong admitting?

"Your complaint in simple terms challenged the way DVA officials had treated you as an employee (hostile work environment, abuse of authority, etc...). As I pointed out in my earlier email today, OSC has another complaint avenue: Whistleblower Disclosures. That is where your allegations of danger to the patients belong. But because those allegations were contained in your PPP Complaint, they never made it to the other side of our house. When I called my counterpart about your situation, that probably was the first time anyone in our Disclosure Unit might have been contacted about potential patient issues at your hospital.

...[O]IG is normally the investigative entity that will investigate whistleblower disclosures that we refer to the Secretary [Shinseki]."

The OIG investigates Whistleblower matters from the OSC? Why wouldn't the OSC send these reports directly to the OIG?

"...[S]o it could very well be that had we referred your initial complaint to the Secretary (Shinseki), the results would not have changed."

Since Lana did not trust the OIG because they whitewashed their report, Lana was stuck with the OIG who she did not trust.

A bureaucratic error was the reason for investigating the abuse of authority and other PPP claims. The bureaucratic error on the part of an agency of the United States. Lana was asked to re-file and Fong would give them all the info she had sent.

These people were scared to do their jobs, and have no conscience.

On June 13, Lana sent an email to Mary Toy, the OIG investigator working on Lana's case, asking why the hostile environment was not investigated.

Later in the day, Lana sent a message to Bruce Fong about Lana's being transferred to the Mental Health area of the hospital.

June 24 was Lana's day to have it out with Human Resources. Lana had been exiled to the Mental Health Department, away from her training, to keep her quietLana received a response form Herb Moisa, asking Lana to submit forms to him within 30 days. Lana then received an email from Mary Beth McCartan, the head of HR. Ms. McCartan wrote that "Leave Without Pay," was discretionary, and the fact that Lana was going to be out for a while, again, raised a question of if Lana was going to be paid.

There was nothing discretionary about Dr. Schuder mandating that Lana take leave because the environment, which Lana endured as she was protecting Veterans, caused Dr. Schuder to make the decision that Lana needed some time away.

On July 14, 2011, Lana emailed Wendy Kemp to find out why Dr. Hagan wrote things about Lana not knowing much about IMRT, which was the letter distributed to Quality Assessment.

Wendy's reply was less hospitable than before, and a bit dismissive.

It was time to have someone write the story, and go over all their heads. Lana knew that anything she would do would seem like a suicide mission, but she was not stopping.

Oddly enough, at the time Lana was sending her "Dear All" letter, Lynne Roy published the following article. It was of no real comfort to Lana, after all she had experienced, but again Lana was validated.

Chapter Nineteen:

Exposing Corrupt Government Agencies

I met Dr. Schuder on August 3, 2010; Dr. Schuder at a breakfast meeting when I gave a talk about my book, "Don't Get Arrested in South Carolina" and she learned I had been a private investigator. A few years later, in the spring of 2012, she mentioned to me that she knew about a doctor who was doing some unethical things at a hospital, and to employees, and she asked what might be done to expose this abuse. I told her that I could write the story. Soon after her inquiry, Dr. Schuder asked that I meet her in her office to meet one of her patients. There I met Lana Miller Boyer.

Lana told both Dr. Schuder and me that she wanted this story told. I told Lana that I would be glad to write the story, probably in book form, and hopefully the story would help save some Veterans. I was not going to be attending any of the sessions which Dr. Schuder scheduled for Lana (I believe Lana was seeing Dr. Schuder twice a week at this time), but I would be meeting with Lana from time to time and exchanging information via email.

Lana told me she was being treated for PTSD because of workplace abuse and harassment. I then learned that Lana had been subjected to abuse and harassment because of corruption at the Long Beach VA Hospital; the reason for the corruption, above abuse of authority and financial improprieties, was to hide the fact that patients were being abused, injured, and neglected at the Radiation Department. Lana told me she had several 3-ringed binders of notes and emails which proved her allegation. The problem was that the administration moved her from her job as Chief Radiation Therapist to a job in the Mental Health area, depriving Lana of using her skills, and keeping her hidden so the secrets of abuse and improper care in the Radiation Oncology Department would remain secret.

J.B. Simms

I met with Lana again on June 7, 2012 at a restaurant, a few days after meeting in the office of Dr. Schuder. Lana's husband came with her.

She went into more detail as she began telling me the story of the doctors in the Radiation Oncology Department misrepresenting information to federal investigators, a former head of the hospital facilitating the hiring of a same sex partner into a position in which that person was not qualified, patients being "fried" during radiation treatment, and the cover-up of everything.

I began working on the material Lana had given me; Lana brought me 3 binders and other bound records. The emails began in 2008 and ended in 2012. The emails were between her and doctors, administrators, and peers within the VA hospital system. Lana was very meticulous in her recordkeeping. I was shocked and amazed at the amount of paperwork she delivered to me.

I checked some resources to determine that the Chief Oncologist, Dr. Azawi was said to have graduated from a medical school in Iraq. It was necessary for her to obtain training the in United States if she were to practice medicine in the United States.

I asked Lana who would have information which we could pursue, a person who would be able to talk with no fear of repercussion. Lana gave me the name of a person who used to be a finance officer at the Long Beach VA Hospital, and was aware of misappropriation of funds. This person was Charles Feistman. Feistman was forced out in order for the hospital staff to be able to protect Norby.

During an email exchange with Mr. Feistman, he stated:

"...[I]n addition there are the issues of spending excessive amounts of funds for the Child Care center on the VA grounds, thus diverting funds from patient care activities. Raul Martinez (chief Materiel management) has lots of information / data on this. And in fact, is putting something together (a packet of information) to send the chair of the senate veterans committee. You may want to try and talk to him, he could be a lot of assistance in getting copies of documents, etc."

Mr. Feistman also suggested sending FOI requests to several agency heads. I knew from my experience that the FOI would probably be ignored, but I went to work on them.

On August 11, 2012 I was attending a breakfast meeting in Newport Beach, California, when a retired US Army colonel friend asked me what I was doing. I told him I was working on book research about abuse at the VA hospital in Long Beach. The retired colonel told me he was a classmate of General Shinseki, head of the Department of Veteran Affairs. How lucky could I get? The colonel contacted his classmate Shinseki, and I received an acknowledgment email from the chief of staff, telling me they would be contacting either Lana or me.

We were rattling some cages, but no direct results were received. We just wanted them to know that, at any time, it all was going to come out, and Lana would be praised for her sacrifice.

Lana and I had many meetings. I told her we would send out Freedom of Information requests, which I was sure the governmental agencies, while mandated to comply, would never give us information which would show complicity in the cover-up. The main reason for sending an FOI Request is to put someone on notice that it is known that they are complicit in an improper or illegal act, but the agency will never give up information which will implicate the agency.

I had a lot of information from Lana, and she stated there were people at the VA hospital who might talk with me. Lana was going to arrange a meeting.

After hearing the allegations from employees of the Long Beach VA Hospital, I sent a Freedom of Information Requests to the Inspector General of the VA on S. I knew these requests are usually ignored, but this was a role of the dice that it would get someone's attention after Lana had sacrificed her health and her job to expose the corruption at this VA hospital.

Holding people accountable, or getting their attention, is better served by using a "shotgun approach," so more letters had to be sent to different regulatory agencies and other persons and/or entities who failed in their responsibilities to protect the Veterans.

J.B. Simms

If you think the Office of Inspector General of the Veterans Administration has any credibility, think again. You will read the FOI request I sent to the OIG, and the date was September 20, 2012.

They responded quickly (the day after the request, September 21, 2012) with an acknowledgement letter, but I would have to wait until May 7, 2013 for the reply.

After receiving the reply from the original FOI, I sent specific FOI requests for information concerning investigations of the inspections of the Long Beach VA Hospital in 2010, and separate requests for information concerning Dr. Szabo and Ronald Norby. Charles Feistman had made a complaint to the OIG concerning the fiscal improprieties of Ronald Norby while Norby was the director of the Long Beach VA Hospital, and there should have been a record of that investigation.

Eight months after these FOI requests, I received a letter from the OIG, refusing to honor the FOI.

Following are copies of the correspondence with respect to the FOI requests to the OIG:

September 20, 2012- Initial FOI to OIG

September 21, 2012- Reply from OIG to FOI

September 27, 2012- FOI request for OIG inspection records

September 30, 2012- FOI request for Szabo information

September 30, 2012- FOI request for Norby information

May 7, 2013- OIG letter, refusing to honor FOI request

J.B. Simms

Darryl Joe
Office of Inspector General
Washington, DC 20420

Fax Transmission: (202) 495-5859
Email to: vaoigfoia-pa@va.gov
Mailed under separate heading

September 20, 2012

Dear Mr. Joe:

This is a formal request by J.B. Simms under the provisions of the Freedom of Information Act, 5 U.S.C. Section 552 for all records held by the Office of Inspector General and all its offices or subdivisions pertaining to the inspection of the Veterans Hospital in Long Beach, California, resulting in the OIG Report Number 10-03861-119. These records should include but not limited to: all drafts, memoranda, staff memoranda, and correspondence with any and all VA Hospital staff and physicians, as well as any other papers requested by the OIG (certification of physicians knowledge of radiation technologies of which they prescribe)

Under the terms of the D.C. Code, Section 2-532(c) and (d), I expect to be able to inspect these records within ten working days, unless there are unusual articulable circumstances under which the Department would require more than ten days to locate these files. Under Section 2-532 (b), I request that these documents be furnished without charge on the grounds that such a waiver of the fee "is in the public interest because furnishing the information can be considered as primarily benefiting the general public."

When these records are available, you may call me at insert your telephone number.

Thank you for your cooperation in this matter.

Sincerely,

J.B. Simms
c/o Dr. Suzie Schuder
901 Dover Drive, Suite 204
Newport Beach, CA 92660
(803) 309-6850

J.B. Simms

September 21, 2012

J. B. Simms
c/o Dr. Suzie Schuder
901 Dover Drive, Suite 204
Newport Beach, CA 92660

Dear Mr. Simms:

This letter is to acknowledge receipt of your Freedom of Information Act (FOIA) request dated September 21, 2012 in which you asked for a copy of all records held by the Office of Inspector General and all its offices or subdivisions pertaining to the inspection of the Veterans Hospital in Long Beach, California, resulting in OIG Report Number 10-03861-119.

We have assigned FOIA Tracking Number 12-00348-FOIA to your request. Please refer to it whenever communicating with VA about your request.

Your request was received in this office on September 21, 2012. We are processing your request and our response will be forthcoming.

Sincerely,

Marvin Williams
Paralegal Specialist, Information Release Office

J.B. Simms

September 27, 2012

Darryl Joe
Chief, Release of Information Office
Office of Inspector General
Washington, DC 20420
Fax Transmission: (202) 495-5859
Email to: vaoigfoia-pa@va.gov
Mailed under separate heading
Dear Mr. Joe:

This is a formal request by J.B. Simms under the provisions of the Freedom of Information Act, 5 U.S.C. Section 552 for all records held by the Office of Inspector General and all its offices or subdivisions pertaining to the inspection of the Veterans Hospital in Long Beach, California, resulting in the OIG Report Number 10-03861-119. These records should include but not limited to:

1. All drafts, memoranda, staff memoranda, and correspondence with any and all VA Hospital staff and physicians, as well as any other papers requested by the OIG (certification of physicians knowledge of radiation technologies of which they prescribe)
2. Any other papers requested by the OIG (certification of physician's knowledge and training of radiation oncology technologies of which they prescribe such as: External Beam Radiation Therapy, Intensity Modulated Radiation Therapy (IMRT), Imaged Guided Radiation Therapy (IGRT), SBRT, and SRS.
3. Proof of knowledge, training and skills required for appropriate contouring of tumor volumes, critical structures and margins prescribed for CTV and PTV as designated in conjunction with the IMRT/IGRT Medical Necessity form, instructions to physicist or dosimetrist and prescription.
4. Proof of training, knowledge and skills required for contouring multiple site/multiple dose head and neck patients.
5. Proof of training, knowledge and skills of shift limitations and strict procedures of shift applications.
6. Training, knowledge and skills related to unnecessary side effects and damage to healthy tissue.
7. Understanding of dose distribution, authorized treatment plan vs. actual treatment delivery and affects created.
8. Evidence of understanding and rationale regarding basic dose distribution of IMRT/IGRT requirements and selection of patients.
9. Names of those who were involved in the review of the patients in this report and any notes substantiating the conclusions.
10. On Patient #1 - Name of outside facility performing the external peer review assessment, specialties of reviewers, names and quantity of reviewers involved.
11. Where did the external peer review assessment occur; was patient's complete chart information presented and reviewed?

J.B. Simms

12. Documents and notes related to OIG conclusion that "substantiated that facility leaders were not aware of adverse patient outcomes in RT."
13. Criteria leading OIG to the conclusion the radiation oncologists were competent.
14. Although listed as a point to be investigated, what were the criteria for not investigating Hostile Work Environment since it can directly affect patient safety?
15. The report states "We did not address the allegation of a hostile work environment in this report." Which report was hostile work environment addressed?
16. Provide year and page number of publication cited as reference #2 in OIG Report Number 10-03861-119.
17. Proof of training, knowledge and skills required to prescribe and manage patients being treated with IMRT/IGRT as previously requested by the VHA Director of Radiation Oncology, Dr. Michael Hagan, prior to the site investigation on 9/1/2010 and incidental to the OIG Report Number 10-02178-120, March 10, 2011 which was a Congressional Mandated Review involving the competency of Radiation Oncologists in the specialty of IMRT/IGRT and Physicists in the maintenance of correct machine parameters and associated materials spurred by the New York Times series on radiation in Jan 2010 – Feb 2010 highlighting a few VA facilities that were closed down.

When these records are available, you may call me at (803) 309-6850 insert your telephone number.

Thank you for your cooperation in this matter.

Sincerely,

J.B. Simms
c/o Dr. Suzie Schuder
901 Dover Drive, Suite 204
Newport Beach, CA 92660
(803) 309-6850

J.B. Simms

September 30, 2012

Darryl Joe
Department of Veteran Affairs
Office of Inspector General
Release of Information Office (50CI)
801 Vermont Avenue
Washington, DC 20420

Fax Transmission: (202) 495-5859
Email to: vaoigfoia-pa@va.gov
Mailed under separate heading

Dear Mr. Joe:

This is a formal request by J.B. Simms under the provisions of the Freedom of Information Act, 5 U.S.C. Section 552 for all records held by the Office of Inspector General and all its offices or subdivisions pertaining to:

1. Reports of incidents related to the conflict of interest of Dr. Sandor Szabo while operating as Chief of Staff, Chief of Diagnostics & Molecular Medicine HCG, and Chief of Pathology.

2. Any report of unauthorized research funding by Dr. Sandor Szabo.

3. Any report of any investigation of sexual harassment/assault incident which named Dr. Sandor Szabo as the perpetrator, and copies of the reporting of said incident(s) to the law enforcement agency having jurisdiction by Isabel Duff, the OIG, or the victim.

4. Any and all reports pertaining to information regarding the transfer/promotion and subsequent unearned pay increases of Michon Dean, employed at the Long Beach VA Hospital.

5. Reports of assignments/tasks given to Michon Dean outside of her functional statement and known expertise resulting in conflict of interest for the benefit of administrative personnel.

6. Reports of funds utilized by Michon Dean for entertainment of physicians and Administration at her home.

7. Reports of documentation of training, knowledge or expertise in the clinical areas of Radiology or Radiation Therapy of Michon Dean.

8. Reports of the investigation of inappropriate lab equipment purchases for laboratories by the Long Beach VA, to be used in locations other than VA Long Beach.

9. Reports of Dr. Szabo's pre-selection of Dr. Samar Azawi as Chief of Radiation Therapy with the knowledge of multiple incidents of her unprofessional behavior toward staff affecting patient safety.

J.B. Simms

10. Reports or documentation relating to his supervision of Dr. Samar Azawi, and the EEO involvement of the discrimination suit of Dr. Azawi against Dr. Szabo.

11. Any and all reports pertaining to the demotion and reinstatement of Dr. Azawi, as the Chief Radiation Oncologist at the Long Beach VA Hospital, including but not limited to records of all communication with Isabel Duff and Dr. Sandor Szabo.

12. Notes, reports, documentation with regard to meetings or communications with Dr. Azawi about her behavior, skills and incidents involving patient care, delays in treatments, and resolution of each.

13. Any correspondence, reports, and documentation of discussions with Isabel Duff, Dr. Sandor Szabo, Dr. Edgar Moran, Dr. Michael Hagan concerning Dr. Samar Azawi and the closing of the department of Radiation Therapy by Dr. Michael Hagan.

Under the terms of the D.C. Code, Section 2-532(c) and (d), I expect to be able to inspect these records within ten working days, unless there are unusual articulable circumstances under which the Department would require more than ten days to locate these files. Under Section 2-532 (b), I request that these documents be furnished without charge on the grounds that such a waiver of the fee "is in the public interest because furnishing the information can be considered as primarily benefiting the general public."

When these records are available, you may call me at insert your telephone number.

Thank you for your cooperation in this matter.

Sincerely,

J.B. Simms
c/o Dr. Suzie Schuder
901 Dover Drive, Suite 204
Newport Beach, CA 92660
(803) 309-6850Da

J.B. Simms

September 30, 2012

Darryl Joe
Department of Veteran Affairs
Office of Inspector General
Release of Information Office (50CI)
801 Vermont Avenue
Washington, DC 20420

Fax Transmission: (202) 495-5859
Email to: vaoigfoia-pa@va.gov
Mailed under separate heading

Dear Mr. Joe:

This is a formal request by J.B. Simms under the provisions of the Freedom of Information Act, 5 U.S.C. Section 552 for all records held by the Office of Inspector General and all its offices or subdivisions pertaining to,

1. Any report regarding the request by Ronald Norby for funds to be used for the renovation of a privately owned bowling alley.
2. The request to move of the VISN 22 office to the beach with required secured internet connection
3. Giving use of warehouse space to a community college valued at over $3 million dollars
4. Design and construction of a child care facility for over $2 million.
5. Any report of the hiring friends of Ronald Norby as employees who were not qualified but were placed in administrative positions to the advantage of Ronald Norby.
6. Any report of any investigation of reverse discrimination in hiring practices.
7. Any report regarding EEO violations committed by Ronald Norby.
8. All records, complaints or incident reports regarding retaliation by Ronald Norby against employees, and forcing the employee to quit.
9. The identity of officials appointed, employed, or otherwise interacting with the VA OIG and other VACO connections making problems "go away" that should have been thoroughly investigated.
10. Official document written as a type of "plea bargain" or agreement to "retire" for Ronald Norby, Director VISN 22, after investigation involving alleged multiple illegal transactions and policy violations.
11. Documents, agreement, or financial instrument drawn up and signed by Ronald Norby for the VA to receive reimbursement of alleged misappropriation of funds.
12. Any and all communication with any law enforcement agency with respect to the report of criminal activity by Ronald Norby.

J.B. Simms

13. Any and all notes, reports and documents, with respect to any investigation or interview with Ronald Norby, Isabel Duff, Mary Beth McCartan, & Herb Moisa surrounding the alleged misappropriation of funds, illegal hiring practices, shredding of HR documents and the altering HR documents, as well as the identity of the OIG personnel assigned to the above matters.

Under the terms of the D.C. Code, Section 2-532(c) and (d), I expect to be able to inspect these records within ten working days, unless there are unusual articulable circumstances under which the Department would require more than ten days to locate these files. Under Section 2-532 (b), I request that these documents be furnished without charge on the grounds that such a waiver of the fee "is in the public interest because furnishing the information can be considered as primarily benefiting the general public."

When these records are available, you may call me at insert your telephone number.

Thank you for your cooperation in this matter.

Sincerely,

J.B. Simms
c/o Dr. Suzie Schuder
901 Dover Drive, Suite 204
Newport Beach, CA 92660
(803) 309-6850

J.B. Simms

DEPARTMENT OF VETERANS AFFAIRS
Office of Inspector General
Washington DC 20420

May 7, 2013

OIG FOIA # 13-00041-APP

Mr. J.B. Simms
jb.simms10@gmail.com

Dear Mr. Simms:

    This is in response to your appeal under the Freedom of Information Act (FOIA), 5 U.S.C. § 552, that the Department of Veterans Affairs (VA) Office of Inspector General (OIG) received April 10, 2013. You appealed the decision of the OIG on March 9, 2013, to release information with redactions relating to your earlier three requests for specific information related to Mr. Ronald Norby and VISN 22 in Long Beach, CA. Your requests comprised 13 categories, which I will not repeat here, but which are listed in the March 9, 2013, response, in which OIG informed you that OIG had no records for items 1,3, and 6–13, and released redacted information on items 4 and 5. Although not addressed in the March 9 letter, Mr. Darryl Joe responded to you separately as to item 2 that OIG had no responsive documents. The redactions were based on exemption (b)(7)(C) (Exemption 7C). We interpret this appeal as encompassing all 13 categories of your requests.

    I have thoroughly reviewed your submission under the provisions of the FOIA, which provides that Federal agencies must disclose records requested unless they may be withheld in accordance with one or more of nine statutory exemptions. 5 U.S.C. § 552(b). OIG has no records on items 1–3 and 6–13. There are no other reports in OIG records. The material withheld from the documents responsive on items 4 and 5 was properly withheld under Exemption 7C. Exemption 7C protects individuals' names and other identifying information contained in the documents from disclosure. When considering the application of Exemption and 7(C), we take into account the interest in protecting the privacy of the individuals against the public's interest in disclosure. The substantial privacy interests protected by Exemptions 7(C) include the individuals' interests in avoiding disclosure of personal matters, while the public interest involves understanding the operations of the government or activities of any Federal agency. Release of information relating to the complainant and OIG agent identified in the report clearly and significantly invades the privacy of these individuals. Moreover, the information you seek regarding the individuals reveals little about VA's performance of its statutory duties or the activities of any Federal entity; that information has already been released. Accordingly, there is no public interest that outweighs the privacy interests compelling release of such information.

2.
J.B. Simms

For these reasons, I deny your appeal.

This is the final decision of the Department of Veterans Affairs regarding your appeal. The FOIA requires that I advise you that if you believe that the Department erred in this decision, you have the right to file a complaint in an appropriate United States District Court.

As part of the 2007 FOIA amendments, the Office of Government Information Services (OGIS) was created to offer mediation services to resolve disputes between FOIA requesters and Federal agencies as a non-exclusive alternative to litigation. Using OGIS services does not affect your right to pursue litigation. You may contact OGIS in any of the following ways:

Office of Government Information Services
National Archives and Records Administration
Room 2510
8601 Adelphi Road
College Park, MD 20740-6001

E-mail: ogis@nara.gov
Telephone: 301-837-1996
Facsimile: 301-837-0348
Toll-free: 1-877-684-6448

Sincerely yours,

JOSEPH M. VALLOWE
Deputy Assistant Inspector General
for Investigations (51A)

cc: Darryl Joe, Information Release Office (50CI), VA OIG

J.B. Simms

*Mike Tilkin
Assistant Executive Director
Chief Information Officer, American College of
Radiology 1891 Preston White Dr.
Reston, VA 20191
Telephone 800-227-5463
x4908 Email Transmission:
mtilkin@acr.org*

September 24, 2012

Dear Mr. Tilkin,

A writing and film project has begun with respect to documenting the reported violations of ACR provisions by the Radiology Oncology Department of the Long Beach Veterans Hospital, Long Beach, California. I have been commissioned to write the story of the violations, the injuries to the Veterans, and the lack of corrective response (or any response) by the American College of Radiology after the publication of Report Number 10- 03861-119, Department of Veterans Affairs, Office of Inspector General.

This report found that deficiencies in 9 of 10 records not only violated the provisions of an accredited radiology department, but these violations of ACR standards were detrimental to the health of the patients, and the Veterans of our military.

I am in possession of emails from a supervisory staff member at the Long Beach VA Hospital requesting the Chief of Radiation Oncology of the Veteran Hospitals contact your office 3 months prior to the first OIG inspection in September, 2010 concerning ongoing violations which could not be stopped. The executive assistant to Dr. Michael Hagan, Wendy Kemp, was requested to submit to Dr. Hagan, information detailing the violations both prior to accreditation and subsequent to accreditation, which was granted on September 9, 2009, after initially being denied. Ms. Kemp's response was that your organization would not make a visit to any accredited hospital, even after a report such as this, unless a fee of $9,000 was paid to the ACR. Evidently, the violations were never reported to the ACR. These violations were, and are, being committed by the physicians in the Radiation Oncology Department at Long Beach VA Hospital. The victims are the patients, the Veterans.

The OIG report is accessible online at the website for the Department of Veteran Affairs, Office of Inspector General. I ask that you please read this report, and then I would like to speak with you concerning the role of the ACR in this matter and the possibility of inspecting this department, along with the incidents which lead up to the request made to Ms. Kemp.

J.B. Simms

Ms. Kemp's response was that if the ACR was contacted, and the problems reported, the ACR's response would be to call Dr. Hagan, and the inquiry would end there.

Quoting from your current website:

"In order to verify that accredited facilities maintain consistent quality during the three–year
accreditation period, on-site surveys may also be performed at any time during the accreditation
period. These surveys provide an excellent opportunity for a positive educational exchange with
experts in the field, as well as providing validation of continued compliance with ACR
guidelines and standards. These surveys will be conducted by radiation oncologists and medical
physicists from the Radiation Oncology Accreditation Program. Any facility chosen for a
random on-site survey will be notified in advance. There is no additional cost to the facility for
the random survey."

I look forward to communicating with you with respect to this project.

Sincerely,

J.B. Simms

As another parting shot at the OIG, I sent the following email, and received no response.

J B Simms >

12/1/12

to privacy, bcc: Lana

from: J B Simms

to: privacy@usdoj.gov bcc: Lana Miller Boyer

date: Sat, Dec 1, 2012 at 4:33 PM

subject: Violation of Confidentiality Hotline complaint at OIG

Dear   Sirs,
A friend of mine submitted a hotline complaint to the OIG, at the suggestion of the OIG. A person, not acting in the best interest of my friend, published information which identified the person who submitted the hotline complaint. . Does this violation of hotline confidentiality at a federal agency fall under your jurisdiction?

JB Simms

Chapter Twenty:

Interview with Dr. Richard Robbins

I did a lot of reading on the issues of the VA hospital system and came upon an article written by Dr. Richard Robbins. I made some inquiries, and on January 10, 2013, I called Dr. Robbins and conducted an interview. Below are my notes from the interview.

Dr. Robbins is a full professor at the University of Arizona. He was employed with the VA for 31 years.

An overview of the involvement of the OIG with Lana and the VA Hospital in Long Beach was given, and the first reply was " The OIG is very interesting. Someone must have been a burr under the saddle to get their attention."

With respect to Lana, "...[i]f they can, they will crucify her. They will harass her to make her leave."

"The OIG whitewashes a lot of stuff. The reports go to Congress, and the Congressmen get their 15 minutes of fame, but do not want to do anything. Patty Murray's committee does nothing."

"The Chief of Staff of another hospital ran a hospital into debt and became the VISN director in the Washington area."

"Peer review is crap; all political."

"Jack Baghdad, Chief of Research at a VA Hospital, sent out emails, trying to lobby and get more money for research. The director of the hospital had him fired, and tried to say he violated the Hatch Act. Jack is a Jewish-Iranian. He now is the county health director in Eugene, Oregon."

I told Robbins about the appointments of Norby, Duff included, and Robbins stated he knew Duff, as well as the stories of her inappropriate personal activities. "Duff might have been at the University of Arizona."

We discussed the accountability of persons, and Robbins stated the VA moves people when problems occur, and she (Duff) might be "designated to move" meaning there could be a change coming. Sometimes it takes 18 months to get this to happen, quietly.

We discussed the situation that removing Duff would not solve the problem; the problem originated with the oncologists. Robbins stated "...radiation oncologists are hard to find, especially those who speak English."

"The use of Peer Review might be a way to get someone out. They use review by peers from outside the hospital (like was stated some months back). The OIG will never crack down on anyone. About the only way you can get any attention is to 'embarrass the VA 'and you need to get the attention of the right congressman."

Another person who used to work with the VA was Tom Grathwaithe, who was at the Los Angeles VA. He now works at the HCA Columbia-Tennessee. He would be a good person to be contacted.

Robbins stated "...[t]he administration will make her 'persona non-grata' and taking them to court would go nowhere."

In New Mexico, a psychiatric nurse at the VA wrote a bad comment about the VA in Albuquerque. A person named Mill Tucker was going to charge her with sedition. They got the US Attorney involved. She contacted a state senator. It was not pretty.

"Much of the bad stuff occurs at the top levels. The good people get run off."

Robbins mentioned his "Medical Courage" series on his website. (under the www.swjpcc.com site, and under General Medicine). Robbins would consider using a profile of Lana on his site. He mentioned Steve Klotz's profile, #9, and what the administration did to get him out. They dummied up his reviews, took away his grants which he had used for many years. Klotz is now at the University of Arizona.

I advised Robbins of the video Lana made. He said he was going to view it.

Chapter Twenty-One:

VA and ACR Put on Notice

Jan 23, 2013, at 11:37 AM, J B Simms >
Dear General Shinseki and Mr. Gingrich,

As I document the happenings at the Long Beach VA Hospital, I have come upon matters of which I can only assume you were not aware. Since Ms. Miller (Boyer) was betrayed by the VA-OIG with respect to their invitation to file a confidential "hot-line complaint", Ms. Miller-Boyer rightfully has no faith that the VA-OIG would conduct any inquiry which would be in the best interest of the patient-Veterans.

This lack of confidence was conveyed to Mr. Gingrich by Ms.

Miller-Boyer, and a request was made for a staff member from Mr. Gingrich's office conduct the inquiry. Ms. Miller-Boyer has yet to be interviewed by any person from the office of Mr. Gingrich.

Subsequent to the "inspection", the same physician consulted with the psychiatrist who is treating Ms. Miller-Boyer for the stress related disability as a result of hostility as she attempted to protect our Veterans from mismanaged care and physical harm. This VA-OIG physician stated that "workplace hostility does not result in poor patient care". In my experience in an industrial undercover capacity on five (5) occasions. workplace hostility always resulted in a dysfunctional environment which always led to inattentive behavior and lack of focus. This same hostile environment is also applicable to other environments, such as a military unit or an athletic team; the focus is diverted, and the results of the task at hand are marginalized. It is beyond the realm of reality that an educated person, let alone a physician, would not know the consequences of a hostile work environment.

I have met with a number of employees and volunteers of this hospital, and have come away with the feeling that these people are resigned to the fact that improprieties, be they fiscal, administrative, or affecting patient care, need not be reported because the layers of bureaucracy smother their voices.

J.B. Simms

The Veterans, the ones who offered their lives, who were carried from the field of battle, or did the carrying, are being treated with disdain by a nucleus of civilians who never served in the military,

and had questionable qualifications when placed into positions of authority by persons who knew that the perpetuation of secrecy would protect the persons who are harming the Veterans. This can be changed.

You will not know the truth if you base your knowledge on a report from the VA-OIG. I am privy to the report from 2010, and it shocks the conscience.

Lip service will not save these Veterans from the pain and abuse, and they do not deserve to be treated in this manner.

Sincerely,

J.B. Simms

From: J B Simms [mailto:]

Sent: Monday, January 28, 2013 2:17 PM To: Shinseki, Eric; Gingrich, John (SES) Subject: Re: Long Beach VA Hospital/OIG Dear General Shinseki and Mr. Gingrich,

As I sat with the group of employees and Veterans months ago, it was apparent that lack of accountability and consequence has allowed unethical behavior which, even with my experience, shocks my conscience. I just this moment said "Good morning" to an former Marine who I see at a local coffee shop. It breaks my heart to hear of his problems being treated for cancer at this VA hospital.

Having the OIG conduct an investigation of matters at the Long Beach VA Hospital confirmed the lack of confidence conveyed to me by the group with whom I met, as well as the misrepresentations and lack of understanding exhibited by the physician who attempted to gather information.

I look forward to Lana being interviewed and the Veterans being protected.

Jim Simms

J.B. Simms

From: "Gingrich, John (SES)" <Johnr.Gingrich@va.gov> Date: Mon, 4 Feb 2013 06:32:41 -0500

Subject: RE: Long Beach VA Hospital/OIG To: J B Simms

Mr. Simms,

The very serious concerns raised by Ms. Miller-Boyle, as communicated by both her and others, have been taken seriously by the Department. I am certain you understand that because of privacy laws, including HIPAA, I am not at liberty to disclose to you certain aspects of the matters raised.

However, I have been fully briefed on the extensive program reviews that have already been conducted and which are still planned.

I am satisfied they have been handled responsibly and that appropriate corrections have been and are being made. What follows are some details of the program reviews that followed an OIG hotline complaint concerning radiation- oncology care at the VA Long Beach Healthcare System (VALBHS).

The VA Office of the Inspector General (OIG), which operates autonomously under the Inspector General Act of 1978, visited VALBHS on November 15-16, 2010, in response to a hotline complaint concerning radiation oncology care. It identified what it believed to be one case of inappropriate patient care out of the 10 cases cited in the hotline complaint, as well as certain deficiencies in medical-record documentation and in the facility's quality-management program.*

The inspectors noted that the Radiation Therapy Service has equipment to provide Intensity-Modulated Radiation Therapy (IMRT), which is state-of- the-art technology.

However, IMRT was not being used by the providers because they lacked confidence and wished to have additional training. The inspectors believed that the use of IMRT for two of the ten patients might have minimized complications.

The inspectors also suggested that VA consider sending more complex patients to other facilities until those issues were resolved.

J.B. Simms

VALBHS Director consulted with VA's National Director of theRadiation Oncology Program who agreed to conduct a consultative visit to Long Beach, which occurred on December 9 -10, 2010. This review in general concluded that Veterans were receiving appropriate-quality care and noted that by that time, IMRT was being performed.

At the invitation of the VALBHS Director, the VA National Director of the Radiation Oncology Program returned on June 27, 2012, to assess the progress of the program. This return visit, while noting implementation of the majority of recommendations of the review conducted the previous December, focused on remaining issues in the area of medical physics and resulted in a recommendation to place the stereotactic program in Radiation Therapy on hold pending resolution of these issues. The items of concern related to quality checks but not to quality of patient care.

The Chief of Radiation Therapy and VALBHS' contract physicists worked with the VA National Radiation Oncology Program Office overseeing physics on these matters and on September 25, 2012, received approval to resume the stereotactic program.

In conjunction with the June 27, 2012 site visit, the VA National Director of the Radiation Oncology Program also visited the Radiation Therapy Service at VA Greater Los Angeles Healthcare System (VAGLAHS).

Recognizing Network 22's emphasis on program coordination and in conjunction with the Network's Chief Medical Officer, a recommendation was made to create a Network 22 combined Radiation Therapy program with treatment sites at VAGLAHS and VALBHS. It was recommended that Network 22 pursue a contract to achieve this program amalgamation with the Radiation Therapy resources of the University of California, Los Angeles.

VALBHS is actively pursuing the development of a contract for this purpose. VA Long Beach Healthcare System plans to resume the stereotactic program once these plans are solidified.

As noted above, the original OIG Hotline complaint regarding Radiation Therapy at VALBHS cited ten examples of allegedly poor-quality care.

J.B. Simms

These cases were reviewed by the OIG, which identified one (1) case as inappropriate care and recommended an external peer review. The external peer review was completed on April 10, 2011 at VAGLAHS and returned the conclusion that the care was at a Level 1 ("Most experienced, competent practitioners would have managed the case similarly in all of the aspects listed.)I am advised that the OIG intends to conduct at least one more site visit to VALBHS involving the current review before issuing a draft report in approximately 45 days. I am assured that in the meantime, the VALBHS Director will continue consultation with the VA National Director of Radiation Oncology to ensure the continued safety of its radiation-therapy program.

In fact, because OIG realizes that workplace satisfaction does impact quality of care, it surveys facility employees on patient safety and quality of care before each of its Combined Assessment Program Reviews and also publishes the facilities' latest VHA Satisfaction Survey results as appendices to its CAP reports.

I hope this information is useful to you. Respectfully,

John

John R Gingrich

Chief of Staff, Department of Veterans Affairs

(O) 202-461-4809 (C) 202-531-6855

This matter was growing more shocking with each day. It amazed me how the matter of abuse of Veterans, and the cover-up, was tolerated by General Shinseki, a West Point graduate, and classmate of my friend.

I decided to contact General Shinseki and Mr. Gingrich directly and advise them that Lana had been exposed as having been the Hotline informant by an unscrupulous person within the OIG; the same OIG which asked Lana for information of patient abuse, and recommended Lana make the Hotline complaint.

Lana understood "politic-speak" and Gingrich gave the typical response to an uncomfortable situation.

Soon after Lana read the response from Gingrich, Lana drafted a reply, had it reviewed by Dr. Schuder, and sent the email below to Mr. Gingrich.

J.B. Simms

Lana Miller Boyer to Mr. *Gingrich Mr. Gingrich:*

Thank you for your response. Your email dated 2-4-2013 to J. B. Simms and copied to me, Suzie Schuder and Michael Connor begs for a response. Although measured and deliberate, it appears you have accepted as truth all of the information you received from various personnel in the VA OIG, VALB, VISN 22, NDRO, and "Randy" Petzel, (as he is known by his friends at VALB and VISN 22) Undersecretary of Health plus any other miscellaneous contributor available to conspire, spin and create facts that allow this situation to continue to the detriment of all involved – Veterans and employees alike. This is a the poveproverbial rbial [sic]"Hydra". The reports and actions have been ineffective and created more difficulties by empowering administrative personnel to not only continue in their abuses of authority but to increase their misguided leadership in the handling of such destructive situations. Employees that assist in the cover-ups or hostilities receive pay increases, bonuses and promotions to and from positions they were not qualified to hold. Also, Ron Norby is still running things in the background but hopes to be a contract consultant to continue in his previous ways. A although of late he "walked out" of his office in Orange County for reportedly "breaking the law" as was alleged at his departure from VISN 22. Unfortunately the other 3 employees deeply involved in similar activities were spared only to allow their continued involvement in unethical perhaps illegal activities. The initial problem was the radiation injury of the patients followed by a hostile work environment, false accusations, lies and then the cover-up involving many key people previously named and new participants recruited or actively seeking participation to receive "favor" from those in the initial core of self-protection. The OIG report from the Nov 2010 site visit did not address the hostile work environment listed in the plan of investigation. In fact when one witness attempted to provide information on the topic the person was told that hostile work environment was not being investigated. If you read the report, hostile work environment was clearly listed in the items to be investigated. You can also read where it is stated that the "hostile work environment was not addressed in this report." Where was it addressed by the OIG? Why was it not addressed as planned?

J.B. Simms

Yes, multiple reviews have occurred but failed to expose the fullness of the truth. Why? Let me address your statement, "I am satisfied they have been handled responsibly...appropriate corrections have been and are being made." If you were referring to a non-medical problem, you may be correct. However, problems involving medical care, treatment, documentation are not a matter that can be dispensed with in the manner of a casual problem as appears to be the case in the reviews. Because the OIG report from the site visit in November 2010 was superficial in its conclusions and limited in scope of performance (in the public document – not Incl ? 2) does not attempt to acknowledge and correct the blatant disregard of the serious patient care problems. Furthermore, there was no sign of a "subject matter expert" in the group. In an email sent to Wendy Kemp, AO for Dr. Hagan, I questioned the knowledge of Dr. Herbers in the field of Radiation Oncology to which she replied "Hi Lana, Funny, Funny you just sent me this. Dr. Hagan just sent me a text that he told your

Director he will be making a visit to the program based on problems the IG found – looking at week after Thanksgiving. You have made an excellent documentation trail that will surely help the IG and OSC conclude there is a serious problem going on. Not to worry about Dr. Herbers if he's not a RO, he's probably looking at the policy and procedure venue and if he needs anything they always contact Dr. Hagan and I. Keep in touch!!"

Dr. Herbers looked at documentation but was not aware of its requirements or implications. He only examined the obvious deficiencies of whether the documentation was there or not. Nothing was noted regarding the date of the patient notes and the date the Drs doctors signed them. The Drs doctors know how to play the game CPRS so it appears the notes were written as required but when you look at the date the note/consult was signed it could be weeks or months after. This is a violation of VHA policies and punishable under the California Board of Medical Examiners and probably under every state. To emphasize the seriousness of just the documentation issue, the National Practitioner's Data Bank has discussed and possibly passed reporting requirements to the NPDB by hospitals, agencies and accrediting bodies of physicians suspended for not completing medical records within the required time of 15 – 30 days after patient discharge.

So the documentation is SERIOUS. However, the required content of the documentation is even more serious. What you might think is minor is not in Radiation Oncology.

The facility's Quality Management Program is only deficient because the radiation oncologists and nurse refuse to adhere to any requirements of standards on a consistent basis. If the QM program has no support from the Director or Chief of Staff due to their agendas, there is no accountability so the Drs doctors and nurse are free to tell QM they will not abide by rules.

They know nothing will happen to them and will never be made responsible or accountable because the Director and/or Chief of Staff will not do anything do nothing to make them accountable or responsible. This is the problem throughout the Long Beach facility and dare I say, the entire VHA.

The next item is beyond outrageous and a blatant lie! The inspectors noted the Radiation Therapy Service had equipment to provide IMRT but it was not being used by the providers because they lacked confidence and wished to have additional training. Which inspector said this? This statement is either (1) part) part of a self-protecting cover-up by Dr. Hagan, (2) an uninformed statement by Dr. Herbers, (3) constant lies spewed by the Radiation Oncologists that were accepted as fact or (4) a way for the OIG and others to explain away the problems... (5) or p Possibly a combination of the above. Both Radiation Oncologists have been prescribing IMRT treatments for patients since the Winter of 2007. Initially, prostate patients were treated with IMRT followed by Head & Neck patients then patients with other treatment sites. Furthermore, A multitude of patients have been injured by the Radiation Oncologist using both IMRT and 3D conformal radiation.

J.B. Simms

"The inspectors believed that the use of IMRT for 2 of the 10 patients might have minimized complications." As stated above no IMRT treatments were being used by the providers however, "the inspectors believed that the use of IMRT for 2 of the 10 patients might have minimized complications." If you refer back to the OIG Report # VAOIG 10-03861-119, it clearly states in the patient reports that 7 patients were treated with IMRT. Another patient was treated with IMRT but this was not stated in that patient's conclusion.

So the inspectors say the providers DID NOT USE IMRT as stated in the previous paragraph or you can pick one from the list of 5 possible answers.

IT CANNOT BE BOTH WAYS. Where are you getting this information? I can substantiate mine – Can you? I think not. At this point you should be very concerned because there is more. The use of IMRT does not automatically minimize complications. If the Drs doctors contour the tumor and adjacent critical structures for specific doses, then it is up to the Radiation Therapists to deliver the radiation accurately and precisely as prescribed by the doctors. If the Radiation therapists do not do this, unnecessary complications can occur. If the Drs doctors do not have the skill to contour the tumor and adjacent critical structures or organs at risk, unnecessary complications can occur. The 9 patients are prime examples of incompetence. Any number of excuses can be stated about the 9 patients but the injuries are the proof. That cannot be explained away. Patient #10 continues to be forgotten. This Veteran with an emergency condition was not treated and told by the Dr that the reason was he could not lie flat for the CT or treatment. Patients are treated quite frequently in the department in semi-upright positions. Breast patients are always treated semi-upright as well as patients with breathing difficulties or problematic anatomy. With the Dr's doctor's history of racism and the use of the "N" word directed at employees, a good argument could be made for the Dr doctor not wanting to treat the patient because of race. There is no legitimate reason this patient was not treated especially considering the emergency nature of the condition.

Now another problematic area – Dr. Hagan, his report from the site visit of 12/2010 and our conversation. My first day back from 3 months of FMLA from PTSD I was presented with Dr Hagan's draft letter during the Radiation Therapy QM Committee Meeting. Due to the content of the draft letter, I contacted Wendy Kemp to schedule a phone conversation with Dr. Hagan.

He told me he had a private conversation with Isabel Duff recommending the Radiation Therapy department be shut down. When I asked him why, he said I was not conversant with IMRT. He told me he wrote what they said - whoever "they" are. Dr. Hagan's VHA – PCS Issue Brief dated 12/14/2010 refers to the VA-OIG investigation 11/15-16/2010 in the first paragraph.

"The investigation raised several operational concerns, which were detailed in the 11/18/2010 IB prepared for VISN 22 leadership (attached as Incl 2)." This could be very problematic if there is any limitation of privileges related to the Radiation Oncologists. That is an automatic report to the NPDB and probably the CA Board of Medical Examiners. I doubt there is any note regarding this in the Dr's doctors' files. During the RT QM Meeting one of the Drs doctors stated that no more head & neck patients could be treated in regards to IMRT. However, that order was not followed either. Nothing was resolved. Why is Incl 2 (?) from the OIG Nov 2010 visit being hidden?

Does that report contain the problems? The OIG report released for the public was a "white wash." Is that appropriate? Is it appropriate to have two separate reports like two sets of accounting ledgers? This does not look good. Was Congress given a copy of Incl 2? (?) Maybe that is where it states the IMRT equipment is not being used. My colleagues at the other VA Radiation Oncology departments could tell you there are major problems in the VALB department. We are not talking about major complex issues that must be parsed in order to determine the problems.

It is that obvious. So when the VA OIG issues a report that explains away the problems or minimizes the issues, the VA OIG is the one with egg on its face along with Dr. Hagan. There is no credibility or integrity in "playing politics in patient care or protecting Drs doctors and nurses who have no qualms about their harmful, despicable actions directed at Veterans or fellow employees."

Dr. Hagan visited VALB 12/9-10/2010. "This review in general concluded that Veterans were receiving appropriate-quality care and noted that BY THAT TIME, IMRT WAS BEING PERFORMED." Is there any credibility left?

Something untoward occurred during Dr. Hagan's visit in 2010. There was an all-out push by the Radiation Oncologists, nurse and one of Isabel Duff's "hatchet minions" to "run me off" upon my return as retaliation for speaking to the OIG. This intensified attack after just returning from my PTSD leave did more damage to me. They knew exactly what they were doing to me in my condition – a directed and purposeful attack.

That is criminal and inhuman. Until Dr. Hagan came to VALB there was an open working relationship with Wendy Kemp and Dr. Hagan through Wendy.

After his visit in Dec 2010 I became persona non grata. A few weeks after my conversation with Dr. Hagan, Wendy told me not to contact her again. Instructions had been given from someone and/or lies were rampant.

Why? To protect the doctors? The VA?

When Dr. Hagan came in June of 2012, the AO was moved from the department of Radiation Therapy because of the hostile work environment. She was continually driven to tears several times a week by the doctors. I have recently heard that she and 2 others are going to file hostile work environment complaints.

Now the "hatchet minion" of Isabel Duff's is stuck in Radiation Therapy as the AO and is getting a good dose of her own medicine courtesy of the doctors. She wants to get out but no one wants her since she has no skills, Grade 11, but she does excels [sic] in bullying, intimidation, "errand" running for Duff and entertaining Administration and Drs doctors at her home. Everyone knows they cannot do anything to her because she is protected by Duff.

Who is over Radiation Therapy? When DMM HCG was split up whenafter [sic]Dr. Szabo had to give up being the Chief of DMM since he also held the position of Chief of Staff, a conflict of interest. Therefore Radiation Therapy had to be under some group. Because of the Drs doctors in Radiation Therapy and all of their problems with patient care, Medicine would not allow the department to be under them, The Chief of Radiation Oncology at GLA would not take the department either for the same reason. Radiology was the next victim. The Chief of Radiology said NO.

He was ordered to take Radiation Therapy with all of the problems in it caused by the doctors. Does that not give you some insight as to the difficulties in the department and that includes the refusal to follow any normal standards or respect basic human interactions ? Radiology is not similar to Radiation Therapy. The only similarity is the use of radiation – The Cardiac Cath lab also uses radiation. It would make as much sense to put Radiation Therapy under them as it is to put them under Radiology.

"The VA Long Beach Healthcare System plans to resume the stereotactic program once these plans are solidified (UCLA)." Was it stopped again? Previously you stated it had already resumed on Sept 25, 2012 with approval of the VA National Director of the Radiation Oncology Program Office.

In reference to the 2010 visit by the VA OIG, I asked who the "subject matter expert" was on site with them because there was not one present. Dr. Herbers would not say. At the recent visit in Dec 2012 there was a "subject matter expert" who sat beside me during the questioning.

However, I was not allowed to ask her questions related to Radiation Therapy. Only Dr. Herbers and the other 2 from the OIG office could ask me any questions or me to them. If the VA OIG truly wanted to get to the bottom of the situation regarding patient care in the department, the best way would be to allow me to converse with the Radiation

Oncologist and exchange questions/answers for clarification. She would know what I was talking about. Dr. Herbers is too invested since he investigated the first time and it did not come out well.

I asked Dr. Herbers why the hostile work environment was not investigated in 2010. He said something to the effect that if I could show a correlation of a hostile work environment and patient safety he would consider it. That is outrageous! He said something similar to my Dr doctor on the phone after the "in person" questioning. Actually, tThe VA has articles and teams assigned to dealing with that subject though it never makes any difference at the facility/employee level. His comment was totally unacceptable and uninformed.

Just to make sure this is clarified: I asked Dr. Herbers why hostile work environment was not investigated in 2010.Dr. Herbers is the VA OIG during the Dec 2012 visit who made the statement that if I could show a correlation of hostile work environment affecting patient safety it might be considered.I asked Dr. Herbers who the subject matter expert was during the Nov 2010 site visit but he would not tell me.

There is no record of one on site nor did anyone see or interact with one. The Radiation Oncologist with the OIG was not involved in these exchanges since
I was not allowed to direct any questions to her at Dr. Herbers' orders. The above was confirmed by my husband who was present with me the entire time.

"Workplace satisfaction" is not mentioned in the above text, therefore the comparison to a hostile work environment has no prior contextual basis. Workplace satisfaction is an attitude that can impact quality of care by low morale resulting from frustrating situations. A hostile work environment consists of actions such as assault, aggression, demeaning, undermining, intimidation, harassment, fear, and obstruction actively directed at a person or persons to elicit a response or achieve the instigator's goals.

There is no comparison, and any attempt to classify it as workplace dissatisfaction is only an attempt to dismiss the harm and injury that a hostile work environment causes. It is offensive to even bring it up in an attempt to minimize it.???

The VA is broken due to attitudes of cover-up exemplified byas [sic]the information contained in your letter. Dealing with Veterans' health and care is not the same as a bureaucracy of paper. These are people's lives and this is not supposed to be a game. Medical care should be medical care – all about the patient. How many times during combat do U.S. military physicians operate and treat enemy soldiers and civilians who are wounded. They do not turn a blind eye and refuse to follow the oath they took and the desire to help others. That is integrity.

That is courage. That is compassion. That is the medical field. What happened to the VA and its primary goal to care for the ones who have borne the battle.? ? Why desecrate and dishonor their sacrifices by incompetence and cover-up.

There are Directives, Policies & Procedures that are not enforced. The only rules followed are the ones made by Admin and carried out by willing employees who benefit for doing unethical things. There is no integrity, ethics, or trust – just "higher-ups" who do as they please and get protected by "higher-ups" so the game can continue. If you believe what you wrote, it would behoove you to go back and get more information. As I stated in my letter sent to Simonette Reyes and Dr. Herbers, I am willing to take a polygraph. Is anyone else willing to do the same? Lana Miller Boyer

Lana knew why the Long Beach VA Hospital had failed certification. It was surprising that they gained accreditation after the Varian Incident, but Azawi, Williams, and Duff concealed the truth that the therapists were found to have lied, and it was revealed to Varian that Azawi and Williams were not certified to give radiation prescriptions of IMRT on the Varian machine.

After Lana explained to me that the radiation oncology department at the Long Beach VA hospital was the last to be certified, considering the Varian Incident and the OIG reports published in March 2011, I took it upon myself to contact the American College of Radiology to get a response.

I called the ACR, and after talking to one of the officers, a follow-up call was necessary the following day. I asked if the ACR knew that the OIG had visited the Long Beach VA in September and November 2010, and that Dr. Hagan, the head of the Oncology Department of the VA visited in December 2010. The representative from the ACR was not aware that the Long Beach VA Radiation Oncology Department had violated ACR regulations. The ACR had not seen the reports from the OIG. The officer to whom I spoke was also told that Dr. Azawi falsified the Correction Action Program (CAP), knowing she was not going to adhere to the policies she was presenting. The ACR officer stated he would have to look at the stated reports.

J.B. Simms

I asked if the ACR had any records of the Varian Incident at the Long Beach VA Hospital. The answer was "no." I advised the ACR that not only had the Varian Incident occurred a few months before accreditation was obtained, but that the doctor who submitted the forms for accreditation had no intention of performing any of the corrective actions mentioned in the submission.

The next questions to the ACR employee was if the ACR had records of the OIG reports of the VA hospitals. The answer again, was "no." Another call to the ACR would be necessary.

On the following day, I received a telephone call from Leonard Lucey, Legal Counsel for the ACR. I confirmed that I was on speaker phone, and the person to whom I spoke on the previous day was one of a group of persons listening to the conversation.

Mr. Lucey had no explanation for not knowing about the Varian Incident, or not being privy to any OIG reports which investigated matters of the radiation oncology department of the Long Beach VA. Mr. Lucey gave me his email address, and I advised him I would be giving his address to Lana.

After telling Lana of my talk with Mr. Lucey, Lana sent a letter to Mr. Lucey, which is below:

J.B. Simms

Lana's Email To The American College Of Radiology

June 12, 2013

Mr. Lucey –

How was ASTRO this year? That is always such a benefit to all involved in our specialty. Hope you survived the hurricane without too much damage. To follow up on my email to you, I thought it appropriate to list a few incidents and method of operation of the Long Beach VA. These are but a few below:

General Items

Dr. Samar Azawi is not practicing under her licensed name of Dr.

Samar Al-Azawi. Neither physician displays any credentials.

Dr Azawi did not complete four years of residency in the same Residency program - Two years at UCI and 2 years at USC County.

Dr. Richard G. Williams is not board certified. Dr Azawi is.

The nurse, Donna Pikulsky RN, and the two Drs work in "cahoots" against everyone else in the department by keeping patient information secret, obstructing or refusing required document requests, entering misinformation in patient charts, not seeing patients at least weekly by saying it's the responsibility of the attending if the person is an inpatient, violation of HIPAA laws by having patient charts spread out in the nurse's office on OTV days and talking about patients in front of other patients, having patients weight themselves while the nurse sits in her chair across the room – even unsteady patients. Not addressing side effects because if they do they will have to manage them. Refusing to give pain medication to patients – for no reason other than having to manage it

J.B. Simms

Not taking into consideration other drugs, chemotherapies or co-morbidities that would complicate the treatment course. Inappropriate instructions for side effects.

Neither Drs are familiar with their patients if a Resident is involved. If you ask a patient who their Dr is they will know the Resident but not the Attending. The Residents do all of the work and all of the contouring of treatment plans. The Drs. will discuss the patient on consult days in their offices with the Resident but the patient usually never sees them unless there is no Resident doing a clinical rotation at the time.

The Chart Documentation Game – As you are aware from reading the VA OIG report from the mid-November 2010 site investigation several documents were missing but it was not specified which ones. The usual missing documents are Radiation Therapy Consult Notes and Treatment Summaries. The Hematology/Oncology Consult Note is placed in the chart until the Dr gets around to completing it – if ever. Treatment Summaries are generally non-existent. Several weekly OTV notes from Dr Azawi definitely do not comply with any standards.

If patients drop in because of problems after treatment completion and they do not have an appointment, a progress note is not written.

Sometimes the Drs choose not to see the patient. That also happens during treatment if the patient requests to see the Dr other than on OTV day. The nurse will speak to the patient, give some reason the Dr cannot see him then send him on his way.

Consults and Consult Notes are handled in a special way. First the VA has a limit on days a patient waits for a consult. The patient will be scheduled for a consult to meet the "day limit requirement" then the appointment will be "cancelled by clinic" and another appointment will be given for a later time. The Drs do not want more than 24 consults a month unless they cannot find a way out of it. When a patient is seen for a consult the Dr will start a Consult Note, usually on the day seen, and save it to record the date of the Note but there is just a brief sentence or nothing in the Note but it appears to be completed. That works well unless you look at the date the Dr electronically signed it. It could be weeks, months or even a year after the consult. This can happen with the summaries as well. So even if there are documents in the chart, check the date at the top and the date signed. Also, there are Consult Notes never written especially if the patient was not treated. These can be found by looking at the consult request, date of appointment without cancellation.

One day, Dr Williams and the current Resident had a patient requiring electron treatment on his finger. Not knowing what to do, I was asked to do a CT simulation of the hand then the dosimetrist ended up with 12 different plans showing the depth of the electron treatment with different energies.

ACR

The ACR Code of Ethics states:

Article XIII, Section 1, "The medical profession should safeguard the public and itself against physicians deficient in moral character or professional competence...."

"...deal honestly and fairly with patients and colleagues."

Section 2, "Members' behavior should conform to high standards of ethical, legal and professional conduct. Any activity that fails to conform to these standards compromises the member's personal integrity and casts aspersions on the College and the medical profession."

"A radiation oncologist should regularly treat patients only in settings where the radiation oncologist reasonably participates in the quality of patient management, utilization review and matters of policy that affect the quality of patient care."

"Members shall relate to other members of the health care team with mutual respect and refrain from harassment or unfair discriminatory behavior."

"Radiologic research must be performed with integrity and be honestly reported."

RTOG

Inaccurate information has been submitted stating the maximum shift is .5 cm. NOT TRUE. During the meeting to "discuss" improper alignment due to "no limits" with Drs Azawi and Williams and the physicist, Dr Williams became irate after I handed them papers (they requested) on allowed shifts and treatment accuracy. At that point he threatened to sue me for libel.

When I mentioned the information being sent to RTOG was not true and showed it to them, Dr Azawi then became furious and said they had never gotten in trouble because of it so it must not be a problem – although excessive shifts always occurred.

Since neither Dr understood IMRT and at times 3-D treatment planning, they had instructed the physicist and dosimetrist to plan all treatments according to RTOG protocols for particular sites although the patients were not enrolled in any research.

Department Operations

Dr Azawi issues instructions/order regarding who staff can speak to. I was ordered not to talk to Dr Szabo, COS & Chief of our medicine group and the Business Manager who approved requests for personnel and equipment. I told Dr Azawi that would not be possible because of attending the weekly Supervisor's meeting and needing to interact with the Business Manager for our department needs. (see #41)

June 2008, Dr Azawi, Chief of Radiation Therapy, was "demoted" pending investigation of her harassment, bullying and doing - "Because I Can." This management style is constant and pervasive in all of her decisions made regarding the department and patients.

Our department received the Directive from the VHA stating that every radiation therapy department in the VA would go through ACR accreditation. Dr. Williams was Acting Chief at the time. Refusing to understand or ignore the fact that ACR is a technical accreditation, he asked the nurse to provide the list of patients by category as requested then to wait for the final list prior to the site visit January 2009. Dr Williams was not familiar with the standards and requirements of ACR so we discussed what needed to be done as far as QA, Chart Rounds, New Patient Meetings, M&M, tracking patients who stopped treatment prior to completion and documentation of everything. I suggested we begin operating according to ACR by having appropriate meetings and followingdocumentation requirements. He was in agreement so we began to schedule the meetings, create forms and write policies that were not previously allowed or complied with by the Drs. or nurse.

The nurse was checking the charts for completeness although she had no idea what to look for. Then the physicist looked through them falsely thinking the site survey was a mock survey then I went through them and got sick.

J.B. Simms

The Treatment Record was severely lacking required information since they were designed and printed in 1989 and made checking the prescription to dose given a nightmare. Some charts could not be deciphered. Since Dr Azawi would not allow the Varian Patient Management software to be used to go part paperless, a new Treatment Record needed to be designed to specification and printed ASAP. At the time of the site survey, I was able to show the physician surveyor the new Treatment Record that I had designed and waiting for the return from the printing company.

The previous contract physicist was not renewed for many serious reasons then we were able to contract with a good physics company. On the physicist's first day he was faced with the transition to ARIA and an upgraded Eclipse Program. We were making progress with the required documents/procedures - Then things changed.

Dr Azawi was returned as Chief in February 2009 because all of the documentation given to the Chief of Staff, Dr. Sandor Szabo, had been "misplaced" according to the Assistant Chief of HR. Incidentally, Dr Szabo, COS, was also the Chief of Diagnostic & Molecular Medicine, the Radiation Therapy Health Care Group, and Chief of Pathology all at the same time. He was the highest official with exception of the Director who knew about all of the issues having been involved in the "demotion" of Dr Azawi.

Dr Szabo, COS, made Drs Azawi and Williams Co-Chiefs and requested a weekly written report from me regarding Dr Azawi's actions and a weekly written report to the nurse's supervisor.

We received notification from ACR that accreditation was denied with instructions for an Action Plan to resolve the deficiencies to be submitted in June (?) 2009.

I had questioned Dr Williams on the "allowed shifts" on IMRT/IGRT. He informed me he had not seen any papers on the subject. Within an hour I provided him 3 different articles much to his distress. He said he would pass them to Dr Azawi.

Instructions had been given previously to the therapists that no more than .5 cm was permitted for a shift and to contact the Dr.

Each morning I would check the Offline Review films from the day before. One particular patient showed an increasing shift distance despite instructions.

J.B. Simms

Dr Williams was consulted about the patient and I asked him if the patient needed an enema since it was pushing on the prostate. He laughed and said no that was not an issue. I then went to the nurse and asked her to find out when the patient's last bowel movement was. She too laughed and walked off.

Another patient had been having shifts approximately 1.5 cm but was now within the parameters of .5 cm. I commented to the therapist (the contract therapist involved in lying about the Varian table movement) that the shifts did not exceed .5 cm. He proudly replied that he was starting from a different spot so it would not be more than .5 cm. I was stunned then told him to align the patient where he was supposed to. More examples of these therapists doing what they want and Dr Azawi tying my hands and they knew it.

Dr Azawi decided to contact ACR to get some idea what they meant on allowed shifts. Dr Williams and I were present while she questioned a dosimetrist at ACR to get an acceptable shift number from her. The dosimetrist told her that was a decision Dr Azawi would have to make. I asked Dr Williams if he had given the papers on "shifts" to Dr Azawi. When he said he had I asked if she had read them. He shrugged his shoulders.

I emailed the required policies to Dr Azawi for the Action Plan that included a shift policy, Peer Review and possibly M&M. The next day she said she had sent it to ACR but used a different Peer Review Policy - one from the ACRO accreditation and even stated ACRO at the top of the policy.

Although Drs Azawi and Williams and the nurse wanted to appear to be in compliance with ACR guidelines, the New Patient Meetings, Chart Rounds and QA meetings were being discontinued in the department.

Chart Rounds had been "downgraded" by the receptionist and nurse going through charts some of the time. On occasion Dr Azawi would invite the physicist and me (Chief Therapist) to Chart Rounds. No one really knew when Chart Rounds would be held. The only notations permitted for Chart Rounds was what she instructed someone to write.

Questions were frowned upon since it would require and answer they did not want to give.

On Tuesday mornings there was a patient meeting (they called it multi- disciplinary) with Hematology/Oncology Drs, sometimes a psychologist or nutritionist and the nurse. No one else was allowed to attend. Later I discovered why. They primarily discussed when certain patients would start chemo so the treatment plans would be ready for us to start the radiation treatment for concurrent treatments or when patients would need a radiation consult.

Because the Drs were especially inept at contouring Head & Neck anatomy as well as knowing what they should do with the critical structures, it was not uncommon for the patient to start chemo followed by radiation 1 to 2 weeks later. Another approach would be to rush the treatment plan they had been delaying and insist the patient start that day. It was crazy. If anyone else knew when the patient was to start their concurrent treatment and the plan was not ready the Drs would get very angry. There were times when patients would come for consult, be seen by the Dr or Resident without all of the patient's information. Later that day or the next they would find out the consult or even simulation was not needed because chemo had entered into the patient record that for some reason radiation would not be needed at this time or sometimes ever - A CT dose for no reason. They would try not to let anyone know they "goofed" and the nurse would lie about it or say she was not going to tell me.

In June 2009, there was an incident involving the movement of the treatment table between treatments. Both therapists claimed it moved on its own. Since the actions of the linear accelerator system caused the table to move and after consultation with the Chief of BioMed, I contacted Varian since this could be an FDA Device Alert. Dr Azawi was glad I caught the problem. Machine was shut down until problem could be found. Approximately 5 Varian NTS team members arrived for a thorough investigation involving the software team in Baden, Switzerland and California and technical engineers. For 2 days I encouraged the therapists to make sure of what they believed happened and if they did not remember to say they did not remember.

J.B. Simms

Both stood by their stories. After it was firmly determined it was operator error and that one of the therapists went inside the treatment room to move the table sideways for gantry clearance but did not move it back as discussed in a meeting twice in the presence of Dr Azawi the situation flew out of control. I had given my recommendation to Dr Azawi the therapists (one staff on probation & one contract) should be terminated for lying, losing 4 ½ treatment days and causing Varian to go to extreme measures to find the problem. I offered to contact another VA Chief Therapist and one in the "outside world." She agreed. The next day I received a written recommendation from the VA Chief Therapist and forwarded to Dr Azawi who then told me to come up with a schedule to replace the therapists. She was in agreement with my recommendation. The next day the nurse had Dr Azawi "cornered" in deep conversation. Later that afternoon, Dr Azawi decided she did not want the therapists terminated. That same afternoon, the nurse told the two therapists I wanted them fired. From that time on, Dr Azawi would not allow me to correct the therapists making "student- level" mistakes and creating their own procedures. Blatant insubordination was encouraged and became a safety issue regarding patient set-ups and shifts for IMRT/IGRT.

There is much more on this topic but you can get some idea of the environment and operations of the department.

After the Varian Incident (June 2009) I showed the Drs images of what the therapists were doing. Patients were on the table for 30-50 minutes trying to get the initial films correct on 2-4 fields involving 15 – 20 films. It was not uncommon for all of the images to be rejected by them or the Drs then the patient would have to undergo the same procedure for confirmation of the treatment plan. The Drs were not bothered with the mistakes and messes only if the wrong body part was treated. Sometimes the therapists would just lay the patient on the table, raise the table then take a film of whatever was in the crosshairs. Lungs in shoulders, pelvis is stomach, and head with one eye. At this point their goal was to "run me off" as they had every Chief Therapist.

The harassment, retaliation and bullying escalated and I received a Letter of Reprimand creating a whole other set of problems since they told the therapists they were going to "level the playing field" by me being one of them.

J.B. Simms

They all laughed. I will not go into the numerous ways they terrorized me but I filed a complaint with Office of Special Counsel for retaliation for whistleblowing (incidents above) and Prohibited Personnel Practices in October 2009.

Patients were not being treated properly. Side effects had increased in ways I had never seen and with total disregard for the patient in addressing those side effects. Their focus was all on my demise.

In January 2010 the New York Times began a series of articles about radiation treatments by Walt Bogdanich causing a Congressional Mandated Review of all VA Radiation Therapy Departments. Questions about the IMRT training of all Drs, how many patients and types had been treated and questions about calibration and QA of linear accelerators were submitted to each department by Wendy Kemp, Administrative Officer of the Chief of Radiation Oncology for the VHA, Dr Michael Hagan.

In June 2010 when the Resident completed his clinicals any form of Chart Rounds ceased. The time from simulation to treatment was 3 – 6 weeks for approximately 12 patients. The dosimetrist said that was the most he had ever seen held up. The department was getting entirely out of hand so I informed Dr Szabo who then immediately forwarded my email to Dr Williams (Dr Azawi was on leave). I wrote him back and asked why he did that because now they were going to make me pay for contacting him. He told me to "calm down."

Dr Azawi asked me to take photos of the patient in the exam room. He had been on break for about 1 ½ weeks for skin breakdown. I walked in and was shocked. All I could say was "I'm so sorry" then asked if he had family here hoping they would do something about the treatment he received. They were. I took the photos and printed them as asked.

Prostate patients were having pain on urination almost a year after treatment. Another patient was in a wheelchair and we treated a very large buttocks area that caused a bad skin breakdown and constant painful bladder problems. These are just a few of the patients that were referred for hyperbaric oxygen treatments to heal the burns. Although the Drs were supposed to be following up with these patients, they were not the Drs who sent the patients for hyperbaric treatments.

It was always another physician/department where the patient had been referred from the long-term care area. Drs Azawi and Williams and the nurse never would manage the side effects appropriately.

Before having to take 3 months of FMLA in the Fall of 2010 due to the PTSD from the environment allowed and promoted by the 2 Radiation Oncologists and the nurse, I met weekly with Dr Szabo in the Supervisor's meeting consisting of Radiology and Radiation Therapy. Each week he would ask what was going on in the department, since he knew how things were, and I would go down the list of patients with problems, how they were being treated, hostilities, harassment, demeaning actions all directed at me. He knew how bad it was since 2008 along with the Director, Isabel Duff; Director and Assistant Director of HR Patient Safety Officer and many more.

By this time more and more blatant inexcusable decisions and injuries were occurring. I asked for a meeting with Dr Szabo and Isabel Duff, Director to discuss what I was planning to do (contact ACR) and wanted their input. They ignored my request. After speaking to some of my colleagues at other VA's the consensus was to contact the Chief Therapist in NJ at the facility that was closed down. She recommended calling Wendy Kemp, Administrative Officer for Dr Hagan, Chief of all Radiation Oncology departments. I did. It was important for her to know this was not a few incidents but many. I described a few patients to her then told her I wanted to call the ACR. Her reply was that ACR would just call Dr Hagan. I had read about the surprise visits that had no fee attached so I was surprised when she said it would cost $9,000. She then told me to let Dr Hagan handle the situation but to keep her up to date and she would do the same. She would pass information between me and Dr Hagan and would give me feedback.

An emergency patient with SVC was brought to the department for treatment on a Thursday and Friday. We were informed the patient would be treated Monday afternoon at 3:30 pm. We were also told he had difficulty lying flat which was not a problem for us. Dr Azawi walked by around 2:30 pm so I asked if the chart was ready for verification and consent signed. She would check.

J.B. Simms

By 3:00 pm there still was no chart so I went looking for her. She said we would not be treating the patient and walked off without explanation.

About a week later I checked on the patient and read the consult note written by Dr Azawi stating the patient would not be treated and that it was "emperative"[sic] the patient be able to lie flat for the CT simulation and treatment. Dr Azawi told the patient he had to be able to lie flat before they could help him. For a week this patient would practice lying flat so he could be treated to help his breathing. I saw Dr Azawi's signature at the end of the consult and the time it was signed. It was Monday at 11:48 am. She knew the patient was not going to be treated when I ask her about the chart at 2:30 pm. She left for the day at 3:30 pm. I suppose she forgot she treated breast patients on a breast board and not lying flat.

Notices were sent to each facility a few days prior to the VA OIG investigators arrival for the Congressional Mandated Review with requirements for their work area and information to have ready. The investigators arrived in Long Beach September 1, 2010 to begin examining documentation. Most of the information was not available to them upon arrival so they considered leaving. The Drs managed to produce the Peer Review documents but the investigators let them know of their dissatisfaction of not being prepared and the Peer Reviews not current.

The investigators asked me to give them 10 patient names to investigate as a Hotline Complaint. I told them the Drs would know I was the one that gave them. I finally consented and gave them the 10 names requested.

Wendy told me the OIG visit did not go well so the OIG would return. Dr Hagan was kept informed.

Between September 15 and December 15, 2010, I was on FMLA for PTSD and therefore not present at the next investigation by the VA OIG the middle of November. That did not go well either so Dr Hagan planned to make a site visit in early December at which I was not present at either.

J.B. Simms

My first day back after FMLA I was greeted with a new intensity of harassment. Dr Szabo asked me to come to the new department QA Meeting. They handed out a draft letter from Dr Hagan dated December 14, 2010 making recommendations for the department.

He then included a couple of sentences basically saying I did not know what I was talking about concerning shifts and IMRT. I had no idea what was going on so after the meeting I immediately contacted Wendy Kemp to set up a phone call with Dr Hagan that day or the next then call me with the arrangements. I spoke with him the next morning and asked him what was going on and why did he write that about me when he knew better. He told me he just wrote what the Drs told him. Then he unfolded his conversation with Isabel Duff, Director in a private 45 minute meeting. He told her they should shut down the department. The department was not shut down, the Drs and nurse felt vindicated since I was "called out" in the letter.

Dr Azawi issued an edict forbidding anyone in the department to speak with me. Unfortunately, the receptionist did and was transferred out of the department the next day.

Although I was "allowed" on the Department QA Committee, it was being run and directed by the Lab Manager and the Lab QA person – people totally unaware of radiation therapy operations, requirements or standards. I was not allowed to be involved in creating another Chart QA form or anything else even when I discussed the deficiencies of the new suggested form designed by the Lab QA person. They had also assigned the Administrative Officer from Radiology to make clinical decisions in the department and yell at me at every corner. No one could touch this person because she was lunch buddies with the Director and was allowed to do anything, go to any meeting and generally not do her job because she did not know how. She had been a Grade 5 and ended up a Grade 11 in about a year – in impossible legal task. Dr Szabo would meet with the AO, Lab Manager and the Lab QA person to take care of problems in the department. The Lab Manager had met with Dr Azawi and asked her to bring the ACR standards the next time they met. She had no idea what he was talking about or where to find them. He was told to document the incident.

J.B. Simms

Soon after at another meeting, the situation with Drs Azawi and Williams and the nurse had reached the point of the ridiculous.

The Lab Manager feeling exasperated asked Dr Szabo "What does Dr Azawi have on you" because Dr Azawi and the others were never made accountable.

Please refer to the VA OIG report 10-03861-119, Healthcare Inspection, Alleged Poor Quality of Care in Radiation Therapy, VA Long Beach Healthcare System, Long Beach, California, Recommendation 3, "The Radiation Therapy Nurse audits the medical records daily to ensure progress notes, treatment summaries, radiation doses, and treatment modifications are completed within 7 days after the last radiation therapy treatment. Documentation discrepancies are addressed in the weekly chart round meetings." The nurse would not know a treatment modification, radiation dose or treatment summary or what is required. (My emphasis) This once again goes to the secrecy and cover-up by Drs Azawi and Williams and the nurse. Recommendation 4 – "The nurse was also responsible for reporting adverse clinical outcomes and treatment interruptions."

The nurse covers for the Drs and typically minimizes the serious nature of side effects or pain (if it is even recorded)

Around January 2011 the physicist went to Dr Szabo to let him know Drs Azawi and Williams did not understand cross-sectional anatomy or how to contour prostate patients and especially head & neck patients. Dr. Szabo listened, made no record of the meeting and nothing happened (as usual).

Need to attach the analysis of what missing documentation can do to affect patient care. Name specific documents.

The falsification of the application to the ACR, the falsification of the CAP submitted to the ACR, and the unwillingness of Hagan to be receptive to a review of the department puts all patients in peril of mistreatment, maltreatment, injury, and pain.

Sincerely,

Lana Miller Boyer

Chapter Twenty-Two:

Catching Up with Lana

During the spring of 2016, I was busy writing two books, and decided to get back into touch with Lana. I had moved from the Newport Beach area and had not heard from Lana in a couple years.

In May 2016, I decided to check on her and remind her that I still had the manuscript of the story of the corruption and abuse suffered by the patients in radiation oncology, as well as the attacks on Lana.

Lana told me that around August 2014, Lana retired from the Long Beach VA Hospital. She had grown weary of reporting to different watchdog and governmental agencies and seeing one cover-up after another. Lana's husband had family in South Carolina, and Lana was currently in a western state visiting her relatives.

I told Lana that I was interested in finishing the story, and she encouraged me to do so.

We talked on the phone for a bit, and I sent her a bit of the manuscript to review. Lana told me she would email me information about what happened after she was moved to Mental Health (after her "Dear All" email), being moved to another area, and being asked to return under a new hospital administration.

It was frustrating for me to see Lana experience the abuse during the years I was compiling this book. Both Lana and I put different agencies on notice, of the wounding of Veterans by the VA Hospital in Long Beach. Emails and conversations were held with the OIG, OSC, ACR, EEO officers, and others.

Lana told me she retired in June 2014. My first thought was that Lana suffered all these years, and worked so hard, to protect the Veterans, and I wanted to know if any

Below are the texts of some of the emails which Lana sent me, all during a couple of days in May 2016. These emails tell the story of what happened because of Lana's determination to save the lives of the Veterans.

J.B. Simms

Emails Sent To Me By Lana: May 2016

May 24, 2016

Sorry for the delay. I had to work myself up to reading it. Will get to the other 2 parts. Hope this helps some. Just some clarification.

Can't remember if I told you this..

I will have to tell you what lead up to my "retirement" which is just another fact of the crap but anyway when I notified my supervisor that I was leaving the next day, Azawi cornered me in my office, asked if it was true and if I would meet her later in the day. She gave me her cell number which she would have died before giving me when I was there before. Asked me to call her around 3p and meet somewhere. What did she want? Why was she acting like I was her new best friend? We met on the patio of the cafeteria all sneaky like. I was already there. She was wearing big sunglasses and looked behind her as she walked toward me. She sat with her back to the building then slinked down in the chair with one hand protecting her face from the side. OMG!

She begged me to stay! Yep. She wanted me to stay and help her fight against the people now trying to get rid of her. Would I be willing to help? CAN YOU BELIEVE THE TOTAL INSANITY OF THAT QUESTION TO ME?
Why should I help after what you have done to me? Please, Please, I need your help. Absolutely not! After about 20 minutes of the nonsense she was heading back to the dept ahead of me. We both walked back to the cafeteria door where she entered the building then turned around. Through the glass door she was making an idiotic, pleading face and holding her hands together begging and mouthing the words "please". I just shook my head no several times. She finally turned and left. WHAT JUST HAPPENED? TWILIGHT ZONE!

A few weeks ago, Cindy told me Azawi had gone up to her office and begged her to help her too. One messed up, heartless woman.

J.B. Simms

May 25, 2014

The new Director, Fisher, has worked diligently to get her removed. She always threatens lawsuits then they buckle. Duff wanted her gone too but could not withstand the pressure. Szabo got caught in his mess so he buckled before that.

Thu, May 25, 2016 at 9:01 PM

They finally addressed the issue of Dr's not seeing patients. It is ridiculous! Some only see patients one day a week. Big BS. I am sure they needed the lawyers to defend against lawsuits for killing vets. Typical stupid administration people. Then they send in reports with false numbers to get big bonuses. Duff used to have luxury catered lunches for herself and her minions. The waste is incredible. I guess they think if more vets commit suicide because there is no MH professional available then that's just fewer to deal with complaint wise. They ate sick puppies. You wouldn't believe what they would do to the vets in physical rehab. Enough to make you sick. One guy the amputated his leg bit by bit 5 different times. The last one they splintered the bone and said oh well you can go home now. Sicko people.

May 26, 2012

While I was working in Mental Health, I was assigned to the Suicide Prevention Program to track suicides, call coroner and see how totally ineffective mental health was for the Veterans. After a year there the Chief of the nursing home, rehab, hospice, home care etc (at one point she was over Radiation Therapy when the health care group got pulled from under Szabo) asked if I would move to her division and become the Business Manager. Told her I would come help. When I went it was a political thing to oust the current one who was out on leave. She even wanted me to move into the BM's office. No. BM came back in a week. Yikes. While there I processed/purchased $500k in equipment for the various dept. There was a rush to spend the money that had been removed from the Veteran vocational dept. They hired Vets with mental/physical disabilities and made things for sale. They had been working with a vendor who had a contract to sell garden hose pressure nozzles at Home Depot. I saw one in Roswell at Walgreen's in the last month. So instead of the program that earned the money being able to spend it on their needs, it was "swept" into a different use. Typical.

J.B. Simms

Duff was transferred to Las Vegas. That was a mess. Equipment & employees had not been taken care of so Duff began detailing employees to Vegas to try to make it operational. Big disaster. Drs. there were furious. In typical Duff form, she boarded up the front entrance to the ER. A patient died there for lack of emergency response. In the LV papers.

No director was at LB so all of the known crooks on the top admin floor continued to run their games on people. I think they each took turns as to who was in charge each week. Crazy. A new director had been names from Washington state, I believe. He had a good reputation and some at LB who had worked with him there said he would straighten things out. By that time, Szabo had be removed as Chief of Staff and detailed to the VISN (district) office and had to sit at a desk without any tasks while he was investigated for buying equipment for his lab in Hungary.

When the new director arrived he was just surveying the land with a lot of input from others he knew before. The Cabal on the top floor thought they could continue to run their "shadow" admin and keep Duff in the loop. Keep things hidden etc. He became wise to that and started putting the clamps on them and letting them know their days were numbered. He even demoted some of the privileged few.

Cindy contacted me and said the new Dr from UCLA wanted me back in the dept but he wanted to get certain things done first. Okay. I was excited.

That was around March. I never spoke with him during that time. Around June-July I was informed that I would be returning to radiation. I was so excited. The Chief in the dept where I was had gone on vacation for several weeks so the acting chief, who I had contact with in Mental Health, interfaced with HR on the move. I told her I was not going back if I had to report in any way to Azawi so that would need to be specified on my job description/functional statement. Got that accomplished. I was also required to update my Supervisor education (40 hrs) prior to returning.
Everything was great.

They had split radiation into 2 sections. One was under Dr Lee and the other was the chief nurse who was over nursing (1 person). This person, Lynette, had been the Patient Safety Officer for the hospital until about 6 months prior. I had also dealt with her over the Varian incident investigation. She had been moved to the health group I was currently in overseeing home care. Our offices were close and frequently ran into each other (when she came to work). Everything had been fine to that point. I discussed going back to radiation with Jeff & Schuder. Both threatened to pull me out if I began having problems.

J.B. Simms

Without notice, Lynette came and got me and said I was going to radiation for the department meeting but stopping at her office to meet Dr Lee. I'm expecting a friendly reception based on conversation he had with Cindy. NO. Right after I was introduced he told me he knew about the video, had not seen it and would not see it. Off we went to radiation. I was a tad bit stunned.

Met the new people in the dept and saw Azawi. She grinned her sicko grin. Saw Gail who was quite pleased with herself. Afterwards I was escorted back to Lynettes office and told I could not do anything unless I asked her first. Then I was given a letter saying that I would be working on the machine for 2 months and not to participate in supervisory activities. I had no idea of the ridiculous plan. Every week I was supposed to report to Lynette with a list of all of the patients I had treated. Dr Lee had already brought in therapists who would become employees and one in particular that was "running" the therapists. She made it clear from her actions that she was the boss. She had worked with Dr Lee for several years and was meeting with him outside of the dept.

It was absolutely ridiculous. I got in trouble for typing out a schedule based on peoples' days off for info only. When they said I could do nothing without permission they were serious. It was construction discharge from day one. It became difficult to go into work and was having to take more meds than prescribed. After 2 weeks, I was done. Saw Schuder on Mon. She said enough and wrote one of her stellar letters to them. It was great. I was supposed to have a meeting with Lynette to give her my list of patients but I gave her the letter instead. Said I was done and was doing the retirement thing.

As I was walking to lunch I ran into the person who was acting chief and who I had worked with in Mental Health. She asked how I was so I gave her Schuder's letter to read. Her jaw dropped and was speechless. Told me to call her later. I didn't. No point but she was blind-sided by the situation too. Later that day was when Azawi wanted to meet.

Dr Lee's agenda was to get me out too it seems so he could put in his therapist. Getting rid of Azawi was still on the agenda. They first caught her for fraud involving Administrative Leave. That was when they detailed her to Surgery to read charts. There was also a patient issue that got reported to the National Practitioners Data Base. Some of the therapists also file hostile work environment with OSC, I think. Sure helps when the hospital is supporting in this. Cindy said Azawi was fighting it like crazy but the hospital was determined. Lawyers, intimidation etc. The director stood firm.

J.B. Simms

A couple of weeks ago, Cindy said she was going to be gone shortly then told me about Azawi coming to her to enlist her help. What a totally clueless, incompetent Dr. Asked Cindy to let me know when she goes out the door because I wanted to have a glass of wine and a pork product to celebrate. Wine & bacon? Haven't heard anymore.

So that's how stuff happened. It was heartbreaking for me since I thought they really wanted me to return to the dept. I even cried when I got the letter saying I would be going back. I was so happy. BOOM!

Williams came back for awhile on contract but then left after a period. Azawi was never able nor willing to learn the skills she needed to practice civilized country radiation. All smoke & mirrors. Although I was unable to get her removed because of my inability to deal with the second onslaught of the PTSD upon returning from the first one, at least more people were aware of her dangerous ways. They just had no balls. I could not deal with the OSC's screw up requiring me to refile for hostile work environment. The lawyer said it was a classic case but there was no paper work. Fell through the cracks and so did I. I am grateful to you, Col, Schuder and Cindy for making an all out assault. It did matter but she lived to fight another day until now. Just think if she had been removed before I even was hired. The patients would have been protected. I don't like to think of the ones who were not.

We did our best. I pray for the others. Veterans deserve more than that.

He[Director Fisher] is not connected to Norby at all. No other contacts except previous people who had worked for him and we're at LB or retired from LB. Those people filled him in reeaall good. This guy is not stupid like most and seems not to be interested in his own kingdom. He has worked at the VA forever. Started at the bottom and has worked his way up. Familiar with actual workings of depth since he worked in many on his way up.

I retired the end of August 2014. She approached me on my last day when she heard I was leaving. Cindy was maybe a month ago.

Epilogue

Lana left the VA thinking all of her attempts to save Veterans had failed. It took new leadership to see the truth, but Lana was not there to see her victory.

As you read the emails from Lana to the hospital (Dear Alll), OSC (Fong), OIG, ACR, and the Chief of Staff of the VA (Gingrich), or Dr. Hagan, the story never changed. None of these people had the courage to protect the Veterans.

None of the changes would have happened without Lana having sacrificed to save the Veterans. The guilty persons at the Long Beach VA just wanted Lana gone, hoping their misdeeds would not be discovered.

A new director comes in, and put the Radiation Department under the supervision of the Los Angeles VA Hospital. That was a good thing. Azawi was plenty nervous, but Lana was not going save her. The bad guys would slowly be eased out, no one was made accountable; not Duff, Szabo, Norby, McCartan, Pikulsky, or Gail Francis. People were transferred, got new jobs, and their misdeeds did not follow them. They were all protected by each other.

When you start to play the leverage game, you better be clean. Szabo thought he could control Azawi, until Azawi had leverage on Szabo. Azawi thought she could control Gail Francis and Doug Hollins, but Gail went past Lana and, behind closed doors, must have let Azawi know that she (Gail) had something on Azawi, and Azawi began dancing to Gail's tune.

All this childish game-playing resulted in poor and inadequate care for the patients, the Veterans.

The bureaucrats, administrators, politicians, and others in authority in the VA hospital system will thump their chests about the changes made in the Long Beach VA Hospital. None of this would have happened without Lana coming forward to attack those who were attacking the Veterans. They knew the story was going to come out. Changes were made, but these changes have Lana's fingerprints all over them.

Thank God, the Radiation Oncology Department at Long Beach VA Hospital is no longer being run by Dr. Azawi.

J.B. Simms

J.B. Simms

Appendix One:

Public Health Service Act HR 2104

112TH CONGRESS
1ST SESSION
H. R. 2104

To amend the Public Health Service Act and title XVIII of the Social Security Act to make the provision of technical services for medical imaging examinations and radiation therapy treatments safer, more accurate, and less costly.

IN THE HOUSE OF REPRESENTATIVES

JUNE 2, 2011

Mr. WHITFIELD (for himself, Mr. BARROW, Mr. BOSWELL, Mr. COHEN, Mr. CONNOLLY of Virginia, Mr. DUNCAN of Tennessee, Mr. GUTHRIE, Mr. HALL, Mr. HARPER, Ms. EDDIE BERNICE JOHNSON of Texas, Mr. JONES, Mr. KILDEE, Mr. KIND, Mr. LANCE, Mr. HEINRICH, Mr. MCINTYRE, Mrs. MYRICK, Ms. RICHARDSON, and Mr. RUSH) introduced the following bill; which was referred to the Committee on Energy and Commerce, and in addition to the Committee on Ways and Means, for a period to be subsequently determined by the Speaker, in each case for consideration of such provisions as fall within the jurisdiction of the committee concerned

---

A BILL

To amend the Public Health Service Act and title XVIII of the Social Security Act to make the provision of technical services for medical imaging examinations and radiation therapy treatments safer, more accurate, and less costly.

1 *Be it enacted by the Senate and House of Representa-*
2 *tives of the United States of America in Congress assembled,*

J.B. Simms

SECTION 1. SHORT TITLE.

This Act may be cited as the "Consistency, Accuracy, Responsibility, and Excellence in Medical Imaging and Radiation Therapy Act of 2011".

SEC. 2. PURPOSE.

The purpose of this Act is to improve the quality and value of health care by increasing the safety and accuracy of medical imaging examinations and radiation therapy procedures, thereby reducing duplication of services and decreasing costs.

SEC. 3. QUALITY OF MEDICAL IMAGING AND RADIATION THERAPY.

Part F of title III of the Public Health Service Act (42 U.S.C. 262 et seq.) is amended by adding at the end the following:

"Subpart 4—Medical Imaging and Radiation Therapy

"SEC. 355. QUALITY OF MEDICAL IMAGING AND RADIATION THERAPY.

"(a) QUALIFIED PERSONNEL.—

"(1) IN GENERAL.—Effective January 1, 2014, personnel who perform or plan the technical component of either medical imaging examinations or radiation therapy procedures for medical purposes shall be qualified under this section to perform or plan such services.

"(2) QUALIFICATIONS.—Individuals qualified to perform or plan the technical component of medical imaging examinations or radiation therapy procedures shall—

"(A) possess current certification in the medical imaging or radiation therapy modality or service they plan or perform from a certification organization designated by the Secretary pursuant to subsection (c); or

"(B) possess current State licensure or certification, where—

"(i) such services and modalities are within the scope of practice as defined by the State for such profession; and

"(ii) the requirements for licensure, certification, or registration meet or exceed the standards established by the Secretary pursuant to this section.

"(3) STATE LICENSURE, CERTIFICATION, OR REGISTRATION.—

"(A) IN GENERAL.—Nothing in this section shall be construed to diminish the authority of a State to define requirements for licensure, certification, or registration, the requirements for practice, or the scope of practice of personnel.

"(B) LIMITATION.—The Secretary shall not take any action under this section that would require licensure by a State of personnel who perform or plan the technical component of medical imaging examinations or radiation therapy procedures.

"(4) EXEMPTIONS.—The qualification standards described in this subsection and the payment provisions in section 1848(b)(4)(C) of the Social Security Act shall not apply to physicians (as defined in section 1861(r) of the Social Security Act (42 U.S.C. 1395x(r))) or to nurse practitioners and physician assistants (each as defined in section 1861(aa)(5) of the Social Security Act (42 U.S.C. 1395x(aa)(5))). Such practitioners shall not be included under the terms 'personnel' or 'qualified personnel' for purposes of this section.

"(b) ESTABLISHMENT OF STANDARDS.—

"(1) IN GENERAL.—For the purposes of determining compliance with subsection (a), the Secretary, in consultation with recognized experts in the technical provision of medical imaging or radiation therapy services, shall establish minimum standards for personnel who perform, plan, evaluate, or verify patient dose for medical imaging examinations or radiation therapy procedures. Such standards shall not apply to the equipment used.

"(2) RECOGNIZED EXPERTS.—

"(A) IN GENERAL.—For the purposes of this subsection, the Secretary shall select recognized expert advisers to reflect a broad and balanced input from all sectors of the health care community that are involved in the provision of services of the type described in paragraph (1) to avoid undue influence from any single sector of practice relating to the content of such standards.

"(B) DEFINITION.—In this paragraph, the term 'recognized experts' includes—

"(i) representatives of all medical specialties and providers that perform or plan medical imaging procedures;

"(ii) representatives of all medical specialties and providers that perform or plan radiation therapy procedures;

"(iii) medical imaging and radiation therapy technology experts; and "(iv) other experts determined appropriate by the Secretary.

"(3) MINIMUM STANDARDS.—Minimum standards established under this subsection shall reflect the unique or specialized nature of the technical services provided, and shall represent expert consensus from those practicing in each of the covered imaging modalities and radiation therapy procedures as to what constitutes excellence in practice and be appropriate to the particular scope of care involved.

"(4) ALLOWANCE FOR ADDITIONAL STANDARDS.—Nothing in this subsection shall be construed to prohibit a State or certification organization from requiring compliance with standards that exceed the minimum standards specified by the Secretary pursuant to this subsection.

"(5) TIMELINE.—Not later than 12 months after the date of enactment of this section, the Secretary shall promulgate regulations for the purposes of carrying out this subsection.

"(c) DESIGNATION OF CERTIFICATION ORGANIZATIONS.—

"(1) IN GENERAL.—The Secretary shall establish a program for designating certification organizations that the Secretary determines have established appropriate procedures and programs for certifying personnel as qualified to furnish medical imaging or radiation therapy services.

"(2) FACTORS.—When designating certification organizations under this subsection, and when reviewing or modifying the list of designated organizations for the purposes of paragraph (4)(B), the Secretary shall consider—

"(A) whether the certification organization has established certification requirements for individuals that are consistent with or exceed the minimum standards established in subsection (b);

"(B) whether the certification organization has established a process for the timely integration of new medical imaging or radiation therapy services into the organization's certification program;

"(C) whether the certification organization has established education and continuing education requirements for individuals certified by the organization;

"(D) whether the organization has established reasonable fees to be charged to those applying for certification;

"(E) whether the examinations leading to certification by the certification organization are accredited by an appropriate accrediting body as defined in subsection (d);

"(F) the ability of the certification organization to review applications for certification in a timely manner; and

"(G) such other factors as the Secretary determines appropriate.

"(3) EQUIVALENT EDUCATION, TRAINING, AND EXPERIENCE.—

"(A) IN GENERAL.—For purposes of this section, the Secretary shall, through regulation, provide a process for individuals whose training or experience are determined to be equal to, or in excess of, those of a graduate of an accredited educational program in that specialty to demonstrate their experience meets the educational standards for qualified personnel in their imaging modality or radiation therapy procedures. Such process may include documentation of items such as—

"(i) years and type of experience;

"(ii) a list of settings where experience was obtained; and

"(iii) verification of experience by supervising physicians or clinically qualified hospital personnel.

"(B) ELIGIBILITY.—The Secretary shall not recognize any individual as having met the educational standards applicable under this paragraph based on experience pursuant to the authority of subparagraph (A) unless such individual was performing or planning the technical component of medical imaging examinations or radiation therapy treatments prior to the date of enactment of this section.

"(C) CERTIFICATION TEST REQUIREMENT.—To be eligible to be certified under this subsection an individual shall, not later than 18 months after the date on which the list of designated certification organizations is published under paragraph (4), successfully complete a certification examination administered by a designated certification organization. During such 18-month period, the penalties provided for under section 1848(b)(4)(C) of the Social Security Act (as added by section 4 of the Consistency, Accuracy, Responsibility, and Excellence in Medical Imaging and Radiation Therapy Act of 2011) shall not apply to such individuals.

"(4) PROCESS.—

"(A) REGULATIONS.—Not later than July 1, 2013, the Secretary shall promulgate regulations for designating certification organizations pursuant to this subsection.

"(B) DESIGNATIONS AND LIST.—Not later than January 1, 2014, the Secretary shall make determinations regarding all certification organizations that have applied for designation pursuant to the regulations promulgated under subparagraph (A), and shall publish a list of all certification organizations that have received a designation.

"(C) PERIODIC REVIEW AND REVISION.— The Secretary shall periodically review the list under subparagraph (B), taking into account the factors established under paragraph (2). After such review, the Secretary may, by regulation, modify the list of certification organizations that have received such designation.

"(D) CERTIFICATIONS PRIOR TO REMOVAL FROM LIST.—If the Secretary removes a certification organization from the list of certification organizations designated under subparagraph (B), any individual who was certified by the certification organization during or before the period beginning on the date on which the certification organization was designated as a certification organization under such subparagraph, and ending on the date on which the certification organization is removed from such list, shall be considered to have been certified by a certification organization designated by the Secretary under such subparagraph for the remaining period that such certification is in effect.

"(d) APPROVED ACCREDITING BODIES.—

"(1) IN GENERAL.—Not later than 24 months after the date of enactment of this section, the Secretary shall publish a list of entities that are approved accrediting bodies for certification organizations for purposes of subsection (c)(2)(E). The Secretary shall revise such list as appropriate.

"(2) REQUIREMENTS FOR APPROVAL.—The Secretary shall not approve an accrediting body for certification organizations under this subsection unless the Secretary determines that such accrediting body—

"(A) is a nonprofit organization;

            "(B) is a national or international organization with accreditation programs for examinations leading to certification by certification organizations;

            "(C) has established standards for recordkeeping and to minimize the possibility of conflicts of interest; and

            "(D) demonstrates compliance with any other requirements established by the Secretary.

        "(3) WITHDRAWAL OF APPROVAL.—The Secretary may withdraw the approval of an accrediting body under this paragraph if the Secretary determines that the body does not meet the requirements of paragraph (2).

    "(e) ALTERNATIVE STANDARDS FOR RURAL AND UNDERSERVED AREAS.—

        "(1) IN GENERAL.—The Secretary shall determine whether the standards established under subsection (a) must be met in their entirety for medical imaging examinations or radiation therapy procedures that are performed and planned in a geographic area that is determined by the Medicare Geographic Classification Review Board to be a 'rural

J.B. Simms

area' or that is designated as a health professional shortage area. If the Secretary determines that alternative standards for such rural areas or health professional shortage areas are appropriate to ensure access to quality medical imaging examinations or radiation therapy procedures, the Secretary is authorized to develop such alternative standards.

"(2) STATE DISCRETION.—The chief executive officer of a State may submit to the Secretary a statement declaring that an alternative standard developed under paragraph (1) is inappropriate for application to such State, and such alternative standard shall not apply in such submitting State. The chief executive officer of a State may rescind a statement described in this paragraph following the provision of appropriate notice to the Secretary.

"(f) RULE OF CONSTRUCTION.—Notwithstanding any other provision of this section, individuals who provide medical imaging examinations relating to mammograms shall continue to meet the regulations applicable under the Mammography Quality Standards Act of 1992 (as amended).

"(g) DEFINITION.—As used in this section:

"(1) MEDICAL IMAGING.—The term 'medical imaging' means any examination or procedure used to visualize tissues, organs, or physiologic processes in humans for the purpose of detecting, diagnosing, treating, or impacting the progression of disease or illness. For purposes of this section, such term does not include routine dental or ophthalmologic diagnostic procedures or ultrasound guidance of vascular access procedures.

"(2) PERFORM.—The term 'perform', with respect to medical imaging or radiation therapy, means—

"(A) the act of directly exposing a patient to radiation, including ionizing or radio frequency radiation, to ultrasound, or to a magnetic field for purposes of medical imaging or for purposes of radiation therapy; and

"(B) the act of positioning a patient to receive such an exposure.

"(3) PLAN.—The term 'plan', with respect to medical imaging or radiation therapy, means the act of preparing for the performance of such a procedure on a patient by evaluating site-specific information, based on measurement and verification of radiation dose distribution, computer analysis, or direct measurement of dose, in order to customize the procedure for the patient.

"(4) RADIATION THERAPY.—The term 'radiation therapy' means any procedure or article intended for use in the cure, mitigation, treatment, or prevention of disease in humans that achieves its intended purpose through the emission of ionizing or non-ionizing radiation.".

SEC. 4. REQUIRED STANDARDS FOR MEDICAL IMAGING AND RADIATION THERAPY.

Section 1848(b)(4) of the Social Security Act (42 U.S.C. 1395w–4(b)(4)) is amended by adding at the end the following new subparagraph:

"(E) REQUIRED STANDARDS FOR MEDICAL IMAGING AND RADIATION THERAPY SERVICES.—With respect to expenses incurred for the planning and performing of the technical component of medical imaging examinations or radiation therapy procedures (as defined in subsection (g) of section 355 of the Public Health Service Act) furnished on or after January 1, 2014, payment shall be made under this section only if the examination or procedure is planned or performed by an individual who meets the requirements established by the Secretary under such section 355.".

J.B. Simms

SEC. 5. REPORT ON THE EFFECTS OF THIS ACT.

(a) IN GENERAL.—Not later than 5 years after the date of the enactment of this Act, the Secretary of Health and Human Services, acting through the Director of the Agency for Healthcare Research and Quality, shall submit to the Committee on Health, Education, Labor, and Pensions of the Senate, the Committee on Finance of the Senate, and the Committee on Energy and Commerce of the House of Representatives, a report on the effects of this Act.

(b) REQUIREMENTS.—The report under subsection (a) shall include the types and numbers of individuals qualified to perform or plan the technical component of medical imaging or radiation therapy services for whom standards have been developed, the impact of such standards on diagnostic accuracy and patient safety, and the availability and cost of services. Entities reimbursed for technical services through programs operating under the authority of the Secretary of Health and Human Services shall be required to contribute data to such report.

J.B. Simms

Appendix Two: OIG Inspection-November 15-16, 2010 Report

 **Department of Veterans Affairs**
Office of Inspector General

Healthcare Inspection

Alleged Poor Quality of Care in
Radiation Therapy
VA Long Beach Healthcare System
Long Beach, California

Report No. 10-03861-119   March 9, 2011
VA Office of Inspector General
Washington, DC 20420

Alleged Poor Quality of Care in Radiation Therapy, VA Long Beach Healthcare System, Long Beach, CA

Executive Summary

The VA Office of Inspector General Office of Healthcare Inspections conducted an inspection to determine the validity of allegations regarding radiation therapy (RT) at the VA Long Beach Healthcare System (the facility) in Long Beach, CA. Allegations included:

- Inappropriate care
- Lack of competence of radiation oncologists
- Lack of communication with facility leadership about adverse events
- Hostile work environment

We substantiated the allegation of poor care for 1 of the 10 patients reported and identified deficiencies in medical record documentation for 9 of the 10 patients. We also substantiated that facility leaders were not aware of adverse patient outcomes in RT and found that action was not taken to correct deficiencies identified in peer reviews.

We did not substantiate the allegation that radiation oncologists lacked competence.

We recommended that the VISN Director require that the Facility Director (1) ensures that an external peer review assessment of the treatment provided by radiation oncologists for Patient 1 is performed; (2) evaluates the care of Patient 1 with Regional Counsel for possible disclosure to the patient; (3) ensures that RT medical record documentation complies with VHA policy and ACR guidelines; and (4) ensures that RT patient outcomes are monitored by the Quality Management program and others external to the RT department to oversee the implementation of corrective actions for all adverse patient outcomes.

The VISN and facility Directors agreed with our findings and recommendations. The implementation plans are acceptable, and we will follow up on the planned actions until they are completed.

J.B. Simms

Alleged Poor Quality of Care in Radiation Therapy, VA Long Beach Healthcare System, Long Beach, CA

DEPARTMENT OF VETERANS AFFAIRS
Office of Inspector General
Washington, DC 20420

TO: Director, Veterans Integrated Service Network 22

SUBJECT: Healthcare Inspection – Alleged Poor Quality of Care in Radiation Therapy, VA Long Beach Healthcare System, Long Beach, California

Purpose

The VA Office of Inspector General (OIG) Office of Healthcare Inspections conducted an inspection to determine the validity of allegations regarding poor quality of care in radiation therapy at the VA Long Beach Healthcare System (the facility) in Long Beach, CA.

Background

The OIG Hotline Division received allegations that the facility's Radiation Therapy Service provided inappropriate radiation therapy (RT) care to 10 patients. Allegations included:

- Inappropriate care
- Lack of competence of radiation oncologists
- Lack of communication with facility leadership about adverse events
- Hostile work environment

The facility, part of Veterans Integrated Service Network (VISN) 22, has 231 acute care beds and 91 long-term care beds. It provides primary, secondary, and tertiary care for 183,000 veterans. Affiliations include the University of California at Irvine, the California State University at Long Beach, and the University of Southern California. At the time of our review, RT was provided by full-time radiation oncologists.

RT is used to treat cancer and other abnormal cell growth while protecting normal cells as much as possible. In the most common form of RT, external beam RT, intense radiation from linear accelerators is directed at tumors. With intensity-modulated RT (IMRT), higher doses can be delivered to abnormal tissue while reducing exposure of adjacent non-target structures, resulting in fewer side effects.[1] The severity of side effects varies depending on the part of the body being treated and whether the patient is also receiving chemotherapy. Common side effects from RT include fatigue, diarrhea, hair loss, and abnormalities of the skin and urinary tract.[2]

With the higher doses of radiation used in IMRT, there is an increased risk of harm to patients. Practice guidelines and documentation requirements aim to maximize patient safety.[3] Examples of documentation requirements include weekly clinical treatment management notes and summaries at the completion of treatment.[4]

Effective quality management (QM) requires an organized, systematic approach to planning, delivering, measuring, and improving health care.[5] Peer review is a key organizational function contributing to quality improvement. In addition to assessments of specific instances of care in response to an adverse patient outcome, peer review encompasses the ongoing evaluation of professional practice.[6]

Scope and Methodology

We conducted a telephone interview with the complainant to clarify the allegations prior to a site visit November 15–16, 2010. We interviewed managers and employees and reviewed pertinent VHA policies and procedures, facility documents, credentialing and privileging (C&P) information, and medical records. We did not address the allegation of a hostile work environment in this report.

We conducted the inspection in accordance with *Quality Standards for Inspection and Evaluation* published by the Council of the Inspectors General on Integrity and Efficiency.

Inspection Results

Issue 1: Quality of Care and Competence

We substantiated the allegation of inappropriate RT care for 1 of the 10 subject patients. We also found deficiencies in the documentation of treatment for 9 of the 10 patients.

We did not substantiate the allegation that radiation oncologists lacked competence. The C&P folders and profiles of the radiation oncologists complied with VHA policy. In

---

[1] American College of Radiology, *Practice Guidelines for Intensity-Modulated Radiation Therapy (IMRT)*, 2007
[2] U.S. National Institutes of Health, National Cancer Institute, "*Radiation Therapy Side Effects.*"
[3] American College of Radiology, *Practice Guidelines for Radiation Oncology*, rev. 2009.
[4] American College of Radiology, *Practice Guideline for Communication: Radiation Oncology*, rev. 2009.
[5] VHA Directive 2009-023, *Quality Management System*, September 11, 2009.
[6] VHA Directive 2010-025, *Peer Review for Quality Management*, June 3, 2010.

addition, peer reviews for ongoing professional practice evaluations were appropriately documented.

Patient 1

Case Review. A patient was diagnosed with squamous cell carcinoma of the right tonsil with metastasis to retropharyngeal lymph nodes. He underwent IMRT and 3D conformal RT in May and June 2010. During and after IMRT, concerns included sore throat, hoarse voice, and moderate erythema of the skin involving breakdown on both sides of the neck.

IMRT treatments were suspended in early June to avoid further skin breakdown. The treatment plan was modified without new scan images, and the patient was started on 3D conformal RT 5 days later with minimal documentation explaining the treatment change. Although the patient's condition subsequently improved, at 3 months after treatment, he continued to have dry mouth and was unable to tolerate solid foods.

Case Findings. We substantiated the allegation that this patient received inappropriate care during the course of RT. The radiation prescription did not spare the parotid gland on the side opposite the tumor, and the patient was not referred for Speech Pathology consultation after experiencing swallowing difficulties.[7] Additionally, progress notes required during treatment were not entered, and the treatment summary lacked details about treatment dates, patient response, and radiation dose.

Patient 2

Case Review. A patient with a past history of prostatectomy and hormone therapy[8] underwent IMRT for prostate cancer in late 2009 and early 2010. The patient had urinary frequency, dysuria, and diarrhea during and after RT. He underwent cystoscopies in September 2009, May 2010, and July 2010. Radiation urethritis[9] was diagnosed, and the patient was treated with hyperbaric oxygen (HBO) therapy. A total of 30 treatments were administered prior to resolution of symptoms.

Case Findings. We did not substantiate the allegation of inappropriate RT care. We found that treatment was appropriate and the side effects anticipated. However, treatment documentation had discrepancies with respect to cumulative dose and type of treatment given.

---

[7] American College of Radiology, *Practice Guideline for Radiation Oncology*, rev. 2009.
[8] Treatment to stop testosterone from being released in order to manage the growth of remaining prostate cancer cells.
[9] Inflammation of the canal through which urine is discharged from the bladder.

J.B. Simms

Alleged Poor Quality of Care in Radiation Therapy, VA Long Beach Healthcare System, Long Beach, CA

Patient 3

Case Review. A patient underwent IMRT for prostate cancer during February—April 2009. Approximately 1 month after initiation of hormone therapy in early September, an oncologist noted that although progression of the cancer had halted, the patient had developed diarrhea, dysuria, and urinary frequency. The patient continues to receive hormone therapy at the facility.

Case Findings. We did not substantiate the allegation of inappropriate RT care. We found that treatment was appropriate and side effects anticipated. However, treatment documentation had discrepancies with respect to radiation doses and dates of treatment.

Patient 4

Case Review. A patient with oropharyngeal squamous cell cancer underwent a positron emission tomography scan that showed a large metabolically active pharyngeal mass. He had chemotherapy & concurrent IMRT to the head and neck area during March—May 2010. The patient experienced mucositis[10] and mild erythema (redness) on the neck. During the course of treatment, the patient required blood transfusions.

Case Findings. We did not substantiate the allegation of inappropriate RT care. We found that treatment was appropriate and side effects anticipated. However, there was no required treatment summary describing the patient's response to IMRT or resolution of symptoms.

Patient 5

Case Review. A patient was diagnosed with low grade prostate cancer. He underwent IMRT treatment under research protocol during July—September 2009. The patient developed urinary frequency, nocturia, dysuria, and rectal irritation. During follow-up visits, side effects were noted to have subsided.

Case Findings. We did not substantiate the allegation of inappropriate RT care. We found that treatment was appropriate and side effects anticipated. However, we found a change in the prescribed dose prior to initiation of treatment and noted the lack of documentation of this change and of the type of treatment delivered.

Patient 6

Case Review. A patient underwent IMRT for prostate cancer under research protocol during December—February 2010. Concerns after RT included a skin reaction in the

---

[10] Painful inflammation and ulceration of the mucous membranes lining the digestive tract.

buttocks area which improved during the course of treatment. The patient also experienced urinary frequency and dysuria which improved with medication 6 months after treatment.

Case Findings. We did not substantiate the allegation of inappropriate RT care. We found that treatment was appropriate and side effects anticipated. However, the prescription was not complete, the isodose was not specified, and the treatment summary was not completed until eight weeks after treatment ended. We also noted that treatment progress notes written by RT residents were not co-signed by an attending physician as required by VHA policy.[11]

Patient 7

Case Review. A patient underwent IMRT under research protocol for prostate cancer during October – December 2009. A cystoscopy[12] performed in July 2010 confirmed the diagnosis of radiation cystitis (inflammation of the urinary bladder). The patient had hematuria (blood in the urine) and required multiple visits to the Emergency Department for bladder irrigation. He did not require blood transfusion, but was treated with HBO and underwent 30 HBO treatments before the hematuria resolved.

Case Findings. We did not substantiate the allegation of inappropriate RT care. We found that treatment was appropriate and side effects anticipated. However, we noted that the radiation oncologist changed the radiation prescription for the patient but did not document the change in the medical record.[13]

Patient 8

Case Review. A diabetic patient with a left above-the-knee amputation required long-term inpatient rehabilitation and wound care beginning in September 2008. In March 2009, he was diagnosed with anal margin squamous cell cancer and underwent surgery. RT was initiated in June 2009 and completed in August 2009.

The patient experienced difficulty with urination which began after the 14th radiation treatment and continued until after the end of RT. In late August 2009, radiation cystitis was diagnosed and confirmed by cystoscopy. Treatment with HBO therapy was not indicated at that time. Residual bladder abnormalities were noted to be slowly improving as of March 2010.

Case Findings. We did not substantiate the allegation of inappropriate RT care. We found that treatment was appropriate and side effects anticipated. However, follow-up

---

[11] VHA Handbook 1400.1, *Resident Supervision*, July 25, 2007.
[12] Examination of the urinary tract using a lighted instrument.
[13] American College of Radiology. *ACR Practice Guideline for Radiation Oncology*, Rev. 2009.

evaluation of the patient was not completed within 4–6 weeks as required. Discrepancies were also found in the documentation of dates and type of treatment delivered.

Patient 9

Case Review. A patient with head and neck squamous cell cancer required RT and chemotherapy. The patient was admitted with open neck wounds and received the majority of his wound care, RT, and concurrent administration of cetuximab (chemotherapy) in the facility's long-term care unit during June—August 2010.

The neck wounds deteriorated soon after the sixth RT treatment, although it was not documented exactly when the worsening occurred. The patient was subsequently transferred to a private facility for treatment of bleeding arteries in the neck. The patient was transferred back to the facility and RT was resumed.

Supportive wound care and intravenous antibiotics were later required for a neck wound infection. The right neck wounds healed and were considered superficial when the patient was discharged home in late September 2010, 3 months after initiation of RT.

Case Findings. We did not substantiate the allegation of inappropriate RT care. The combination of cetuximab and RT was necessary in the management of this patient's advanced malignancy. However, the combination imparted a high risk of skin complications. Facility staff reported that this case had been reviewed by an interdisciplinary team to determine the appropriateness of reporting to the U.S. Food and Drug Administration. The team concluded that reporting was not necessary for an expected reaction.

Although we did not substantiate poor RT care, we found inadequate documentation of the patient's response to treatment, including the status of neck lesions. In addition, the treatment summary was missing.

Patient 10

Case Review. A patient had metastatic non-small cell lung cancer unresponsive to chemotherapy provided at a private facility. The last dose of chemotherapy was given in June 2010. In July, the patient was found to have a large pericardial effusion, and a pericardial window was placed.

The patient was transferred to the facility in mid-July 2010 for RT. He was seen by the radiation oncologist on the day of admission, but treatment was not initiated because the patient was unable to lie flat. The plan was to initiate second-line chemotherapy, with RT to be attempted again if and when appropriate. Chemotherapy infusions were initiated but stopped due to the patient's shortness of breath. RT was never contacted again for re-evaluation. The patient's condition continued to deteriorate, and he expired in mid-August 2010 after electing palliative (end-of-life) care.

Case Findings. We did not substantiate the allegation of inappropriate RT care. The patient had very advanced disease and could not tolerate the positioning requirements for RT. There was no further request for RT, and the patient expired after choosing palliative care.

Issue 2: Communication with Facility Leadership

We substantiated the allegation that senior leaders were not aware of RT patient outcomes. VHA expects that "peer review done for quality management fosters a responsive environment where issues are identified, acted upon proactively, and in ways that continually contribute to the best possible outcomes and strong organizational performance".[14] Facility staff confirmed that RT peer reviews had been performed. However, results had not been communicated to facility leadership nor was action taken to correct deficiencies identified in peer reviews.

During our onsite visit, facility staff provided evidence of plans for a new "Radiation Therapy and Oncology Quality Management Committee" which would focus on clinical care monitors such as unplanned interruptions during treatment, unusual, severe, early, or late complications of treatment, and unexpected deaths during RT care. The committee is to meet quarterly and report to the Medical Executive Council. Staff also provided a 2010 charter for a Comprehensive Cancer Program which is expected to work in concert with the committee and assume responsibility for the "continuous overview of the quality of cancer care, evaluate its safety and long-term results, and assure timely reporting to the [facility] Executive Leadership Board".

Conclusions

We substantiated the allegation of poor care for 1 of the 10 patients reported and found deficiencies in the medical record documentation for 9 of the 10 patients. We also substantiated that facility leaders were not aware of patient outcomes in RT nor was action taken to correct deficiencies identified in peer reviews.

We did not substantiate the allegation that radiation oncologists lacked competence. The C&P folders and profiles of the radiation oncologists complied with VHA policy. Peer reviews for ongoing professional practice evaluations were appropriately documented.

---

[14] VHA Directive 2010-025, *Peer Review for Quality Management*, June 3, 2010.

J.B. Simms

Alleged Poor Quality of Care in Radiation Therapy, VA Long Beach Healthcare System, Long Beach, CA

Recommendations

Recommendation 1. We recommend that the VISN Director require that the Facility Director ensures that an external peer review assessment of the treatment provided by radiation oncologists for Patient 1 is performed.

Recommendation 2. We recommend that the VISN Director require that the Facility Director evaluates the care of Patient 1 with Regional Counsel for possible disclosure to the patient.

Recommendation 3. We recommend that the VISN Director require that the Facility Director ensures that RT medical record documentation complies with VHA policy and ACR guidelines.

Recommendation 4. We recommend that the VISN Director require that the Facility Director ensures that RT patient outcomes are monitored by the Quality Management program and others external to the RT department to oversee the implementation of corrective actions for all adverse patient outcomes.

Comments

The VISN and facility Directors agreed with our findings and recommendations. The implementation plans are acceptable, and we will follow up on the planned actions until they are completed.

(original signed by:)
JOHN D. DAIGH, JR., M.D.
Assistant Inspector General for
Healthcare Inspections

J.B. Simms

About the Author

J.B. Simms is a former private investigator of over 25 years. He is the author of three books, and lives in California.

Don't Get Arrested in South Carolina, which was awarded a bronze medal for true crime books by the Independent Book Publishers in 2009.

Incest Within the Criminal Justice Family, which was his second book, is anexpose' of the intricacies of the criminal judicial system in the United States

Yeah, My Dog Did That, Too, is a book of stories about a dog Simms had from his college years through the first years of his investigative career.

Additional information about J.B Simms and his publications can be found at www.erikpublishing.com

www.ingramcontent.com/pod-product-compliance
Lightning Source LLC
Chambersburg PA
CBHW052012290426
44112CB00014B/2214